THE
MOSSAD

THE MOSSAD

Israel's Secret Intelligence Service

INSIDE STORIES

Dennis Eisenberg • Uri Dan • Eli Landau

PADDINGTON PRESS LTD

NEW YORK & LONDON

Library of Congress Cataloging in Publication Data

Eisenberg, Dennis, 1929–
  The Mossad–inside stories.

  Includes index.
  1. Intelligence service—Israel. 2. Secret service—Israel. 3. Israel. Sherut ha-bitahon
ha-kelali.
I. Dan, Uri, joint author. II. Landow, Eli, 1939–joint author. III. Title.
UB271.18E37   327'.12'095694   78-18824
ISBN 0 7092 0145 1
ISBN 0 448 22201 9 (U.S. and Canada only)

Filmset in England by SX Composing Ltd., Rayleigh, Essex
Printed and bound in the United States
Designed by Patricia Pillay

IN THE UNITED STATES
PADDINGTON PRESS
Distributed by
GROSSET & DUNLAP

IN THE UNITED KINGDOM
PADDINGTON PRESS

IN CANADA
Distributed by
RANDOM HOUSE OF CANADA LTD.

IN SOUTHERN AFRICA
Distributed by
ERNEST STANTON (PUBLISHERS) (PTY.) LTD.

IN AUSTRALIA AND NEW ZEALAND
Distributed by
A.H. & A.W. REED

Contents

Publisher's Note

Every story and every incident in this book is true.

The only facts knowingly altered are the names and, in a few instances, the biographical details of some of the Mossad agents involved. These alterations have been made for the simple reason that to identify an agent still in the field would be to endanger his or her life.

Even while changes have been made, however, great care has been taken not to detract in any way from the truth of the stories. In all important respects, their accuracy and authenticity remain intact.

Acknowledgments

This book was written with the cooperation of countless men and women who supplied us with background information and previously unpublished material. Their identities cannot be revealed, but they trusted us with their secrets and we are deeply grateful.

We also thank Dick Ehrlich of Paddington Press for his editorial support and guidance.

DENNIS EISENBERG
URI DAN
ELI LANDAU
Tel Aviv and London
April, 1978

Introduction

There will come an age of small and independent nations whose first line of defense will be knowledge.

Charles Proteus Steinmetz, the man who wrote this statement, was a German-born Jewish scientist. In trouble with the German authorities for his socialist beliefs and activities, he emigrated to the United States, where he made a brilliant career in electrical engineering. Today he is remembered for the important research he did in this field.

Yet Steinmetz might as easily have been a prophet, for the prediction quoted above summarizes with astonishing accuracy the situation in which the state of Israel has found itself since its beginnings. More than artillery, more than fighters or high-speed sea craft, Israel relies for its military strength on accurate and comprehensive knowledge of its enemies' activities.

A look at the map of the Middle East will explain instantly why this should be so.

To the north, south and east, Israel is surrounded by nations which are hostile to her. At the moment of her statehood, five of these nations—Syria, Egypt, Iraq, Jordan, Lebanon—declared their opposition to her right to exist. Together with Libya and South Yemen (both violently anti-Israeli in outlook) they have almost fifty times the land area* and twenty times the population of Israel. They have been armed and advised by powerful allies sympathetic to their aims. Today, though relations have improved

*These figures are based on Israel's post-1967 borders.

somewhat, they still present a constant threat to Israel's survival.

Moreover, Israel's enemies do not always attack her in a conventional manner. Terrorist activities aimed at unarmed civilians, like the operation carried out at the 1972 Munich Olympics, or the 1976 hijacking that ended so dramatically at Entebbe airport, cannot be fought solely with military might.

The founders of the Israeli state could hardly foresee the diversity of threats to which their nation would be susceptible. But they did recognize from the beginning—even in the chaotic days of the War of Independence—the necessity for maintaining a strong and efficient intelligence service.

It would have to be small, both in human and in financial resources, because Israel is a tiny country. It would have to operate in secrecy and be answerable to the Prime Minister. It would have to act in a way that would assure it popular support. Nor could it take the law into its own hands without careful checks and safeguards.

Above all, it would have to be the match of the best intelligence organizations in the world. Israel's survival would depend on it.

Thus, even in the earliest days of independence, Prime Minister David Ben-Gurion concerned himself with establishing Israel's intelligence service. Working within the institutional framework inherited from pre-independence days, he set up five major intelligence branches.

One of these was the Shai, the intelligence division of the Haganah, the underground army formed by the Jewish settlers in Palestine. Even after the Haganah itself was incorporated into the official Israeli Defense Force, the Shai remained intact to gather and analyze intelligence.

The second major branch was the Shin Beth, which officially had responsibility for internal security. The third, Aliyah Beth, had been set up during the period of the British Mandate to smuggle "illegal" immigrants into Palestine. After independence Aliyah Beth turned its attention to helping Jews escape to Israel from hostile Arab countries.

The Foreign Ministry had taken responsibility for establishing a fourth intelligence group, whose sole purpose was to establish links with intelligence officials in other countries. A fifth branch dealt exclusively with police intelligence matters.

For the few years following the 1948 War of Independence, these five branches made up the entirety of Israel's intelligence community. Like so many other aspects of Israeli life in this period, they were plagued by confusion. There was neither an absolute definition of responsibility nor a clear set of guidelines for action. Everyone involved had to feel his way along as best he could. To complicate matters further, there was a certain amount of competitiveness and jealousy among the different branches.

In 1951 Prime Minister Ben-Gurion undertook to alleviate this confusion by reorganizing and consolidating the intelligence services. The Aliyah Beth and police intelligence force remained intact and kept their original, limited areas of responsibility. The Shin Beth also maintained its role of watching over internal security.

All other responsibilities were divided between two major organizations. One of these was a branch for military intelligence, sometimes called Aman. This branch was to concern itself exclusively with matters of military interest, primarily in the gathering of data, and was to work closely with the armed forces.

The final major branch of the intelligence community was given responsibilities more loosely-defined, more varied, and more wide-ranging than any of the others. This branch was called the Mossad—short for the Institution for Intelligence and Special Assignments. Its primary task was to gather and analyze information abroad, in any area that might be of interest to Israel.

But Prime Minister Ben-Gurion, who is generally acknowledged to have had a superb understanding of intelligence affairs, recognized that the Mossad's execution of its tasks would involve it in a multitude of difficult and dangerous activities. It was for this reason that he included the phrase "Special Assignments" in its official title. The Mossad would be called upon to perform any unusual operations that fell outside the realm of other arms of the government, whether military or civilian. In Israel's struggle for survival, Ben-Gurion knew, the Mossad would be one of her most valuable weapons.

Today, after thirty years of existence, the Mossad is rated by *Time* magazine as one of the four finest intelligence agencies in the world, ranking along with the numerically and financially superior KGB, CIA and Britain's D16.

In its brief life, the Mossad has had its share of both triumph and failure. Ironically, it is on those occasions when something does go wrong that it tends to attract the most attention. For instance, in 1973 a Mossad team assigned to execute those responsible for the Munich Olympic Games terrorist attack bungled one mission. They killed the wrong man, and through carelessness, made it relatively easy for the police to capture them. This bungled operation attracted worldwide attention and gave the Mossad considerable publicity.

The Mossad does all it can to avoid such publicity. Most of its missions, though equally or more dangerous than the so-called "hit team" operation, are concerned with genuine intelligence work. Such missions, as the Mossad recognizes, can only be performed in quiet obscurity. By recruiting, as its long-time chief Isser Harel laid down, "only those who are highly motivated by patriotism and idealism," it avoids making heroes out of the extraordinary men and women who work for it. Its sole purpose, as all operatives are taught, is to safeguard the state of Israel.

The Two Issers

On July 1, 1948, three years before the Mossad was even created, an event of fundamental importance for its future took place in the small Arab village of Beit Je'ez, located on the road between Tel Aviv and Jerusalem. The few villagers, mostly children and old men and women, who had stayed behind there despite the fierce fighting of previous weeks, watched in astonishment as a strange scene was enacted.

There, in a stony field, against a 400-year-old olive tree, stood a handcuffed prisoner.

He was clearly a Jew.

Facing him in a ragged line were six armed men. One had a British army rifle, another a Czech submachine gun; two others held museum pieces that had first seen the light of day in Germany, just before the First World War. Some of the soldiers were dressed in patched khaki, others in sports jackets. Another wore what he proudly boasted was a "Russian Army ski-troop anorak."

This motley collection of soldiers consisted of members of the newly-created Zahal, the Israeli Defense Force.

The villagers of Beit Je'ez found nothing unusual in the sight of armed soldiers. Israel's declaration of statehood only weeks before, on May 14, had provoked a bitter war between the new nation and invading armies from Jordan, Syria, Iraq, Egypt, and the Lebanon. Palestinian villagers and guerillas had joined in the fight under the rallying cry of "Death to all Jews."

On June 11 a ceasefire had been declared, but in effect it was nothing more than breathing space. The Arab forces were regrouping for renewed attack. Israel, under the leadership of David Ben-Gurion, was trying to organize itself. Arms, supplies and new immigrants—many of them survivors of the concentration camps—were pouring into the country. The various underground organizations forces were being integrated into one army despite the opposition of some of their members.

In the hills surrounding the road from Tel Aviv to Jerusalem, however, the fighting had never let up. After some of the fiercest battles of the war, the ancient city of Jerusalem had fallen to the troops of King Abdullah of Jordan.

In order to bring food and arms to the beleaguered defenders of that part of the city which still remained in Jewish hands, convoys of improvised armored vehicles had run the gauntlet from Tel Aviv to Jerusalem.

Arab forces, based in the hills dominating the road, poured down a merciless barrage every time a supply column tried to fight its way through. In a bid to outflank their attackers, groups of Jewish soldiers were battling with armed bands of Arab villagers in the hills, and the sound of shooting could still be heard everywhere.

But here amidst the ruins of Beit Je'ez, a squad of Jews was about to execute one of their fellow countrymen.

An hour earlier a senior officer had arrived and told the local commander to organize a firing squad to execute a traitor. Mopping-up operations were suspended and half a dozen men chosen. Of these six, two asked not to take part. They were replaced by two others.

Now, in the barren and rocky field, the reluctant executioners faced the condemned, Captain Meir Tobianski.

The scores of Zahal men who watched the scene were momentarily stunned. From group to group an incredulous cry feebly echoed: "See what they are doing to a Jewish traitor!" Their hearts were heavy, for traitor or not Tobianski was a fellow Jew. He had served long and well in the Haganah army. As the firing squad took aim, that service counted for nothing. There was silence among the observers, Arab and Jew alike.

Two volleys of shots rang out, and the lifeless body of Meir Tobianski fell to the ground. Blood oozed through his shirt into the barren earth of Beit Je'ez. For a few moments he lay there, slumped against a cactus plant. Then the soldiers carried his corpse down the slope, away from the village, for secret burial. Soon they were back at their regular duties.

When news of Tobianski's death reached Isser Be'eri, he wrote in his diary: "Mission accomplished." Be'eri was the man who had ordered the execution.

Born in Poland in 1901, Be'eri (originally named Bernzweig) had come to Palestine as a twenty-year-old pioneer. After doing manual labor in Haifa he set up his own contracting business, but went bankrupt within the year. Disillusioned, he returned to Poland, but shortly afterwards was back in Palestine.

In 1938 Be'eri became a full-time underground fighter. The tall, slenderly-built pioneer served well and was quick-witted. By 1948, the year of independence, he was a lieutenant colonel and chief of the Shai, the Intelligence Service of the Haganah. Dealing primarily with security matters, he was known to be a brilliant officer.

The War of Independence presented Be'eri and those under his command with massive problems. He had to constantly enlarge his network of agents who would tell him of enemy troop movements and strategies. He slept little and was under enormous pressure from all sides.

To complicate things even further, it immediately became obvious that there was a major breach of security in Jerusalem. Jordanian artillery units stationed on the hills overlooking the city had time and time again directed a murderous barrage against key Jewish military installations. Even when the defending units moved under cover of darkness to take up new positions, Jordanian shells would come crashing down on their heads at daybreak.

There was no doubt about it: a spy inside the Jewish lines was signaling precise information to the enemy artillery every few hours.

Ben-Gurion summoned his Chief of Intelligence. In three brief sentences he presented the facts to the loyal Be'eri and added curtly: "What are you doing all the time? Find that spy immediately!"

The mission to close up the security leak became priority number one, even after the ceasefire was declared. The situation was desperate, for clearly hostilities would be resumed as soon as both sides had rearmed.

Suspicion finally fell on Meir Tobianski. He had served with the British Army before joining the Haganah and was known to go drinking frequently with British officers. Through them he could easily pass on information to the Jordanians.

On June 30, Be'eri received a report on Tobianski—meager information gathered from the field and a standard intelligence dossier.

He ordered his arrest.

Early the next morning a team of agents picked up Tobianski at his home. He told his wife Lena that he would only be gone a few hours.

Obviously he had no inkling of the charges he was about to face. At an immediate ad hoc "court martial" he was interrogated for several hours by a group of senior Israeli officers. The prisoner admitted that he *had* mixed with British military men and counted many among his personal friends.

But he denied spying for the British, and he vehemently rejected suggestions that his drinking pals had passed information about Haganah military positions to the Jordanians.

The "court martial" curtly rejected his defense, and within hours the lifeless body of Meir Tobianski lay on the barren field outside Beit Je'ez.

Lena Tobianski reported her husband's disappearance to the police immediately. They, of course, had no idea where he was. Attempts to contact him through army friends proved equally fruitless.

Finally, official acknowledgment of his death came in the newspapers. He had been executed, it was said, for passing information to the enemy.

Absolutely convinced of her husband's innocence, Mrs. Tobianski appealed to all the authorities she knew of for help in clearing his name. Everyone sympathized, but no one could help.

Finally she wrote personally to Ben-Gurion.

The Prime Minister was still working desperately on the problems crowding in on him day and night, but even so, he could not ignore the anguished widow's claims of a "terrible injustice." One of his aides later said the Prime Minister "sensed in his bones that something was wrong. He knew it immediately."

In his own hand Ben-Gurion wrote to Lena Tobianski and promised her he would look into the matter. "I cannot say if he was guilty or not guilty," he wrote. But something, as he put it in Hebrew, was *lo beseder*—"not OK." There would be an official investigation, he told her, and in the meantime she and her son would be cared for by the state.

The investigation culminated in the arrest of Isser Be'eri, the very man who had ordered Tobianski to face a court-martial.

When brought to trial in August 1948, Be'eri stoutly maintained his innocence of the charges of improper conduct.

"I appointed three judges to try Tobianski," he said. "I was the prosecutor. They listened to the evidence and agreed with my request for the death sentence. We knew that Tobianski, who was a heavy drinker, was living well above his means. The gravity of his crime was such that the death sentence had to be carried out immediately. You will remember this was in the middle of a war. A war to the death. I did my duty."

The court listened to descriptions of how Tobianski pleaded for mercy as the firing squad aimed their rifles at him. "I served in the Haganah for twenty-two years. At least allow me to send a message to my son," he asked.

His request was brushed aside.

Now Isser Be'eri's judges decided that the field court martial had been totally illegal. Tobianski had not been given the elementary right of a lawyer to defend him. The sentence had not been confirmed by any higher authority and no appeal had been allowed.

The court also knew, however, that the incident had occurred during an agonizingly difficult period. Both Be'eri and Tobianski were victims of the spy-hysteria prevailing at the time. The tension was compounded by the lack of guidelines for action. There were no rule books, no precedents, no traditions to dictate what was to be done with men suspected of treason.

Nor was Isser Be'eri an evil man. He had been totally dedicated to his job. His patriotism was beyond question. Not a trace of corruption had ever been associated with him. Clearly he had ordered Tobianski's execution because he was convinced that the man was a spy.

Nonetheless, said the court, justice must prevail.

Be'eri was found guilty. His sentence was "imprisonment from sunrise to sunset," which meant he would avoid the disgrace of spending a night in jail.

To a man like Isser Be'eri, however, his sentence might as well have been death. Even though President Chaim Weizmann pardoned him and he never served behind bars, he felt disgraced in the eyes of his countrymen. Forcibly retired from public life, he died in 1958 a broken-hearted man.

The execution of Meir Tobianski is important in the history of the Mossad because, in bringing about the downfall of Isser Be'eri, it also led to the rise of another man who eventually took control not only of the Mossad but of the whole of Israel's intelligence service. This extraordinary man, Isser Harel, did more than any other individual to make the Mossad what it is today.

Isser Harel emigrated to Palestine from Latvia in 1930. His family, with whom he had moved to Latvia from the Russian city of Vitebsk, preceded him to Palestine by a couple of years. When he joined them as a youth of seventeen, he already showed a penchant for undercover work: Isser smuggled a revolver through the rigorous British customs search. The customs officials never suspected that such an innocuous-looking youth—he stood barely four feet eight inches tall and had enormous ears—was an arms smuggler.

Soon after his arrival Isser went to work on a kibbutz near Herzliya, a few miles up the coast from Tel Aviv. So diligently did he toil among the orange groves that he earned himself the title of "Stakhanovitch," an allusion to the Russian coalworker Alexei Stakhanov, whose name was synonomous with high productivity. Isser learned Hebrew quickly but never quite lost his Russian accent. He was known among his fellow *kibbutznikim* as a serious, somewhat stern personality.

By contrast, the Polish-born woman named Rivkah whom Isser married at the kibbutz was a gay and exuberant character. She loved singing, dancing, and horseback riding. They stayed at the kibbutz for some thirteen years, living at first in a tent pitched on the sand dunes. In 1943 they left when some other members refused to apologize to Isser for what he thought was an insult aimed in his direction. Walking off with no possessions other than the clothes on their backs, Isser and Rivkah set up house in Tel Aviv.

Both of them worked during the day, but Isser also joined the Haganah, the Jewish underground army which was fighting at the time against bands of hostile Arabs. Within months he found himself working in an intelligence unit.

Isser was good at his work and his superiors marked him for promotion. Soon he became leader of his group and later, after the end of the Second World War, commander of the Shai for the Tel Aviv area. He was to retain this post for several years.

It was during this period that Isser Harel came to be known as Isser "the Little." His height was an obvious reason for this nickname. But more important a reason was the need to distinguish him from the other Isser, Isser Be'eri. The two men were widely known in the same circles, and confusion between them became a problem in conversation among military and intelligence leaders.

Isser the Little served bravely and diligently in the period between the Second World War and Israel's War of Independence. He was unswervingly devoted to Ben-Gurion, whom he worshipped beyond question. And he expected, not surprisingly, that with Isser Be'eri's fall from grace in December of 1948 he would be appointed to take his place as head of the Shai.

But the post went instead to a Polish-born officer named Chaim Herzog. Isser the Little had to content himself with commanding the second major branch of the intelligence service: the Shin Beth, which was responsible for internal security.

Isser worked diligently as ever in his new post. But he was a proud, arrogant and ambitious man—too ambitious to be content for long. Almost immediately after Ben-Gurion's reorganization of Israel's intelligence community, Isser the Little began a one-man campaign to gain complete control over it.

Incredibly enough, his campaign worked. Within less than a year he had convinced the head of the Mossad to resign; five months later, Isser stepped into his shoes. Not long after that he took over the still-active Aliyah Beth. Soon he became chairman of the security services committee, which had responsibility for over-seeing the activities of the different security branches.

Isser was now truly the "memuneh"—the Big Boss of Israel's intelligence services. For over a decade he controlled intelligence operations virtually single-handed. Answering only to Ben-Gurion, he was effectively the second most powerful man in Israel.

Isser had an obsession with secrecy that began in his days as com-mander of the Shai for the Tel Aviv area. After the Second World War he had amassed an enormous archive containing a variety of different kinds of information about internal security, Nazi war criminals, everything he thought might one day be useful.

Fearful that the British might discover his precious archive, Isser rented a small apartment in Tel Aviv and employed a bricklayer to build him a false wall with a concealed entrance. Here he stored his documents for many months. The apartment was searched several times by British troops and they never found the compartment.

But even that wasn't good enough for Isser.

Driving around the countryside near Tel Aviv one day, he saw a gang of men doing construction work on what was going to be an apartment house. This gave him an idea. He stopped his car and, approaching the work supervisor, made discreet enquiries about the men on the work crew. After talking to a few of them, Isser picked one he thought he could trust and asked him for a small favor.

He wanted a room built in the heart of the building as a storage space for his archives. The room was to be a secret to everyone, including the builders and the architect. The worker built the room, and it was here that Isser hid his archive until the British left the country and he was able to establish proper headquarters in Jaffa.

Isser's secrecy became something of a legend. The joke went around that one time he hailed a taxi in Tel Aviv and, when asked by the driver where he wanted to go, replied abruptly that his destination was a secret.

For many years his neighbors had no idea what his job was. They knew he was involved in some way with military matters, but never suspected either his branch of service or his rank (which was Lieutenant Colonel). A shopkeeper who spotted him once on a rare occasion when he was wearing his full uniform blurted out: "Such a quiet little guy like you, how can you be such an important officer?"

On the whole, neighbors felt sorry for the diminutive bald gentleman they occasionally saw shopping for his wife, whom they called "The Amazon." They assumed that he must have a hard time at home. Indeed, it is known that the only people who have ever given him orders are Rivkah and Ben-Gurion.

But in his office "Isser the Little" became a giant. His agents respected and feared him.

"When Isser looks at you," said one of them, "you feel like you're already in prison."

Another expanded: "He had cold piercing blue eyes which seemed to cut through to your innermost thoughts like a sharp knife. He always looked people he dealt with absolutely straight in the eyes. He never averted his gaze. The longer he looked at you the more menacing he became.

"You were always guilty. The urge to break down and confess— even if you were innocent and there was nothing to confess—was at times overwhelming."

Isser Harel was a born spy. During the decade when he was Israel's chief spy-master, Isser planned his country's most daring espionage coups. Not content with sitting behind a desk and giving orders, he frequently went out into the field to direct operations on the spot, and plainly enjoyed the excitement of hunting down a quarry.

Again and again his intuition led him to the correct interpretation of events when all logic seemed to point in the opposite direction. His closest colleagues even suspected that he had some kind of inbuilt antennae which never let him down, especially during moments of crisis. He was particularly adept at recognizing talent, and promotion came rapidly to men with flair and determination.

He was always aloof, always the lone operator. In all the years she knew him, even his wife Rivkah never dared ask what operation he was busy with, when something was clearly troubling him.

Only once, worried about his unexplained absence, did she ask the Prime Minister: "Tell me what will happen to my husband. Where is he?" On that occasion, however, not even Ben-Gurion could give her an answer: he did not have the faintest idea where his secretive intelligence chief was.

Rivkah learned very early not to ask her husband any questions about his work, but she had her own espionage techniques. Whenever important business was being conducted in the living room of their home, she would make frequent visits with fresh coffee and plates of sandwiches. "Eat, you look hungry," she would scold Isser and his visitors. From wisps of conversation she would draw her own conclusions.

Isser had little respect for what he considered to be any kind of frivolity. He believed that wearing a tie was a sign of "bourgeois decadence," and refused even to own one. Not until he was going to Europe to meet leading government officials did he consent to this compromise of his principles. One of his men bought the tie for him, and had to teach his boss how to knot it.

Isser's sole concession to social niceties was a weekly gathering which he held at his house. Every Thursday evening some of Israel's most important personalities, generals, ministers, statesmen and others whose jobs nobody was ever quite sure about, would gather there for coffee and poppy-seed cakes.

Asked if his personal friends also came to those weekly gatherings, a member of his family looked puzzled and said: "Friends? He knows everybody, and they know him. But I don't think he has any actual friends. He never confides in anyone, not even in us."

Not the faintest hint of moral or financial scandal ever touched Isser's name. A devoted family man, his attitudes were almost fanatically puritanical. Once he discovered that a valued agent had used the excuse of "going on a mission" to explain his absence to his wife, when in fact he was spending a week with his lover at a seaside resort. Isser promptly fired the man.

He scorned material things, and it is as well for Israel that this was so. For he was answerable to nobody, not even government ministers, on how he spent the Mossad budget. To this day, still residing in the same modest house with its small neat garden which he has occupied for most of his career, his simple way of life underlines the incorruptibility of the man. Isser had the total confidence of his agents, particularly those who had to carry out dangerous missions abroad. He made a point of knowing their private lives and personally helping when he could over domestic problems. Yet nobody could take the slightest liberty with him. He had no sense of humor whatsoever. The nearest anybody ever came to hearing him make a joke was when he said, "The only people who are not afraid of my blue eyes are dogs and children."

His manner when displeased was frightening. One agent who had inadvertently blundered through carelessness had to undergo a grueling cross-examination at the hands of Isser. His mistake had caused public embarrassment to the government but Isser did not fire him. When the man emerged from his chief's office, pale and shaking after a severe rebuke, he commented: "If Isser had remained behind in Russia he would have been head of the KGB and eaten even that monster Beria for breakfast."

Isser was a tough master, but he repaid dedication in kind: he never abandoned an agent who was in trouble, and if ever any of his men were caught he made superhuman efforts to gain their release. He was ready to pay any price in gold or almost anything else requested in exchange. Isser opposed totally the traditional secret service view that an imprisoned agent was expendable.

European and American security chiefs who knew Isser the Little had the utmost respect for his professional talents. He was cunning and devious, and reveled in the world of intrigue and espionage. His only known hobbies were opera and the detective novels of Agatha Christie. Spy novels, with rare exceptions, brought forth his contempt: "My boys make so-called heroes like James Bond look like amateurs."

This was the man who ran the Mossad in its formative period. The standards he set, and the style he established, remain with the organization to this day.

The Eichmann Kidnapping

LATE AUTUMN, 1957. Isser Harel had stayed up all night reading a single dossier. It was a thick dossier, one of those he had assembled after the Second World War and hidden so carefully from the British.

Its subject: Adolf Eichmann.

At times Isser had had to force himself to read on. The enormity of the man's crimes was sickening.

From the time of his appointment in 1934 to the Jewish section of the security service of the SS, as an "expert" on Zionism, Eichmann had played a key role in the formulation and execution of the so-called "Final Solution to the Jewish Question." He outlined the idea of "forced emigration" as a method of concentrating the Jewish population of Europe into easily-dealt-with units, and proposed the establishment of a single agency to carry out that policy. Throughout the war his role was more one of administration than of policy-making—but he carried out his orders with a murderous and enthusiastic efficiency.

Eichmann had taken immense pride in the smoothness of the operations he organized. At the Nuremberg war trials evidence was produced that he had boasted of his part in the liquidation of millions of Jews, which included a major role in the expansion of Auschwitz to become the largest center for mass extermination. Approximately two million Jews died at Auschwitz.

Eichmann's activities in Hungary, where, in March 1944, he was given responsibility for administration of the Final Solution, typified the cold-blooded efficiency with which he went about his tasks.

Dividing the country into six zones to facilitate deportation, and then importing troops specially for the purpose, he began to round up and deport as many of Hungary's 650,000 Jews as he could get his hands on. By July, barely four months after he had begun, 437,000 Jews had been dragged off to Auschwitz. Later, when the war was going badly for Germany, an offer was made to supply desperately-needed equipment in exchange for Jewish lives. Even while the negotiations were going on, Eichmann continued the deportation.

Many of the top Nazis were captured after the war and tried at Nuremberg. Others were dealt with more informally by men who decided to take the law into their own hands.

Even before the war was over, a group from the Jewish Brigade of the British Army organized itself into a revenge squad whose sole purpose was to track down Nazis. The group called itself the *Hanokmin* (Avengers), after a biblical reference to the avenging angels of God.

Putting together their own lists from testimony given by survivors of the camps, these men set up a network of agents and contacts throughout Europe. Sympathetic military men from the French, British, American and other occupying forces aided them. They located and captured hundreds of Nazis, especially the SS men who had organized and run the concentration camps.

At first they handed over the captured Nazis to Allied military authorities. But frequently the prisoners escaped in the chaos that followed the war or were released.

On one occasion in 1944, two high-ranking Nazis were captured and presented to the Russians occupying Hungary. To the horror of the men who had captured the pair, however, the Soviet commander said he would need more proof than simply the word of biased concentration camp victims that these men were criminals. He ordered their immediate release. The two Germans walked out laughing into the street.

They did not get far.

The Avengers who had captured them cut the men down with a burst of sub-machine gun fire.

From then on it was official policy simply to kill Nazis immediately upon capture. When the man was tracked down to a particular house, he would receive a visit from a small party of British soldiers politely asking him to come and answer a few questions. He would be taken to a nearby field or woods, have his crimes and sentence read to him, and would then be executed.

Over a thousand such corpses were discovered in the first year after the war.

Somehow Adolf Eichmann had managed to escape both the Nuremberg trials and the swift arm of the Hanokmin. He was known to be an intelligent man and was experienced in police and security affairs. He had managed perfectly, it seemed, to cover his tracks.

Managed, that is, until autumn of 1957.

Isser Harel had received reliable information from a Dr. Fritz Bauer, Public Prosecutor of the province of Hesse, Germany, that Eichmann was living in Argentina.

And so it came to pass that Isser spent the night studying Eichmann's dossier. By morning he knew that the man had to be brought to justice.

To capture the great criminal—who was certainly living under an assumed name, and surrounded by friends in and out of the Argentine government—would be one of the most difficult tasks he had ever faced. And once he was caught there remained the problem of what to do with him. It would be easy enough to execute him in the style of the Hanokmin. But Isser the Little was not going to kill Eichmann. He was going to bring him back to Israel, to make him stand trial before the Jewish people he had tried so hard to exterminate.

This would make the job far more difficult, but there was no alternative. Perhaps remembering Meir Tobianski, the officer whose death had disgraced Isser Be'eri, Isser wanted this operation to conform as nearly as possible to legal standards. Eichmann was too important a criminal to have summarily executed in a deserted field.

It was a daunting task with massive consequences whether it failed or succeeded.

Isser studied the problem at length, assessing all possibilities. Finally when he was convinced that he would have a good chance of pulling it off he went to see his boss, David Ben-Gurion. The two men never discussed anything important over the telephone.

Their meeting was characteristically brief. Isser walked into the office and told Ben-Gurion he had information on Eichmann's whereabouts.

"I would like the green light to bring him back to Israel."

"Do it," said Ben-Gurion.

From that moment on the mission was Isser Harel's number-one priority.

His lead had come to the German Prosecutor Fritz Bauer from a blind Jew in Buenos Aires whose daughter was being wooed by a young man who called himself Nicolas Eichmann. This was the name of one of Adolf Eichmann's sons, born to him and his wife in Germany. The lead gave an address for the Eichmann family: 4261 Chacabuco Street in the Buenos Aires suburb of Olivos.

An agent was sent there early in 1958 to organize a surveillance of the house.

But something went wrong. Perhaps Eichmann, with his well-developed fugitive's sense, knew he was being watched. In any event, the family no longer lived there.

The trail went cold.

In March of that year Isser sent to Buenos Aires an experienced officer named Ephraim Elrom. Isser had hand-picked the man himself.

Elrom was not, in fact, a Mossad agent. He was a police officer, born in Poland but raised in Germany. He had worked for British police after emigrating to Israel and became a senior officer in the Israeli police almost immediately after its founding in 1948. Isser chose him because of his fine record and because he could easily pass as a German.

Also, Elrom had lost almost his entire family in Nazi concentration camps.

On arriving in Buenos Aires Elrom immediately paid a visit to Lothar Hermann, the blind lawyer whose daughter had been dating Nicolas Eichmann. He heard how the lawyer's suspicions had been aroused when the young man boasted of his father's important role in the German war effort.

Inquiries about the man they thought was Eichmann proceeded delicately and slowly. The investigators could not risk the danger that their prey would learn he was being followed. Even more difficult was the necessity of identifying their man beyond the slightest doubt. The only thing worse than losing the real Eichmann would be capturing the wrong one.

Agents were armed with dossiers containing every scrap of information by which Eichmann could be identified: physical characteristics, his rasping voice, even the date of his wedding anniversary. The ex-Nazi had taken care to destroy every photograph of himself he could get his hands on, leaving the investigators with only blurred pictures dating from before the war.

Leads went cold, others proved to be red herrings. The Mossad had also to deal with complications such as a widely publicized report that Eichmann was posing as an oil executive in Kuwait.

Some senior men worried that they were wasting the Mossad's limited resources. Being a small organization they were hard-pressed to continue the hunt for Eichmann *and* keep an eye on military and political developments in Syria, Egypt and other Arab countries.

Still, the search went on. Isser the Little had made up his mind.

In December 1959 some of the Mossad agents identified Eichmann as a man who was living under the name Ricardo Klement. He had run a laundry business which was now bankrupt. After trailing the man's son the team succeeded in tracing the family to a house in Garibaldi Street, in the low-lying San Fernando district of the city. They surveyed the house constantly, photographing it from every angle with a telephoto lens, making notes about its lack of a fence, its fiberboard door, its unplastered walls. They observed the habits of the balding, bespectacled man who lived there with his family. They felt certain he must be Eichmann. Now all they needed was positive proof of his identity.

Finally, on March 21, 1960, the agents got their proof.

At dusk on that day, Ricardo Klement got off the bus and walked slowly toward his home. In his hands was a bouquet of flowers.

Ducking under the strand of wire that marked off his plot of land, Klement presented the bouquet to the woman who greeted him warmly at the door. The couple's youngest child, who usually dressed scruffily or played naked in the garden, was neat and well-turned out.

Later, from behind the house's shuttered curtains, came the sound of celebration laughter.

What was this celebration about? One of the agents looked through his copy of the dossier. He discovered that March 21 was the Eichmanns' silver wedding anniversary.

All remaining doubts about Ricardo Klement's real identity were swept away. He was Adolf Eichmann.

The chase was well and truly on.

Not long after his agents positively identified Eichmann, Isser decided to go to Argentina himself to personally supervise the capture. He said later that "It was the most difficult and most delicate operation the Mossad had ever countenanced. I felt I needed to assume personal responsibility on the spot."

One of his agents put the matter in a slightly different light: "Isser could not resist it. He just had to be there."

Preparations began to speed up. Isser and his lieutenants devised a plan for capturing Eichmann and flying him out of Argentina with forged documents. Every detail was worked out and every contingency planned for. Minor changes were made in accordance with new information supplied by the team in Argentina, who by this time were shadowing Eichmann's every move.

Each man for the mission was hand-picked by Isser Harel from his very best operatives. All had been on assignments abroad with their "boss" before. All had risked their lives in Arab and other countries.

Knowing that the mission would be difficult and dangerous, Isser insisted that there be no recruits: each member would be asked to volunteer.

As it turned out, according to one Mossad man, "Nobody had to be asked three times."

The leader of the group was an Israeli-born commando who had first seen action at the tender age of twelve. He had helped free a large party of Jewish illegal immigrants from an internment camp, and later blew up an "impregnable" British radar station on Mount Carmel. Wounded in action against Arab marauders, he became a scout and joined the intelligence service under Isser.

All the other members of the squad were survivors of Nazi persecution. They had seen brothers, sisters, fathers and mothers being led away to the concentration camps, never to be seen again.

Some were the sole survivors of families who had been wiped out.

One such member was Shalom Dani (whose name meant "forger"). Dani had been brought up in ghettoes and then moved from camp to camp after the Nazi invasion of his native Hungary. His father had been sent to die in the gas chambers of Bergen-Belsen.

Even after his rescue at the end of the war, Dani had known further imprisonment when a British warship intercepted the illegal immigrant ship he was sailing on to Palestine. What remained of his youth he spent in Cyprus, this time in one of His Majesty's internment camps there.

Now it was Dani's task to prepare documents for the other team members and for Eichmann, to facilitate his "vanishing act" from Argentina.

Another of the men chosen by Isser had lost his sister and her three children at the hands of the Nazis. When he learned of their deaths he swore that one day he would avenge them.

Isser had chosen him to be the man responsible for grabbing

Eichmann and physically overpowering him.

He broke down in tears when asked whether he wanted to volunteer.

"Just try and keep me away," was his only reply.

Another man was one of the original Hanokmin; he had already engaged in several killings of Nazis after fighting with the British Army in Italy. His only regret was that his would be a support role, and that he would not be the first to lay his hands on Eichmann.

In all there were over thirty people in the team: a round dozen in the "active" team and another twenty or so serving as aides in Argentina.

Nothing was left to chance. To ensure that there were no problems with documents, plane connections, visas, health certificates, character references for the unit, a miniature travel agency was set up by the Mossad in a European city. (Which city it was remains a secret to this day.)

Special care had to be taken to avoid the impression that the group was organized and sent from Israel, for there were bound to be serious political repercussions if the plan failed. The Argentinians would be understandably angry when they discovered that the Israelis were violating their sovereignty by seizing a man in their capital.

Yet Isser had no real alternative. He knew very well that if he simply passed on his information to the Argentinian police, there was no guarantee that Eichmann would even be arrested, let alone brought to justice. Nazi sympathizers with great influence abounded in Latin America. The continent has, in any event, a long history of giving sanctuary to men on the run from Europe—whether they are simply bank robbers, idealistic political emigrés or full-blooded Nazi criminals.

The operation began innocuously at the end of April. Agents flew in on different dates from all parts of the globe—no two from the same city, few from the same country. They began immediately to rent "safe" houses as bases for their operation and a fleet of cars which they changed constantly to avoid being noticed.

Arrangements had been made beforehand to fly the prisoner out in an El Al airplane which would be going to Buenos Aires to drop off a delegation of Israelis attending celebrations in honor of Argentina's 150th year of independence. It was a major bit of good luck that Isser was able to take a strong hand in dictating when the plane would be allowed to take off from Argentina. The alternative to plane travel—if it could even be arranged—was a sixty-day trip by boat.

By May 11, all was ready. On that day, it was decided, Eichmann would be overpowered as he returned home in the evening, and spirited off to one of the Israelis' "safe" houses.

It was a classic operation.

At 7:34 two cars were parked in Garibaldi Street. One had its hood raised, and two men were studying what appeared to be a breakdown. On the floor of the back seat was another man, ready to spring out.

By the other car, about thirty yards away, another man was trying to figure out why his motor wouldn't start.

Eichmann usually came home on a bus that dropped him off at 7:40. They would grab him as he walked to his house.

The 7:40 bus pulled up, on time.

Eichmann wasn't on it.

The tension ran high. The men decided to wait for the next bus, thinking Eichmann might have missed the one he usually took. But he wasn't on the next one, either.

Nor was he on the third. Had he got wind of the plans against him?

The agents held a hurried conference. If their cars remained on the scene much longer they would begin to arouse suspicion. This could ruin the whole mission. Still, they had come too far to turn back so easily. A few more minutes. . . .

Then, at precisely eight o'clock, another bus came into view. When it stopped a lone figure got off. As it walked slowly toward the agents they recognized that this was their man.

Silence. They waited for Eichmann to reach the right place.

Suddenly Eichmann was blinded by headlights. Two men tackled him and he let out a single panic-stricken cry. Before he had time to make another sound he was being thrown into the back seat of one of the cars, his head jammed between the knees of one of the Mossad men.

He was bound and gagged. Dark goggles were placed over his eyes so he would not recognize his captors, and would have no idea of where he was being taken. He was covered with a blanket and placed on the floor of the car.

One of the Mossad men leaned over and spoke to him in German: "If you make one move you will be shot."

Eichmann said later that he didn't doubt the seriousness of the threat.

Within an hour of his capture Eichmann lay blindfolded on a bed in a house situated in another part of the city. One leg was shackled to the bed frame. His clothes had been taken from him and he was dressed in a pair of recently purchased pyjamas.

His hosts expected from wartime records to find Eichmann's SS number tattooed in the usual place, just under the armpit. Instead there was only a scar. Eichmann explained that when he was briefly in American hands after the war he had tried to remove the number with a blade.

The Mossad men went through his other identifying features one by one, noting that all matched their records.

To their surprise, and disgust, Eichmann obsequiously cooperated with them. Gone was the arrogance of the SS officer who once had hundreds of men to carry out his commands. Now he was frightened and nervous, at times pathetically eager to help. He told his captors whatever they needed to know.

"My membership number of the National Socialist Party was 889895.

"My SS numbers were 45326 and 63752.

"My name is Adolf Eichmann."

The Israeli agents could barely believe that his ordinary-looking man had been responsible for hundreds of thousands of deaths. Some of them later described feeling almost physically ill. One of their worst moments came when their prisoner began reciting in perfect Hebrew the *Sh'ma Israel*, one of the holiest of Jewish prayers. "Hear oh Israel, the Lord our God, the Lord is one. . . ."

Eichmann explained that he had learned Hebrew from a rabbi.

For a week Eichmann was kept in that room, guarded twenty-four hours a day.

The Israelis never let him out of their sight. They accompanied him even when he went to the toilet next door. The light in his room was kept on around the clock, the only window having been blacked-out with nailed-down curtains. In the garage a car waited, ready for a quick getaway in case their hideout was discovered.

For a week the Mossad men interrogated their prisoner, determined, at Isser's orders, to be absolutely certain that he really was Eichmann.

At times the ex-Nazi came close to panic when he became convinced that his captors were going to shoot him. For a while he refused to eat his food, fearing that it had been poisoned. He insisted that someone else taste the food first.

That long week of captivity was an ordeal for the Israelis as well. Eichmann's presence brought to their minds the nightmare in which their families had died. Even the toughest of them had to leave the house occasionally for a walk. When Isser saw what tension they were suffering under, he ordered them to take turns "sightseeing" in Buenos Aires.

Even so, hardened agents who had killed men in their duties had to hide their heads in cupped hands when tears came forth at unexpected moments.

The agent whose job it was to cook Eichmann's simple daily diet of soup, eggs and boiled chicken with mashed potatoes admitted that she was tempted once to poison the man who had acted as the angel of death to so many of her fellow Jews.

But discipline held, as Isser knew it would. Not for nothing had he carefully chosen his team after studying their records of action under pressure during operations.

When Isser himself looked at Eichmann for the first time (four days after his capture) the captive aroused in him neither anger nor disgust. "All I could think of was how ordinary he looked." Never for a second did he allow his emotions to cloud his judgment on how to execute the next stage—the "getaway."

The El Al plane was due to leave Buenos Aires on May 20, nine days after the capture of Eichmann. Its departure could not be advanced for fear of arousing the suspicions of the Argentinian authorities.

Isser Harel had anticipated that Eichmann's family would not go straight to the police after they realized he had disappeared. If they admitted they suspected a kidnapping, the family would have to explain that Ricardo Klement was in fact somebody quite different. A worldwide hue and cry would certainly be raised if the name "Eichmann" leapt into the headlines. This might result in his immediate execution.

As the Mossad chief anticipated, this was just the way the Nazi's family did react. They called hospitals and clinics in the area to check whether he had been involved in an accident but avoided contacting the police. Instead they turned to friends and sympathizers for help.

Here too, Isser's suspicions proved correct. He thought that other ex-Nazis, who were themselves in hiding, would not lift a finger to help Eichmann. And he was right. Most of them ran for their lives and scattered all over the continent. Some even headed for Europe—just in case the group who had seized Hitler's henchman were also on their tracks. For they knew precisely who the hunters were. Only Israelis would have gone to all that trouble in seeking them out in Latin America.

Eichmann's son Nicolas later admitted: "The other Nazi friends of my father just melted away. Most of them went to Uruguay for safety. We never heard from them again."

Joseph Mengele, another top Nazi on the wanted list of the Mossad, was also discovered to be in Buenos Aires at the time. Eichmann's capture warned him off, however, and the slight hopes that the Mossad team would be able to grab him as well were not realized.

Mengele had good cause to flee. His notorious medical "experiments" on women and children at Auschwitz, carried out without any form of anaesthetic, marked him as a man of particularly sadistic cruelty. It was Mengele who also sorted out new arrivals at the concentration camp, deciding who should die immediately, who should work, or who should be carried off as raw material for his operating theater.

The method of smuggling Eichmann out of the Argentine had been carefully planned well in advance.

An agent was planted in a local hospital supposedly suffering from brain damage after a fake accident. He was visited daily by a "relative" (the Mossad doctor) who told him how to describe his symptoms. The plan was for him to make slow but steady progress.

On the morning of May 20 the patient had recovered sufficiently for his pleased doctors to order his release. They provided him with medical certificates and, at his request, gave him written permission to fly home to his native Israel.

No sooner was the patient released from the hospital than his papers were whipped away from him and Eichmann's photograph and personal details substituted. By this time the Nazi was so submissive that he even signed a document revealing his true identity and declaring that he was prepared to travel to Israel to stand trial there: "I make this declaration of my own free will. I have been promised nothing nor have any threats been made against me. I wish at last to achieve inner peace. I understand I shall receive legal aid."

Later, in Israel, he was to comment:

"My capture was carried out in a sporting fashion and was out-standing for its organization and exemplary planning. My captors took special pains not to hurt me physically. I take the liberty of expressing my opinion on the subject because I have had some experience in police and intelligence matters."

The critical period when Eichmann was to be smuggled past the customs and passport officials, as well as the security network around the airport, was the most difficult in the life of Isser Harel.

He moved his mobile headquarters to a table at the airport staff canteen and sat there all day. The hundreds of soldiers, police, and airport staff who used the canteen would have been astonished to know that the inconspicuous little man was issuing orders and weighing up progress reports from the relay of agents who kept coming and going from early morning to late at night.

At his side, under the very noses of the Buenos Aires authorities, Shalom Dani sat putting the last touches to fake passports and ensuring that the documents brought to him were correctly marked with "official" Argentine Government stamps.

Meanwhile Eichmann was being carefully washed and shaved, and then dressed in an El Al airline uniform. Using a special needle, the doctor in the squad administered a drug designed to blur Eichmann's senses so that he would be totally unaware of what was going on around him, yet would be conscious enough to walk if supported on either side by two men.

The Nazi prisoner cooperated so fully that at one stage he reminded his captors that they had forgotten to put on his airline jacket. "That will arouse suspicion for I will be conspicuously different from the other members of the squad, who are all fully dressed," lectured Eichmann.

Seated in the second car of a convoy of three vehicles, all filled with "air crew," Eichmann was driven to the staff entrance of the airport. As the convoy approached the guardhouse, the men in the first car began singing and laughing loudly. Their driver, visibly embarrassed, explained to the guards that they had enjoyed the night life of Buenos Aires so much they had nearly forgotten they had to fly home that very evening. By the way some of the men were dozing off, the guards joked that they would never be able to fly the plane in their befuddled condition.

"They are OK," said the driver. "They are only the relief crew, so they can sleep it off on the plane." The two men winked at each other. With a grin the guard waved the convoy through. He even pointed out to a colleague the way three men in the back seat of the second car were huddled together with their eyes closed. Clearly Buenos Aires had been very much to their taste!

With Eichmann firmly wedged between them, and supporting him on either side with their arms, two sturdy crew members "helped" him climb the gangway to the plane. There was one frightening moment when an obliging airport official turned a powerful search-light onto the Britannia, lighting up the gangway steps to help the crew.

Eichmann was pushed and pulled aboard and placed at a window seat in the first-class section of the plane. Surrounding him were "crew" members, all pretending to be fast asleep. The captain of the plane aircraft then doused the lights in that area. One by one the other crew members passed through customs and passport control. Everything was going smoothly.

Finally Isser himself presented his documents and climbed aboard the plane.

Everything was ready for takeoff.

Suddenly a group of important-looking officials started running from a terminal toward the plane. Isser and his men stiffened.

Whatever the officials wanted, they were too late. With a roar from its engines the plane was thundering down the runway. In a moment they were airborne.

It was five minutes past midnight.

The atmosphere relaxed a little. The genuine crew members were told who their "passenger" was, and the doctor examined him to make sure that the mild drugging he had undergone was doing him no harm. All was well. Everyone settled down for the twenty-two-hour flight to Israel.

But even now the drama was not over.

The plane's mechanic came originally from Poland. When he was eleven years old a German soldier held a dagger to his throat and then threw him down a flight of stairs. Later he hid in his house when the Germans rounded up all the Jews in his home town and shot them; later still he used the same means to escape being dragged off to Treblinka. Finally he and his family were captured and taken to a work camp. When they got there, the old men and young children were executed. One of the children was his six-year-old brother. He watched him being led away.

Several times the mechanic had been marked for death but had managed to avoid it. On one occasion he had had to stand and watch while the camp commander gouged out the eyes of some prisoners who were caught stealing food.

It was only by a miracle that he survived the war.

Thus, when the plane's mechanic learned that their passenger was Eichmann, he lost control of himself. Only when he had calmed down did the Mossad men allow him to sit across from Eichmann. There he sat, staring at him and weeping silently. After a while he stood up and walked away.

Twenty-four hours after leaving Buenos Aires, the plane touched down at Lydda airport in Israel.

Isser Harel drove directly to Ben-Gurion's office. For the first time in his dealings with the man he allowed himself a little ironic joke.

"I have brought you a little present."

Ben-Gurion was speechless for several seconds. He knew that Isser was on Eichmann's trail, but had no idea he was so close to bringing him in.

Isser had been away twenty-three days. When he got home that night, Rivkah asked him where he had been.

"Somewhere" was the only reply she got.

But she learned more of the story the next day, when Ben-Gurion made a short but momentous speech in the Knesset.

I have to announce that a short time ago one of the greatest of Nazi criminals was found by the Israeli Secret Service: Adolf Eichmann, who was responsible, together with the Nazi leaders, for what they called the "Final Solution of the Jewish Problem" —that is, the extermination of six million Jews of Europe.

Adolf Eichmann is already under arrest in Israel, and he will shortly be brought to trial in Israel. . . .

Ben-Gurion's voice shook with emotion.

As he spoke, the eyes of every man and woman in the Knesset turned to a place in the nonmembers section. Isser Harel was seated there, making a rare appearance in public.

No one needed to be told who was behind Eichmann's capture.

In the moment of his greatest triumph, Isser sat perfectly still. His blue eyes stared straight ahead. He said nothing.

No one, even in private conversation, referred to him as Isser "the Little" ever again.

Jossele

ISSER HAREL WAS FINISHING a speech to one hundred of his top agents.

It was the end of February, 1962, nearly two years after the spectacular mission that brought Adolf Eichmann to justice in Israel.

Now Isser was telling his men about another mission.

"Although we are operating out of our usual range of tasks," he concluded, "this is nonetheless a highly important case.

"It is important because of its social and religious background.

"It is important because the prestige and authority of the Israeli government are at stake.

"It is important because of the human question which the case involves."

The speech was over. Isser's men walked silently out of the briefing room at Mossad headquarters.

If they were perplexed, one cannot blame them. A Mossad agent has to expect danger and difficulty in every moment of his work, but this case was most unusual.

Isser Harel was sending out the elite of Israel's secret service to find a nine-year-old boy.

His name was Joseph ("Jossele") Schumacher, and at that moment he was, without knowing it, at the center of a cultural and political battle with profound implications for the entire state of Israel.

Jossele was born in Israel in March, 1953, to Arthur and Ida Schumacher.

Ida's father, Nahman Shtarkes, was an intensely religious old man. He had lost three toes and an eye when living in Siberia at the orders of the Russian government. One of his sons had been murdered by an anti-semitic gang and the authorities had done nothing. His hatred of the Russians was almost as strong as his religion.

It was Nahman who had convinced his remaining sons and his daughter Ida to emigrate to Israel after the Second World War. Nahman emigrated with them.

Ida and Arthur found that life was rough in the Promised Land. Israel was still suffering in the aftermath of her hard-fought War of Independence. Work, food and money were scarce.

Unable to practice his occupation of tailor, Arthur Schumacher got a job in a factory and Ida worked in a photographic studio. They were desperately short of money and when their first child, Zena, was born they had to send her to live in a village of Hasidic Jews.

In 1953 they had a second child, a boy. His name was Joseph but he soon became known as Jossele.

Jossele they sent to live with his grandparents in the Mea Shearim section of Jerusalem, an area inhabited by the most religious Jews.

Nahman Shtarkes belonged to the sect called Neturei Karta, the Guardians of the Walls of the City. Strictly, fanatically orthodox, the sect refused to acknowledge the state of Israel; its young men would not serve in the army.

Shtarkes and his grandson quickly became devoted to each other, and it was the grandfather's hope to raise Jossele as a strictly orthodox Jew.

Ida and Arthur, however, were more concerned with practical affairs. On one of her numerous visits to see Jossele, Ida suggested that she and Arthur might emigrate to America. It was so difficult to make ends meet in Israel, she explained.

Nahman Shtarkes was horrified.

"Jossele will never leave Israel," he vowed. And thus ended the conversation.

Finally, after nearly five years of struggle and hardship, things began to improve for the Schumachers.

They even managed to buy an apartment near Tel Aviv, and were at last able to bring their children home to live with them. Ida collected Zena from the village where she had been staying and then went to Jerusalem to get Jossele from her parents.

But Nahman Shtarkes had his suspicions. He disapproved of the way Arthur and Ida were becoming modern, secular Israelis. They had little time these days for the full demands of daily prayer and ritual. Worse still, he could not forget Ida's awful threat that they might leave the Holy Land altogether.

After hours of trying, he finally convinced Ida that the boy might benefit from staying a little while longer in Jerusalem.

For a while Jossele remained with his grandparents, but finally Ida went back, begging with tears in her eyes.

"Please, father, give me back the child."

Old Shtarkes relented and, with sadness in his voice, promised to give back Jossele the following weekend. He just wanted a few more days with the intelligent boy he loved so well. On a cold December day in 1959 Ida happily kissed her son goodbye before she got on the bus for Tel Aviv. She spent the ninety-minute bus ride thinking about how wonderful it would be to have her whole family together at last.

Ida was not to see her son for nearly three years.

Nahman Shtarkes had decided to bring Jossele up as a devout Jew, and if he had to take the boy forcibly from his mother to achieve his aim, then he would do just that. The boy would be better off with the rabbis of the Neturei Karta.

When Ida returned to Jerusalem, Jossele had simply disappeared. Her father would not tell her where he had gone.

After weeks of vain pleading with her grandparents, Ida went to the police. They paid a visit to Nahman Shtarkes, but the old man told them nothing.

"To save a single soul is to save the whole world. I will not tell you where the boy is."

A high court order sent Jossele's grandfather to prison until he would promise to release the child from wherever he was hidden.

But this was "no big hardship," as he put it, for an obstinate old Jew who had spent eight years in Siberia. The prison officials disapproved of his actions but respected his religous conviction, and they treated him more like an honored guest than like a criminal.

The High Court, on the other hand, called Jossele's disappearance a "shocking crime." But there was little they could do. The ranks of the Neturei Karta, aided by other extreme religious sects, closed tightly in a protective cocoon. The police spent weeks visiting every religious establishment—schools and synagogues of all kinds—throughout Israel. They searched everywhere and interrogated everyone.

They came up with nothing. Not a trace.

Ida meanwhile told her story to journalists and the scandal burst into the headlines. Mocking cartoons derided the efforts of the authorities to track down the little boy. Every time a policeman issued a parking ticket he had to put up with insulting comments. "Instead of wasting your time giving me a fine, why don't you go find Jossele?"

On police stations were chalked up the three words which enfuriated the forces of law and order: "Where is Jossele?"

Months of hard work by detectives and uniformed men brought no results whatsoever. Jossele had apparently vanished from the face of the earth.

In the spring of 1960 the Jossele controversy took a serious political turn.

Virtually from the founding of the state, there had been a split between the devoutly religious Jews and those Israelis who wanted to run their country like any other modern secular state. They wanted to free themselves from the shackles of ancient rules they regarded as overly rigid and inapplicable in modern times.

The Jossele controversy brought all these disagreements to the surface.

One of the first to recognize the explosive issues involved was Rabbi Shlomo Laurenz, a member of the Agudat Israel party. Agudat Israel was an orthodox religious party but more moderate than the Neturei Karta. Their leadership feared a civil war if Jossele wasn't returned soon.

Rabbi Laurenz traveled around the country, putting pressure on the leaders of the Neturei Karta. Other religious leaders followed his example. They pleaded, argued, threatened.

Nothing happened.

A group of religious leaders went to see Rabbi Amram Blau and his brother Moshe, who were the spiritual heads of the entire Neturei Karta. They appealed to them to be reasonable and give up the boy.

"We know nothing" was the reply they got.

The national leaders, police, and politicians who visited them received the same treatment.

It became apparent that the Neturei Karta were not going to budge. This was the same obstinate spirit in which Jews had chosen to be burnt at the stake rather than give up their religion. They would die before they gave up Jossele.

Police efforts to find the boy continued to prove fruitless. The Jerusalem police chiefs knew when they were beaten.

The prison authorities responsible for Nahman Shtarkes realized that it was futile to keep the old man any longer. His lips remained sealed in defiance; he was unbroken; he was not going to tell them anything.

In April, 1961, after a spell in the prison hospital, he was quietly released on "health grounds."

The old man's supporters now regarded him as a martyr. In the religious quarter slogans chalked onto the walls told of the fury of the inhabitants:

"The Israeli government is as bad as the Nazis."

Military leaders worried because of the proximity of the Mea Shearim, where the Neturei Karta lived, to the Jordanian side of the city. In case of a war between Israel and Jordan, that entire quarter would be easily overrun. It was a weak, undefended link in the Israeli front line.

Summer of 1961, a year and a half after Jossele disappeared. A general election was approaching.

The unsolved mystery of Jossele was now a national issue that threatened the ascendancy of David Ben-Gurion's ruling Mapai party. The Prime Minister relied on a coalition with a number of smaller parties, including some of the religious ones, to stay in power. Because of Jossele the religious groups were questioning their continued support.

It was a delicate situation.

In the end, Ben-Gurion's Mapai party won the election. But his coalition was definitely weakened. Fundamental disagreement on the questions raised by Jossele's disappearance—"Who is a Jew? What is a Jewish state?"—was eating at the unity of Israel.

Young people with a secular outlook began to attack the children of the Neturei Karta as they made their way to prayers at synagogue or at the Western ("Wailing") Wall.

In retaliation young orthodox men threw stones at cars that desecrated the Sabbath by riding through the streets on Friday night or Saturday.

Tens of thousands of citizens opposed to the Neturei Karta signed a petition organized by the "Public Committee to Save Jossele."

In her apartment near Tel Aviv, Ida Schumacher wept for her son. He had been gone two years.

At the end of February, 1962, Ben-Gurion decided that drastic action was necessary. He sent a message to Isser Harel: come and see me.

When Isser arrived he simply sat down across the desk from Ben-Gurion. The two men never shook hands. They never exchanged gossip or inquiries about each other's health. Even when the most momentous subjects were being raised they concluded their dealings in a matter of seconds.

Ben-Gurion looked at Isser and asked:

"Where is Jossele?"

"I don't know," replied the Mossad man.

"Can you bring him to me?"

Ben-Gurion didn't even wait for a reply to his second question. He looked back down at his papers and Isser quietly left. He had his orders.

Isser understood full well the significance of what lay ahead of him. That night he said quietly to his wife, "You know what I think? We have to save the prestige of the country."

It was a rare confidence that he shared with Rivkah. He didn't even tell her what he was referring to: she had to guess.

Isser took the entire file amassed by the police in their fruitless two-year search. He began to study the case from beginning to end and soon discovered that the police were no closer to knowing where the boy was than when they had started.

The challenge of finding Jossele was clearly going to be immense.

The police were well-trained and conscientious men, but they had found nothing.

And Isser knew that the assignment would not be popular among his men.

They were trained at espionage and counter-espionage. They were trained to gather information under perilous conditions and to kill, if necessary, in the course of their duties. At times they, like other secret service organizations, used methods of doubtful morality. They could justify such methods by telling themselves they were fighting enemies of the Israeli people.

But was this little boy an enemy of Israel? Were the religious Jews who protected him a threat to the Jewish state? Even the most irreligious among the agents respected those who carried the observance of their faith to an extreme.

Quite possibly they would feel humiliated by the assignment. They were used to dealing with Nazis, KGB, ruthless men like themselves. Now they were looking among essentially peaceful fellow-Jews for a ten-year-old boy.

Isser knew they wouldn't like it.

But he also knew his men. If ordered to do so they would pursue Jossele as thoroughly as they had pursued Eichmann.

This was what he told them at his speech the next day.

He and some top aides had already formulated a strategy and within a few days of receiving his orders from Ben-Gurion his men were in the field.

They began with an intensive search of Israel. From north to south and east to west they visited every religious school, synagogue and settlement.

Crack agents dressed in the traditional garb of religious Jews and went to the Western Wall to mingle with the crowds of praying men.

Almost immediately they ran into problems: not being religious themselves, these agents had no idea how to go through the prayers. The truly pious sensed what they were up to and showered them with abuse.

The agents left in embarrassment.

Even with setbacks like this it didn't take long for Isser's intuition to tell him that the boy was not in Israel. The strategy shifted accordingly.

His agents were now deployed all over Europe. Some went as far afield as Hong Kong, Japan, South Africa, Latin America.

They did the same kind of surveillance they carried out in Israel. The same kind of surveillance they would have done to catch a spy or a terrorist. In Jewish centers like Golders Green in London, the Pletzl in Paris, the Williamsburg section of Brooklyn, they walked the streets, visited schools, made inquiries.

And frequently they tied themselves up in knots.

On one occasion three agents spent a day parked near a religious school in a tiny community not far from Paris. They peered through binoculars at every child in the school, on the chance that Jossele might be one of them.

At the end of the school day, having decided that their quarry was not among the school children, they prepared to drive off. But the car, a rented one, had a flat tire. And no spare in the trunk.

They were miles from any phone or garage. It was winter and getting colder by the minute.

Suddenly the door of the school opened and a rabbi approached the car. He was timid but polite:

"I see you have a flat tire. Can we be of any assistance?"

Sheepishly the agents followed him into his little school. They had never thought of asking the unwitting objects of their surveillance for help.

They were more worried about being noticed by the French police, for they were strangers to the area and held foreign passports. Worse still, their passports were not even Israeli.

One of the agents said afterwards that they all felt "like nasty bastards."

But the rabbi had no idea of their true identities. He made them hot coffee and arranged for someone from the nearest garage to come and help them. When they left the rabbi invited them back "to have a look at our little school."

Another agent, renowned in the Mossad as an expert executioner, was assigned to keep watch over a Jewish school from the cover of a nearby wood. He complained bitterly about it.

"I felt ridiculous sitting there with owls and bats keeping me company. What was I doing? Tracking down a terrorist? No, looking for a little boy. I felt like an idiot!"

One agent "infiltrated" a group of Hasidic Jews going from Switzerland to Jerusalem so they could bury one of their dead near the walls of the old city. He was quickly found out.

In London a group of ten agents went to an orthodox synagogue for Saturday morning services. They too were exposed as frauds and noisily expelled. The congregation followed them down the street, yelling insults at them. When violence threatened, the rabbi called on the police. Nobody at the station quite knew how to handle the mob of bearded men with their *yarmulkes* yelling about "religious imposters" trying to infiltrate their community.

Finally the ten agents, who had on false beards, were arrested. Scotland Yard intervened, and the men were speedily released.

In other instances the Mossad's methods went to bizarre and almost brutal extremes.

A famous orthodox rabbi living in London was invited to Paris, where a very rich family said they wanted him to perform a circumcision. His first-class air fare would be paid for, and he would receive a fat fee for his trouble.

The rabbi asked only for his expenses, and in total innocence he took a plane to the French capital. There a party of religious Jews invited him to come to a "nice little respectable café" they knew where they could drink a cup of tea and relax a few minutes before the ceremony.

The "friends" took the old man to the red-light district, the Pigalle.

Suddenly two ladies with very short skirts and low-cut blouses came up to the startled rabbi and flung their arms around his neck. One sat on his lap and then posed with thighs in black net stockings wrapped around him.

The Mossad agents took Polaroid photographs of the whole thing. They showed the frightened rabbi the incriminating pictures and told him point-blank:

"If you don't tell us where you have hidden Jossele, we will take these photographs back to London and distribute them to the entire congregation of your synagogue."

In great distress the rabbi cried out: "I don't know anything. I don't know anything."

Finally he convinced them that he was telling the truth. As his "friends" walked away in frustrated anger, he ran after them calling out: "But the circumcision. Don't you want me to do it?"

He returned to London on the next plane. To this day he has a low opinion of the Mossad.

Several months had passed since Isser sent his men out into the field. There were no results. Morale was low among the agents assigned to the case. They knew what a large portion of the Mossad budget must be going into the search for Jossele.

But Isser would not give up what he had begun. He would not go back to Ben-Gurion empty-handed.

Finally, after five months on the case, the break came.

When Isser had had his intuition that the boy was not in Israel, he had spoken to the military censor who has the right to open and read mail passing in and out of the country. He asked the censor to pay attention to all mail going to and from religious institutions in Israel and abroad. If there was anything suspicious, he was to let him know immediately.

Something had been picked up by one of the censors.

A soldier serving in an army camp in the Negev had written a letter to his mother in Brussels. In the middle of the letter, completely out of context, there occurred an innocent-sounding question:

"And how is the boy?"

When the censor showed this to him Isser knew he was on the right track. He called one of his lieutenants and showed him a photostat of the letter.

"The boy is here," he said. "Get onto this lady and our problem is solved."

The Mossad chief began making plans for a trip to Europe.

Meanwhile, more than a dozen agents were sent scurrying to Brussels to locate the woman. She had moved to France but was easily traced to the city of Aix les Bains in the south. There the agents kept constant watch over her.

One morning she went to the local post office and asked to place a collect call to England. She read out the name of the person she was calling as well as her own.

These details were gratefully noted by the gentleman who happened to be standing behind her, waiting to place a call to Paris.

The man was a Mossad agent.

When the woman's call came through, two men sitting in the booths next to her listened to every word she said. They followed her when she left the post office and tailed her when she drove off in her car. She was a fast driver and they were hard-pressed to keep up with her while avoiding being spotted.

The woman reached the outskirts of Paris that night, still tailed by the two Mossad men.

Suddenly, after emerging from a long tunnel, she was gone. Whether she had spotted her pursuers is not known, but she vanished without a trace.

Two of the agents' colleagues in London paid a visit to the man—a rabbi—whom she had called in London. He would reveal nothing and threatened to throw out the agents and call the police. They left, frustrated again.

Isser Harel was rushing to Paris to take personal control of the situation. On the plane he reviewed his dossier on the woman who had given his agents the slip.

She was Madeleine Frei, the daughter of an aristocratic French family. Intelligent and ambitious, she had studied at the Sorbonne and at Toulouse University. In her youth she had worn expensive fashionable clothes and had been known as a great beauty. She led a hectic social life, was courted by dozens of men.

Then came the Second World War.

Madeleine had served in the Maquis, the French underground resistance movement. Here she came into contact with Jews for the first time, and won a reputation for her courage. She chose to participate in the particularly dangerous task of helping to rescue

Jewish children from ghettoes before they could be taken off to the concentration camps. For her wartime exploits she had been awarded a resistance medal.

After the war she married a fellow Catholic and gave birth to a son whom she named Claude.

Then something strange happened to Madeleine Frei. She had a revelation—and determined to become a Jew. She divorced her husband and, with the help of a young rabbi who was in love with her, converted to Judaism. Her son had emigrated to Israel and she was planning to join him.

As Isser contemplated finding this woman again and getting her to lead him to Jossele, he was troubled.

He and his agents were, he knew, treading on dangerous ground. They had been using ruthless and underhand methods to find the boy. Now they were trampling on the convention that each country recognizes the sovereignty of every other.

This could be justified when they were tracking down ex-Nazis, depraved men who were responsible for countless deaths, but if the prey was just a little boy. . . .

Nonetheless, he pressed on with his mission. He was going to find Jossele, and his intuition had told him the boy was in Paris.

On his arrival there, he booked into a small, modest hotel. The rest of that day and far into the night he reviewed the case with his men.

On returning to his hotel in the small hours of the morning, the desk clerk winked at him and asked:

"Enjoy yourself, monsieur? You can always bring her back here, you know. . . ."

Isser was a puritanical man. The desk clerk outraged him.

He checked out of the hotel immediately and moved into the Israeli embassy in the Avenue Wagram.

The ambassador looked forward to having such a distinguished visitor, and had a large room prepared for him at his own home.

To the ambassador's discomfiture, however, Isser insisted on sleeping in a humble iron cot tucked away in a small room at the back of the embassy. He had no use for the niceties of protocol, and anyway, as a former pioneer he was used to sleeping in a simple camp bed.

When his agents heard where the boss was staying they hurriedly moved out of their already-modest hotels and found lodgings in the cheapest rooms they could find.

With more than forty men now in Paris, the group spent all their time trying to pick up the trail of Madeleine Frei. There had been no sign of her since she lost the Mossad agents in a tunnel days before.

She did not keep them waiting long.

One of the agents whose task it was to look through all the Paris newspapers saw an advertisement she put in one of them. Madeleine Frei wanted to sell her villa outside Paris.

Within hours of the ad's appearance she had a telephone call from two Germans who were interested in the house. They asked if they could come and have a look at it. Happy to find prospective buyers so soon, Madeleine readily agreed. She picked up the men at a prearranged location and drove them to her house.

Once inside they slammed the doors and revealed their identities. They were two of Isser Harel's agents.

Furious at having been tricked, Madeleine Frei screamed for help and physically attacked the two agents. They quietly restrained her. One apologized but informed her that she was their prisoner for the time being.

"We are not going to harm you. We will not touch you. Please, sit down. Make yourself comfortable—after all, this is your house. Let us be civilized about it.

"You are not going to leave here until you give us the information we need."

The agents telephoned Isser at the embassy and told him they had the woman in custody. He immediately sent over one of his most valued men.

This was the Mossad's most experienced interrogator, a man nicknamed "the Spanish Inquisitor" even by his friends in the Mossad.

He was the man Harel had chosen to interrogate Adolf Eichmann when Eichmann was first brought into custody.

A stockily-built man with a monotonous voice, he had broken the will of scores of men during his long career.

Now he faced the Frenchwoman.

For hours he questioned her, looking directly into her blue eyes, going over the same ground again and again, trying to trip her up with all the skills in his repertoire.

Not once did she make a mistake. She met every awkward question with the correct answer. Never did she admit that she was in any way connected with Jossele.

This went on for four days.

At the end of it "the Spanish Inquisitor" was ready to quit. He phoned Isser and told him.

"I am convinced we have the wrong person," he said. "She is totally innocent in this matter and knows nothing about the boy."

He and his fellow officers were getting worried about the mistake they thought they had made of keeping a totally innocent woman locked up in her own house. If the French police were told there would be a terrible outcry.

Isser hurried over to the house. He would not accept his agents' word. He wanted to confront the woman himself.

When he got there Madeleine Frei was as adamant as ever. To her Isser was just another bully trying to make her life difficult.

He questioned her for hours. They went through her alibi again and again. It matched perfectly what she had been telling the interrogator.

Isser Harel had always believed that if he really wanted to he could squeeze anything out of anyone.

But there was no squeezing Madeleine Frei. She flung his questions back in his face.

Meeting total failure for the first time in his life, Isser got up and left the room. He had spent hours with the woman. His men, certain that she was innocent, pressed him to leave her alone.

Isser was equally certain she was lying to them. That she did know where to find Jossele. That she was, in fact, the one who had smuggled him out of Israel.

But how would he prove it?

While his men talked among themselves Isser leafed idly through the woman's documents. Her passport was among them. He glanced at it, turning the pages.

Suddenly he stopped.

Calling one of his men over he asked to see the picture of Jossele.

The man produced it. Isser looked at it closely, then looked back at the passport. Then he called all his men over.

"You see this woman's daughter? I did not know she had a daughter. Look carefully at her. Now forget she has blonde curls. Look at her face. Now look at Jossele's face. What do you see?"

The men were dumbstruck. They were looking at two photographs of the same child.

Isser stood up.

"She is the woman," he announced. "Now do your work."

And with that he turned on his heels and walked out of the room. Soon he was back on the road to Paris.

When the Mossad men showed her the two photographs Madeleine Frei turned pale. She knew they had discovered her secret, but she remained defiant.

"Do what you want. You will never find out where Jossele is. You will have to kill me first, and then you will never find out."

The Mossad men, already worried because they had lost face with the boss, knew they had to produce results.

Reluctantly they put into action a contingency plan they had worked out before the interrogation began.

All but one of the agents left the room. The one who remained pulled out a folder. It was Madeleine Frei's dossier.

The agent began reading. He read everything they knew about her. Details of her love-life during her carefree student days in Paris. Things she barely remembered herself.

When he was finished the agent put the dossier down.

"As you see," he said, "we have a full list of your indiscretions.

"Personally, I believe that is your own private business. But your friends in the Neturei Karta might not think so. They might be surprised if we gave them this information. You know how strict they are about such matters. Already they have their doubts about accepting a former Catholic into their ranks.

"This would damn you for all eternity in their eyes." He tapped the dossier with his forefinger.

"We know you smuggled Jossele out of Jerusalem. We know you dyed his hair to disguise him. Tell us where you took him. Tell us where he is. Then we will destroy these papers."

The French woman was silent for several seconds. Then she angrily blurted out: "This is shameful! It's dirty blackmail!"

"I know," replied the interrogator.

"The future of my country might be in danger unless we find this boy. In the streets of Jerusalem Israelis throw stones at one another.

"And I want to remind you of something else. You are a mother, so you know what I am talking about. This boy has a mother too. She loves him as much as you love your son. She has not seen him for nearly three years because of your actions.

"Think carefully of your own sin before you lecture me about dirty blackmail."

Madeleine Frei was broken. The Mossad had found her weak point.

She explained to them in full how the kidnapping of Jossele had been organized.

Some Neturei Karta friends asked her to help them in taking the boy away, and she had devised a plan for doing so herself.

First she sailed for Haifa on her own as an ordinary tourist. On the boat she deliberately befriended a family of new immigrants— a family with an eight-year-old daughter. As they walked down the gangplank together to disembark, Madeleine innocently asked the young girl if she could hold her hand.

The immigration officer assumed that the French woman came in with her daughter. He duly noted this down in his notebook.

In her passport Madeleine had already skillfully changed the name of her son Claude to "Claudine."

Thus when she boarded a plane a week later to fly to Zurich there was no suspicion about passengers "Madame Frei and daughter."

The daughter was Jossele. His hair had been dyed and he had been persuaded to dress in girl's clothing. It was all part of a lovely game his new "aunt" had made up for him.

The plan was audacious, even desperate, but somehow it worked.

For a time Jossele lived in a religious school in Switzerland. Then when the Mossad chase began to heat up, Madeleine and "Claudine" went to France by way of Brussels. It was only when Isser's men began making inquiries among the religious Jews in Paris that Madeleine knew the boy was in danger of discovery. So she flew with him to New York and put him in the hands of a couple in Brooklyn, members of the Setmar Hasidic group.

"He is there now," she quietly told the Mossad agents. "I will give you the address."

September, 1962. Two years and ten months since Jossele disappeared.

A top priority call came for Attorney General Robert Kennedy. It was Isser Harel, calling from Mossad headquarters. In his heavy accent he spoke briefly and to the point.

"My agents are on their way to New York. They have come to take Jossele home.

"Your cooperation would be appreciated."

Kennedy heard a click. The conversation was over.

For several seconds he was flabbergasted. He knew and respected the name of Isser Harel, but why were his agents flying to New York? On whose authority were they carrying out a mission there?

And who, or what, was Jossele?

He immediately contacted the American ambassador in Tel Aviv, who drove to Jerusalem to see Ben-Gurion. He also sent a message to the Israeli ambassador in Washington, Abe Harman. Harman knew about Jossele but had no idea what Isser Harel was up to. Naturally, he too was worried about the serious breach of protocol involved in Harel's mission. He sent off a frantic message to Israel.

The clever Ben-Gurion was not to be dragged into discussing Isser's actions with anyone. When the American ambassador arrived he was received by Ben-Gurion's military secretary Colonel Haim Ben-David. Ben-David was polite and sympathetic; he promised to mention the matter as soon as possible to the Prime Minister, who unfortunately was in a "Cabinet meeting" at the time. He fixed a meeting for later in the day.

Meanwhile, Isser Harel was not to be found. He was "out of touch," as his secretary patiently explained to the dozens of people who were suddenly trying to get in touch with him.

In Washington, Robert Kennedy had gotten hold of a report on the Jossele affair. He confided later to a CIA official that he was utterly astonished when he read it.

The Mossad was sending agents to collect a ten-year-old boy.

What was he going to do about it?

Kennedy was inclined to let the agents do what they had to and leave without a fuss. Isser Harel wouldn't have sent them without some very good reason. And the Israelis were always exceedingly cooperative with US law officers and intelligence agents. Besides, if the Mossad men were already airborne the only way to stop them would be to shoot the plane down.

On the other hand, Kennedy had his own political worries.

There were Congressional and gubernatorial elections coming up soon, and controversy over this action could lose some of the critical Jewish support that Democratic candidates traditionally rely on. If anyone got hurt in the Israelis' operation . . . or if Jossele proved *not* to be at the address they thought he was at, then what?

Kennedy made one more call to find out whether the boy was really at that address. His informant was certain of it.

Robert Kennedy's mind was made up. He would lodge a protest at Isser's high-handed action in the mildest way possible.

In the meantime, the FBI was to cooperate with the Mossad in every way.

Later that day an El Al flight from Tel Aviv touched down at Idlewild Airport in New York. Standing on the runway was a squad of FBI agents with a fleet of cars.

As the passengers got off the plane several men detached themselves from the crowd and went over to the waiting FBI men. They were hospitably greeted.

Within an hour the cars were pulling up outside a humble apartment house at 126 Penn Street, in the Williamsburg section of Brooklyn. Waiting for them was a further party of plainclothesmen.

A group of agents went into the apartment house and climbed the stairs to the apartment of Mr. and Mrs. Zanwill Gertner. They knocked on the door. Mrs. Gertner, bewildered and a little frightened by the sight of so many serious-looking men, invited them in.

Inside Zanwill Gertner was at prayer. Beside him, holding a prayer book, stood a ten-year-old boy with a *yarmulke* on his head and dark side-curls lining his pale face.

In Hebrew one of the Mossad men said:

"Pack your things, Jossele. You are going home."

Ida Schumacher was flown from Tel Aviv to New York to make sure that the boy really was her son. She didn't need to look for a birthmark to know. She flung her arms around him. He whispered that he had missed her.

Within a couple of days of his being found, Jossele stood blinking in the bright sunshine on the runway at Lod Airport near Tel Aviv. The huge crowds who had gone to the airport to welcome the reunited mother and son cheered as they got off the plane.

Sitting in a car a discreet distance from the crowd was a short, unexceptional-looking man with clear blue eyes. Even Isser Harel had come to welcome Jossele home.

He couldn't resist a chance to observe first-hand the results of his success.

Over forty of his top agents had worked full-time on the case for almost eight months. A hundred had been involved at one time or another. Most of the Mossad's budget for 1962 had been swallowed up in the efforts to find this boy.

Isser watched the celebrations for a few minutes and then drove to see Ben-Gurion.

He had already reported back to his boss as soon as he heard that the boy was positively identified. Now he walked into the Prime Minister's office and said simply, "Jossele is back."

There was no immediate reaction.

For a moment he thought Ben-Gurion might, for the first time since he had known him, ask a question or two on how it had been done. Maybe a word of congratulations. . . .

Ben-Gurion said nothing about Jossele. But Isser swears that the old man had a twinkle in his eye as he asked:

"Tell me. And what about the woman?"

The woman today calls herself Ruth Ben David.

After the Jossele affair was over the Mossad offered her a job in their ranks. They knew that anyone who could elude them so long had the makings of a first-class spy.

Ruth rejected their offer.

After moving at last to Jerusalem she married a man twenty-seven years her senior, Rabbi Amram Blau, the leader of the Neturei Karta whose wife had died two years previously.

Today Rabbi Blau is dead and Ruth Ben David has to be grandmother to his fifty grandchildren. They visit her often in the little stone house where she lives by herself. Like other houses in the Mea Shearim quarter of Jerusalem, hers has a sign outside that announces:

"I am a Jew. I am not a Zionist."

Even in that religious community the Rabbi's widow is known as a *frume*—a religious one. She wears black all the time and covers her shaven head with a scarf. She never goes out in the street without heavy black stockings, even in the hottest weather. She prays frequently, and is well known for her meticulous observance of even the minor rituals of her adopted faith.

Among the visitors to Ruth Ben David's house is a sturdy young man who sometimes, when he is on Army duty, carries his Uzi submachine-gun with him. Jossele no longer wears the black clothing and curling sideburns of an orthodox Jew.

But Ruth welcomes him anyway whenever he comes to visit. And perhaps when they are together they reminisce about their days "on the run" in Europe, outwitting singlehanded the best men in Isser Harel's Mossad.

The Six-Day War

ON THE MORNING of June 5, 1967, war broke out in the Middle East when Israeli forces made preemptive air strikes against military targets first in Egypt and subsequently in Syria, Iraq and Jordan.

Within six days, the war was over. Israeli forces had taken thousands of Egyptian prisoners in the Sinai and annihilated numberless armored units; they had advanced to within miles of Damascus, and recaptured the old town of Jerusalem from the Jordanians.

The world was amazed by the swiftness and precision with which Israel had vanquished her numerically and militarily superior opponents. What no one realized was that Israel had been preparing for such a war years in advance. With great care and complete secrecy it had long been gathering voluminous information about the war capabilities of its enemies. Thus, when war finally came, Israel used its superior knowledge to compensate for its military disadvantage.

Much of the credit for acquiring this knowledge belongs to the Mossad. The three stories that follow relate only a few of their exploits—skirmishes in the secret campaign that helped win the Six-Day War before a shot was fired.

Stealing a Mig

IN AUGUST 1966, newspapers the world over carried the sensational story of an Iraqi pilot who safely landed his Mig 21, the most advanced airplane in the Soviet arsenal, at a landing base in Israel. Like all news stories, it stayed in the papers a few days (with constantly shrinking headlines) and was soon forgotten by most people.

Among those who did not forget were military leaders of the United States, France, Britain and other Western powers. They pressed the Israelis for a glimpse of the aircraft, the first to fall into the hands of a nation friendly to their interests.

Nor did the Russians forget the incident. They were furious. It was a heavy blow to the prestige of their security chiefs, who had assured the Kremlin that every Mig 21 in foreign hands was closely guarded by KGB agents. It was also a major military setback. Air Force commanders feared that within months the effectiveness of their front-line squadrons would be seriously diminished. Every Western air force would know the Mig's secrets.

In Moscow and Jerusalem the Russians made ferocious threats to the Israeli government. They wanted their plane back immediately.

The Israelis happily played down the incident. They explained that the plane had arrived out of the blue one day and simply landed. The incident had surprised, embarrassed and perplexed them. They were trying to decide what the proper course of action was.

In the meantime, the Israeli government was "considering" the Russians' request for their plane.

To soften Russian anger they refused all requests—even that from the United States—to have a look at the plane. This "appeasement," as it was called, brought bitter criticism from the military and intelligence communities. The controversy went on for months.

The scandal in Baghdad was made all the worse by the knowledge that Munir Redfa, the pilot who defected, was not just an "unbalanced immature cadet," as announced over the radio. He was one of the country's best pilots, and he had been very thoroughly screened by Soviet and Iraqi security before rising to his position as a privileged member of the military hierarchy.

Munir had first been selected for training in the United States by the American Air Force. After that he went to the Soviet Union for special instruction in advanced jet-flying. Only then was he entrusted with a Mig 21.

He had won the reputation of being one of Iraq's most competent and experienced aviators, holding the rank of deputy squadron leader.

While their governments were making vain attempts to get the plane back, the Russian advisers and Iraqi military chiefs were trying to figure out how Munir Redfa had planned and organized his defection.

Some Israeli sources talked vaguely of how he might have lost his way and been forced by shortage of fuel to land. Later a report was leaked describing how the Iraqi airman had written a letter to the Israelis, telling them he wanted to leave his homeland.

The Iraqis and their advisers quite rightly dismissed these explanations. The pilot's action was no accident. Nor was it simply the impulsive brainstorm of a disgruntled airman. It was espionage, they maintained: highly organized, carefully planned and executed with the utmost in professional thoroughness.

Years passed before Russian intelligence officials pieced together how the theft of the Mig had been planned and executed. But from the start they were certain of one thing: the Mossad was behind it.

They were right.

The desire to get their hands on the Russians' newest Mig was hardly something new to the Israelis. Since its introduction to the Middle East in the early sixties both the Mossad and the military intelligence had been giving this aim top priority.

The Israeli military command had always placed a premium on complete familiarity with every weapon their enemies might use against them in combat. One of the first to emphasize this was

General Dan Tolkowsky, the commander who built up the Air Force in the early fifties. He said again and again that "It is a basic principle of warfare that to know the weapons the enemy has is already to beat him."

Tolkowsky never let Israel's intelligence commanders—both military and the Mossad—forget his dictum. He constantly pressed them for arms information. And the principle he established has remained a central one to this day.

For the Israelis, the information they get is vital in national defense. But they also use it in top-secret barter with the United States. In exchange for the information and weapons they get through espionage, the Israelis demand new equipment which the Americans might not otherwise be willing to give them.

Thus, the Israelis' weapons intelligence is important to the United States military as well. Somewhere in America there are two full squadrons of genuine, fully equipped Russian planes. The American military uses these units, code named TOP GUN, to simulate a real dogfight.

Much of the equipment in TOP GUN has come from Israel. When Prime Minister Menachem Begin said on American television in 1977 that his country played a role in promoting American security, he was referring to this secret cooperation. He declined to elaborate when questioned, but the military leaders in Washington knew exactly what he was talking about.

Today this Israeli policy of obtaining the latest equipment in the hands of their enemies is known as "Electronic Counter Measures Strategy" (ECM).

When Dan Tolkowsky propounded the idea he certainly didn't use that phrase for it. But he did want to achieve the same ends. Particularly important to him in the first half of the fifties was the Mig 17, at that time the newest Russian fighter.

He told military intelligence that "We must by some means or other, and I don't care which, get hold of that plane. . . ."

With the high command pressuring them so intensely, the entire intelligence service concentrated on the problem. It was not easy. How could they get their hands on a plane so zealously guarded?

Various ideas were investigated.

Could pilots be bribed? Would it be easier to try and intercept the plane as it was unloaded at a port in Egypt? Could secrets be obtained by placing an agent on one of the airbases? Could the plane be lured over Israeli soil and then shot or talked down?

As it turned out, the problem was solved for them by a bit of good luck. When the Israeli forces swept into the Sinai peninsula in the 1956 Suez campaign, they found one of the prized Russian aircraft sitting deserted in an abandoned airfield. Its pilot and crew had fled in the retreat and left it, intact, in lordly isolation.

The Israelis had their plane.

Within five years, however, the military bosses were making fresh demands on their intelligence counterparts. Russia had introduced the new Mig 21 to Egypt, Syria and Iraq, and was supplying the plane in increasing numbers. The Israelis wanted to see what their pilots would be up against if they fought another war.

The new commander of the Air Force, Ezer Weizman, began applying the same high pressure that his predecessor Tolkowsky had applied.

The intelligence services went yet again through all the options open to them: bribery, intercepting a plane at its unloading point in an Arab country, planting an agent on an airbase, all the rest of the possibilities outlined in the fifties. None seemed more likely to work than they had originally.

As the Mossad and its military counterparts gave more and more time to the problem, some of the intelligence officers began to think that their best bet might be to persuade a pilot to actually fly a plane to Israel.

They based their reasoning on the simple fact that they knew so much about the pilots, much more than about anyone else in the Syrian, Egyptian or Iraqi military. It is no secret that major military establishments spend a great deal of time and effort monitoring the flights of their enemies. Arabs, Americans, Israelis and Russians all engage in this routine exercise.

Linguistic and other experts spend their entire working lives analyzing tapes of the messages sent by pilots. Whether reporting back to his home base or conversing with fellow pilots during air exercises, each pilot has every word he speaks taped.

In this way a complete dossier is built up for every pilot. Not only do the experts come to recognize his voice, but they note and analyze details of his behavior and personality.

Field agents supplement this information. They find out whatever they can about the pilots: their home lives, backgrounds, military careers and possible weaknesses. Wherever possible they get to know the pilot himself in order to include personal observations in their reports.

In building this kind of dossier the Israelis have a striking advantage that few other intelligence services, if any, can claim. Many of the people who now call themselves Israelis actually grew up in Arab countries like Syria, Iraq, and Egypt. They look and talk like Arabs. They know local accents and regional nuances. Trained in intelligence work, they can more quickly and accurately puzzle out the background and psychological makeup of the pilots who fly in the Arab air forces.

Israel has an added advantage in the frequency with which Arab pilots travel abroad. Often their own countries lack the advanced training facilities they need, and they have to make up for it in the United States, or Britain, or France or Russia. The host countries then have excellent records of the Arab pilots, and they usually find their way into the hands of Israeli intelligence.

Examining the dossiers they compiled on Arab pilots, both Mossad and military analysts conjectured that they might have the greatest chance of success with those pilots who were not Moslems. Christians and members of small sects were a minority in the Arab states, and were perhaps more vulnerable than their Moslem counterparts. These men became the object of intense scrutiny in the intelligence offices.

At the same time every other avenue was still being explored.

For months there was no breakthrough.

Late in 1965 it was decided to ask military intelligence to concentrate on the job. The Mossad was to play only a secondary role.

This decision stung the Mossad. Getting their hands on a Mig was, of course a top professional and military priority, but now it was a matter of prestige.

The Mossad doubled its investigations into the problem.

Experts combed again through their files. More attention was paid to the interrogation records of pilots who, whether in war or in minor skirmishes, had fallen into Israeli hands as prisoners of war.

When they had compiled a list of likely prospects for persuasion, they reviewed the possible methods of approach. This was a critical problem, requiring immense delicacy so that Arab and Soviet counter-intelligence would not be put on the alert. It had to be done right the first time or the entire project could be ruined.

Meanwhile, at official meetings and private parties, the military leaders continued to press their intelligence men:

"Where is the plane?"

Early in 1966 Mossad headquarters got in touch with one of their top agents, operating at the time in the Iraqi capital of Baghdad.

The agent had been sent there on several jobs, but now the Mossad chiefs were giving absolute priority to the job of making contact with an Iraqi Mig pilot. They supplied a list of several potential "victims," and left the rest up to their agent.

The agent was a woman. Born in New York, she carried an American passport but had been working for the Mossad for some time. In fact, her American passport was an advantage in providing a cover when she went into countries where Israelis weren't allowed.

She was lively and intelligent, and she mixed easily in military and political circles wherever she went. She also had the advantage of being beautiful.

As it happened, she already knew, at least by reputation, most of the pilots on the list provided her by the Mossad.

Within a couple of weeks of getting the assignment the American had made discreet inquiries and decided that she knew the right candidate for friendly persuasion. He was Munir Redfa, a Christian who was considered one of the best pilots in the Iraqi Air Force.

She passed on the message to her superiors in Israel. They quickly gave her the go-ahead.

A few weeks later the Mossad agent went along to an elegant cocktail party attended by many of Iraq's high-ranking military and political leaders. Noticing a good-looking man dressed in an Air Force officer's uniform she asked her host who he was.

The host smiled. "That's Munir Redfa, a great pilot. Would you like to meet him?"

The answer was yes.

Munir and the Mossad agent hit it off immediately.

She knew how to turn her considerable charm on and asked question after question designed to draw him out. It did not take long for their conversation to become open and intimate. Soon he was pouring his heart out to his sympathetic listener.

Redfa was a troubled man.

He was an Arab, he explained, and as patriotic as anyone. But at the moment he found himself in violent disagreement with the current war being waged by his government against the minority Kurdish tribesmen in northern Iraq.

The Kurds were a sturdily independent mountain people who had never fitted into the mainstream of Iraqi life or culture. Recently, led by their chief Mulla Mustapha Barzan, they had risen in revolt against the Baghdad government. A vicious war was now in progress against them. The Iraqis were using modern planes and every other sophisticated weapon at their disposal in a bid to settle the Kurdish "problem." They were trying simply to wipe the Kurds out.

Munir Redfa's Mig was only one of many to blast tiny mountain villages with cannon fire, rockets and napalm. This slaughter troubled him deeply.

As a Christian, he explained, he had a particularly strong sympathy for any minority group. But a war of genocide that required him to bomb women and children was a complete outrage.

The pilot even confessed that he had a "sneaking admiration" for the Israelis, who were "so few against so many Moslems."

To all of this the American woman listened sympathetically. She occasionally dropped a comment about how guilty she felt at the war of genocide her own country had waged against the native American Indians. But for the most part she said very little, eager to hear Redfa relieve his tormented conscience.

The pair talked together the entire evening. It was late when Redfa offered the Mossad agent a ride home. As he dropped her off at her apartment he invited her to have dinner with him in a few days. She willingly accepted.

Redfa, she knew, was the right man.

In her next report to Mossad headquarters she expressed her opinion that he would cooperate with them.

In the weeks and months that followed, Munir Redfa and the American woman saw a great deal of each other. Their intimacy grew. Redfa was a happy and dedicated family man with a wife and two children, but with his new companion he could talk in a way that was impossible with anyone else. She was eager and lively— and she understood his torment at flying missions against the Kurds. The subject came up frequently in their conversation, since it constantly troubled him and provided her with an easy route to his deepest confidence. She meticulously cultivated that confidence, knowing that at the right moment she would use it. In the meantime she slowly nourished the idea that Redfa might have an alternative to participating in slaughter.

In July, months after their first meeting, the Mossad woman decided her moment had come.

She suggested that they take a trip to Europe together. He needed a holiday, she said, and after all he did have some leave coming to him. He agreed, and they flew to Paris.

It was there, after two exhilarating days together, that the American woman opened up. She suggested that Munir fly to Israel with her. She had friends there who might be of service to him.

They could make the trip in total secrecy, with tickets provided free. Out of her handbag she pulled a brand-new passport under a false name and nationality.

"You can use this to travel. If my friends can't help you satisfactorily, no one except you, me and them will ever know about the trip. I guarantee it."

Redfa was not completely surprised. He had suspected the American might have connections with some kind of foreign government activity. But the professional manner in which she made her offer . . . and that perfect false passport. Clearly this had all been planned to the hilt.

He knew now that the woman had not been attracted to him solely because he was a pilot.

But he also knew that she was making a genuine offer. He agreed on the spot, and within twenty-four hours he was being given VIP treatment at a military base in the Negev.

A group of Mossad agents went to see him. They didn't waste much time before asking bluntly:

"Will you return to Iraq and then bring your plane with you to Israel? You will be paid handsomely. We will guarantee full protection for you and your family. We will provide you with Israeli citizenship, a home, and a job for life."

Redfa was willing to accept their offer immediately, but worry about his family preyed on his mind.

"I cannot take the chance unless the safety of my wife and children is assured. You know, in Baghdad they hang people. They would hang my wife and kill my children."

The Mossad men smiled at each other.

"We know they hang people in Baghdad. We have personal experience."

They assured Redfa that he would not be required to make his move until his family's safety was unquestionable.

"We will see to that," they promised.

Redfa's mind was made up then and there. Soon after his conference with the Mossad men he received a visit from General Mordechai "Motti" Hod, Commander of the Israeli Air Force. Hod personally went over his escape plan with him, pointing out on a map the zigzag route he would take to avoid radar stations and Iraqi and Jordanian air bases.

"You know how dangerous this is going to be. The flight is 900 kilometers. If your own colleagues guess what you're up to they may send planes to blow you out of the skies. If they don't succeed, the Jordanians may try. Your only hope is to remain calm and follow this route. They do not know it, we do.

"If you lose your nerve you are a dead man. Once you have left your ordinary flight path there is no turning back."

Redfa seemed perfectly aware of this.

"I will bring you the plane," he replied.

During the remainder of his stay in the Negev, Redfa and other Air Force officers reviewed constantly the details of his escape. He was amazed to see that they knew almost as much about the goings-on at his airbase as he did. They knew the names of all personnel, both Russian and Iraqi, and the layout of the entire base. They knew minutely the routine of training flights: long flights on certain days, short on others.

It was on the days reserved for long flights that the Russians ordered extra fuel tanks to be fitted to the planes.

The extra fuel would be enough to get Redfa to Israel. He would have to leave on one of these "long-range days." At various stages of the flight he would make pre-arranged signals to the waiting Israelis. As long as he did this they would know exactly where he was and could be sure that everything was all right.

During his stay at the airbase some Mossad men, eager to impress upon Redfa the danger of his undertaking, told him the cautionary tale of an Egyptian pilot named Mahmoud Hilmi.

Hilmi had defected to Israel early in 1964 with his Soviet-built Yak training airplane. He was protesting, he said, against the war being waged by Egypt in the Yemen. He objected to attacking villages which supported the Royalist cause in that country's civil war.

The Israelis were delighted: they had no use for the plane itself, but the propaganda value of the Egyptian's defection was immense. The Air Force gave him red carpet treatment and he willingly broadcast on the radio about the reasons for his defection.

But Captain Hilmi wanted to travel. He had heard about Buenos Aires, and asked his hosts whether they could find him a job there. The Mossad hesitated to comply with his request: reports reaching their headquarters indicated that the Egyptians had sworn revenge on the pilot—if they could ever get their hands on him. Hilmi laughed off their warnings never to reveal his identity.

"You have more faith in the Cairo secret service than I do. I know them. Don't worry about me, I'll be OK."

Soon he was flying off to Buenos Aires, where the Mossad had found him a job in a civil aviation firm. He quickly made his first mistake: forgetting that Egypt had complete postal censorship, he sent a postcard to his mother from somewhere in Europe. Thus, Egyptian intelligence knew that he was no longer in Israel.

On his first night in Buenos Aires he made his second mistake. At a local Arab restaurant he met a Cairo-born woman to whom he boasted that he had "money to burn." It did not take long for him to unravel before her his entire story. Visibly impressed, the woman took him back to her apartment and invited him to spend the night with her.

He never returned to his hotel room.

In the early hours of the morning, while he was soundly sleeping, the woman slipped out of bed and made a hurried telephone call. Ten men arrived almost immediately and dragged Hilmi to the Egyptian Embassy. Ten days later, as the local Mossad agents reported back to Israel, he was smuggled aboard an Egyptian freighter and taken back to Egypt.

After a secret trial he was executed by a firing squad.

The Mossad men who told Hilmi's story to the Iraqi Munir Redfa had a clear warning in mind: don't leave Israel if you want to stay alive.

Redfa, who had known Mahmoud Hilmi, got the message.

Before he left, General Hod paid him another visit and wished him good luck. Soon Redfa and the woman agent, who had been away for the few days when he was in the Negev, were back in Europe.

They flew to Iraq the next day.

The Mossad kept their word. Soon after his arrival in Baghdad Redfa's son was "taken ill," and his doctors decided that the boy required special medical treatment which he could get only in London.

Arrangements were made for Mrs. Redfa and their other child to accompany him. They went to Iran, where the officials found nothing unusual in an Iraqi pilot's family going to Europe for medical treatment. In Tehran they boarded a plane destined for London.

They never arrived. At a stop somewhere in Europe they left the flight and within hours were in Tel Aviv. They went into hiding under an assumed name.

Now Munir Redfa's challenge began.

Precisely twenty-seven days after saying goodbye to Mordechai Hod in the Negev desert he was taking off in his Mig. Extra fuel tanks were in place for the routine long-range flight he was going to make.

It was late in August, 1966. One of the days on which the Israeli Air Force would be expecting him.

All morning he had had to carry on business as usual, working with men he was never going to see again. He had tried to act as casual as possible, even when he watched the ground crew servicing his extra fuel tanks to make sure they were filled to capacity.

For the last time he had watched the Russian advisors going about their business. Like the other Iraqis on the base, he disliked the Russians. They took all their meals separate from the Iraqis, whom they held in contempt. There was little mixing between the two groups.

It was this resentment of the Russians that enabled Redfa to get his extra tanks filled so easily. Normally one of the Russians had to give his signed approval. But they were all breakfasting and the ground crew were only too willing to take orders from one of their own officers, especially a star like Munir Redfa.

"That's all behind me now," thought Redfa as his jet roared into the sky.

After takeoff he headed toward Baghdad, as was normal on routine flights. Within minutes he was out of sight of the base.

As soon as he knew those on the ground could no longer see him, he cut sharply and headed southwest toward Jordan . . . and Israel. He began following the zigzag course laid out by the Israelis.

It was a terrifying moment for Munir Redfa.

In the next few minutes he might be shot down. If he survived he could never go back to his native land.

He was heading off to a new life in Israel, the land of the enemy as far as his friends were concerned. They would condemn him as a traitor, he knew. They would try to kill him even if he made it to sanctuary in Israel.

With an angry crackle his radio came to life. Frantic orders came through from the base to return. He kept going. Again the message came, but this time telling him he would be shot down if he didn't return at once.

Redfa turned his radio off.

He knew that at that very moment the Russians might be sending planes up—piloted by his friends—to shoot him down. They might alert the Jordanians, whose air space he was approaching, and ask them to intercept him.

Redfa shuddered. King Hussein's pilots had a good reputation.

But there was another problem worrying the Iraqi pilot as he escaped over what was now "enemy" territory.

That American girl. He was more attached to her than he had realized. Of course, he loved his wife and children, and would never leave them. Only on the assurance that they would be safe had he undertaken to fly his plane to Israel.

But the Mossad agent understood his anguish and his worries so well. True, she had used Redfa to get what she—her bosses— wanted from him. But when he confronted her in Paris, telling her that she had aroused his deepest emotions only for political purposes, she had looked him straight in the eye.

"All right. But spies have emotions too."

And besides, she had risked her life by going back with him to Baghdad after their secret trip to Israel.

Nothing prevented him from walking up to the first policeman they saw and denouncing her as an Israeli spy. She had trusted him, literally, with her life.

And now she was getting farther and farther away as she headed for Israel. She had been compelled to stay behind for reasons she would not explain. Munir knew that sooner or later, if she stayed there too long, she would come under suspicion: his friends had seen him in her company often.

She had promised that she would be heading for the frontier, and safety, within minutes of his arrival in Israel.

But how did he know for sure? Something could go wrong, she might be delayed. . . . If she was caught, he knew what she would have to endure. Hanging would be a relief.

Munir forced himself to concentrate hard on his flight plan. He was still over Jordanian territory and still potentially in danger. Only a couple of minutes and the Dead Sea would be in sight.

Hundreds of miles away Israeli radar picked up the lone aircraft flying at the prearranged altitude in the correct flight pattern. Minutes later a squadron of Israeli Mirages was in the air to meet Redfa and escort him across the border.

When Redfa saw them his heart quickened with excitement and

fear. He went through the agreed maneuvers to identify himself and suddenly the Mirages were flying alongside him. For a moment when they were coming straight toward him he couldn't believe they would be able to react so fast. Now he knew he was safe. He was with his new countrymen. The landing at the Negev air base went perfectly.

For several days Munir Redfa walked around in a daze. He remembers feeling only tired and depressed, and it was a week before he smiled again.

A Mossad agent whose job it was to protect him in the months ahead told him that his Mig had been given a nickname.

Munir asked what the nickname was.

"007," replied the agent. "You know, like the secret agent you see in the movies."

Then with a mischievous grin the agent added, "Maybe they should have called it 'Miss 007'."

Redfa blushed and smiled at the same time.

Today Munir Redfa leads an uneventful life as an Israeli citizen. Few people know his new identity, or where he lives. He was given the promised reward for bringing his plane to Israel and has an ordinary job.

The Iraqis branded him a traitor, as he knew they would, but he insists it isn't true. He flew his plane to Israel, he says, for humanitarian reasons: his act was a protest against the war of genocide waged against the Kurds.

The people on whose behalf he protested are no longer being bombed. After being betrayed with promises of peace (promises made by Henry Kissinger, among others), they were forcibly resettled in the desert areas of the southern part of Iraq.

Munir Redfa does not see much of the American woman who initiated his flight to Israel. She did escape, and they did meet once when she was on leave. But their paths diverged once she was safely in Israel. He had his family, and she had her work.

Certain employees of the Iraqi and Russian government would desperately like to know her identity. They continue to this day to try and discover who she is.

It is one of the Mossad's most closely guarded secrets.

Eli Cohen
Master Spy

IN 1939 THE JEWISH COMMUNITY of Palestine (the Yishuv) and the
Zionist movement internationally were outraged by the British
government's White Paper outlining its policy for the future of
Palestine. Britain would support gradual independence for the
Palestinian state but would limit the immigration of Jews to 75,000
for the first five years. After that, any immigration was to depend
on approval by the Palestinian Arabs and the Arab states.

At the Twenty-first Zionist Conference, held in Geneva in
August 1939, the general mood was for active opposition to the
British.

That mood was to be short-lived: a few days after the conference
ended, Hitler's armies invaded Poland and war broke out. Over-
whelmingly the Yishuv declared its support for the British war
effort against Nazism, and made efforts to cooperate with them fully.
They contributed technical skill in a number of fields, including
intelligence, and tried, initially with little success, to set up their
own fighting force.

In the spring of 1941, however, with General Rommel's forces
advancing steadily toward Egypt, the British took full advantage of
the Jews' offers of military assistance. The Jewish Army, the
Haganah, set up a special strike force called the Palmach to carry
out special operations. Even the Irgun, an extremist group organized
to retaliate against Arab terrorist attacks, lent its cooperation.

The military situation improved in the second half of that year,
but at the beginning of 1942, Rommel again advanced toward the
Egyptian border. There was a real possibility that Palestine would

be invaded. Again the Jewish forces set aside their disagreements both with each other and with the British, and organized and recruited against the likelihood of invasion.

That likelihood was forestalled in autumn of 1942 by the decisive victory at El Alamein.

With the Germans no longer a threat to Palestine, the British began taking a harder line against the Jewish settlers there, whose political aims worried them. They began confiscating arms even from the Haganah, which had fought with them from the beginning of the war, and attempted to restrict political activity. Anti-British sentiment was aggravated by the apparent indifference of the British to the destruction of European Jewry, reports of which became more frequent and more urgent through 1942 and 1943.

In this climate of hostility extremist groups initiated active and violent opposition to the British. One of the vanguards of this movement was the Lechi group, led by a scholar named Abraham Stern, which had split from the Irgun in 1940. The Lechi remained anti-British throughout the war.

Stern was captured by the British in February 1942 and executed immediately; his group was thereby effectively destroyed. But members continued to carry out desperate attacks on the British, and in January of 1944 were joined by the Irgun. The leadership of the Irgun had changed in 1943 and had abandoned their policy of cooperation for one of "revolt against the British conqueror."

The revolt reached its height of extremism on November 5, 1944. On that date, two young Lechi members named Eliahu Beit Zuri and Eliahu Hakim stalked and shot the British Minister of State for the Middle East, Lord Moyne, outside his home in Cairo.

The assassination brought forth a universal outcry. British and world opinion were outraged. In Palestine and Egypt, Jews, Christians and Moslems condemned the act. The Yishuv, including the Irgun, cooperated fully with the British police in rounding up those associated with the Lechi.

In Egypt, the Jewish population of some 300,000 worried about the effect the assassination would have on its already troublesome situation. Throughout the thirties and into the forties, the clashes between Moslem and Jew in Palestine had generated growing animosity in Egypt toward the Jewish population. Thus when the Zionists sought help from the Jewish community there, they were indignantly refused.

When an agent named Ruth Klieger visited a leading Jewish

merchant at his home, she was lectured: "It is better for Jews to be quiet and keep out of the public eye." She was told that dogs would be turned on her if she tried to get their help again.

When the two young Lechi men who had assassinated Lord Moyne went on trial, however, their behavior made a deep impression even on some of those who had opposed them most strongly. Foreign journalists reported with admiration their dedication and bravery. They frequently interrupted the legal proceedings to make political speeches, claiming that their act was a patriotic duty and that they had turned to violence as the only way to win their country's freedom. Repeatedly the two men accused the British government of "abandoning thousands of Jews to their death" in Nazi concentration camps by not allowing them to emigrate to Palestine.

Even Arab nationalists sympathized with the pair, roaming through the streets carrying placards demanding the release of "the killers of Moyne." The Chief of British Security declared: "I never saw captured men who looked less beaten than these brave, arrogant, brutal and heartless young fanatics."

Nonetheless, the two assassins were condemned to death by hanging. Their sentence was carried out on March 22, 1945. The two condemned men carried their bravery to the very last minute of their life. On the scaffold they sang the anthem *Hatikvah* (Hope), which would later become the Israeli national anthem. With the noose around their necks they refused hoods, preferring to face death with their heads uncovered.

The drama of the execution profoundly moved many Egyptian Jews, whatever their religious or political beliefs. For some it was a crucial turning point in their attitude toward Palestine and Zionism.

One such Jew was a twenty-year-old Alexandrian named Eliahu Cohen.

Eli Cohen was born in Alexandria's Jewish quarter on December 16, 1924. His parents, Shaul and Sofie Cohen, had emigrated to Egypt from Aleppo, Syria. Shaul made his living selling ties, handcrafted from silk imported from Paris, to rich customers. The family got by, but with eight children to feed and clothe they did not live extravagantly.

Eli, like his brothers and sisters, was brought up strictly as an orthodox Jew. Unlike them, he observed his faith meticulously. While his brothers were skipping their prayers and spending Saturday afternoons with friends, Eli was at the synagogue. During religious festivals he was always to be seen worshipping with his elders.

Eli excelled in school and won a coveted scholarship to the French Lycée. He was a brilliant pupil, especially in mathematics and languages, and gained an early fluency in both Hebrew and French. During playtime he preferred reading or working at his lessons to joining in games. He also studied the Talmud, learning enormous tracts by heart. He had a spectacularly good memory, which he loved to test. Often he would sit on the balcony of his apartment and write down the license numbers of the cars in the streets below. Then, handing the list to his parents or one of his brothers, he would recite every number without making a mistake.

"Eli was always first class in every subject," said one of his school friends. But he never aroused the jealousy or resentment that often attaches itself to such "high achievers." He was an excellent athlete, and went every day for a swim in the Mediterranean; afterwards he would go for long runs along the beach and easily outdistanced any companions who tried to keep up with him. In class he would always help his fellow pupils by passing his notes around, or letting them read what he had written during an examination.

For Eli's bar mitzvah his parents gave him a Kodak box camera, and photography became his new obsession. He wandered around the city taking photographs which he would carefully mount in his scrapbook. He read dozens of books on photography and became an expert at developing and printing. Every spare minute of his time he spent in the darkroom.

Because of his scholarly inclinations and his deep interest in Judaism, Eli was sent first to the Maimonides School in Cairo and then to the Midrash Rambam, a center of Talmudic study run by Moshe Ventura, the chief Rabbi of Alexandria. There too he proved himself a star pupil.

At the same time he was fascinated by the way of life of his fellow Egyptians, Jew and non-Jew. He would walk around Moslem areas with his camera, talking to people and taking their picture. He had no trouble getting along with everyone he met.

But Eli was, by choice, a loner. He had few good friends among his classmates, seeming to prefer his own company or staying at home with his family.

One possible reason for this was his family's financial position. His parents were rarely (if ever) able to give him pocket money, and during holidays he took odd jobs to help balance the family budget. Every penny he earned he gave to his parents.

During Eli's teens his greatest interest switched from religious subjects to mathematics and physics. As a result he gave up his plans to become a rabbi, and determined to go into science instead. This decision was deeply regretted by the rabbi who had taught him, who said simply: "He has the brains of a genius. He could have become one of the great Talmudic scholars."

When war came to Egypt in 1940, Eli acquired a new hobby: weapons. He was particularly fascinated by different kinds of airplanes, and would paste illustrations of them into a scrapbook. When the Germans flew over on bombing attacks aimed at destroying the British rear lines of support, he would ignore pleas to run for shelter and would stand outside identifying the aircraft. His attempts to photograph dogfights ended, sadly, in failure: his little Kodak wasn't up to the task.

One of his classmates remembered Eli during one of the air raids which took place while they were at school:

"He was always calm, always reassuring. He would turn to the frightened little ones and speak to them soothingly, telling them not to be worried. He would lead them to shelter, and then go out again and, totally oblivious to his own danger, just stood there watching the aerial battles. Eli seemed to be devoid of any fear for himself. He was very strange to us. . . ."

But war had other, more momentous ramifications to claim Eli's attention now.

In the spring and summer of 1942, with Rommel's division advancing toward Cairo and the Allies in retreat, a strong pro-Nazi sentiment grew up in Egypt. Coupled with the desire to throw off British rule, this provoked turbulence and political unrest.

Eli, though a religious Jew, considered himself a full-blooded Egyptian and sympathized with the nationalist, anti-British cause. He even joined in demonstrations against the foreign masters—an activity that brought stern warnings from his parents. Like most of the older generation of Egyptian Jews, they did not want to attract attention to themselves. This meant, among other things, avoiding any participation in the struggle going on in neighboring Palestine. Eli was aware of that struggle, but it seemed to have little to do with him. He was an Egyptian; Alexandria was his home. What went on in Palestine did not concern him.

The trial and execution of Lord Moyne's assassins changed all that.

Eli felt a bond between himself and the two young terrorists. They were almost the same age as he, and all three shared the name of the great prophet Elijah. The courage with which they faced death opened his eyes to the significance of their cause, and prompted him to seek an active way of expressing his sympathy with the Zionist cause.

He did not have to wait for long.

For several years there had been an Egyptian branch of the Mossad Aliyah Beth, the organization set up in Palestine to smuggle immigrating Jews past the British authorities. Set up and organized by Ruth Klieger, the group used ships, trucks, even camels for its smuggling activities. Eli had done some work for the group, acting occasionally as courier. This was part of his activity in the Egyptian Jewish youth movement, the Hacherut.

By 1944, however, the chiefs of the Haganah intelligence service had decided to expand their network in Egypt. With the end of the war in sight they had to look forward to the resumption of their own full-time struggle for independent statehood. The increase of anti-Semitic feeling in Egypt necessitated a stepping-up of the drive to get Jews out of the country. They also wanted to get their hands on some of the vast stockpiles of weapons amassed in Egypt by the Allies.

More generally, they needed information. Cairo was the British headquarters for the Middle East, and therefore the best place to learn what the British plans were for the area. The attitude of the Arab leaders had also to be investigated: what were their views on the establishment of a Jewish state in Palestine? What would they do in the event that a Jewish state *was* established?

The man they chose to organize and run the expanded operation was a top agent named Levi Avrahami, a native-born Palestinian. Avrahami was sent to Egypt in the spring of 1944 under cover as a British officer.

The first place he visited was the home of an Egyptian socialite named Yolande Gabay. Yolande came from a wealthy family of Alexandrian Jews; she had lived in Paris and had acquired Western ways. She was not a Zionist, but she did enjoy the thrill of acting as a spy. Most important to Levi Avrahami, she had innumerable contacts in the highest echelons of Egyptian military and political life.

Soon the two had rented a villa outside Alexandria and were using it, disguised as a health resort for Allied soldiers, as the base for their smuggling operations.

After the execution of Lord Moyne's assassins Eli went to work for Levi and Yolande's underground network with a new dedication. No longer simply a courier for them, he took on more important— and more dangerous—jobs.

To facilitate the emigration of Egyptian Jews to Palestine, the Grunberg Travel Agency was set up with the sole purpose of procuring visas, exit and police permits, and income tax releases. Officially these were denied to Jews.

Eli had the responsibility of greasing the palms of local officials to obtain their "cooperation." Using his mastery of languages— which by now included Italian and German as well as French and Arabic—he bribed both embassy officials and the local Egyptian authorities. With money in their hands they were far more willing to provide documents or look the other way when smuggling operations were going on. Many Egyptians even became friends with Eli after his displays of good will in the nightclubs of Cairo and Alexandria. To them, Eli was a Jew but he was also a good Egyptian.

Through his work for "Operation Goshen," the code-name given to the smuggling network, Eli helped send thousands of Jews to Palestine. From 1945 to 1948 he worked tirelessly at his appointed task.

In the meantime, Eli himself was coming under the pressure that afflicted all Egyptian Jews. In 1946 he enrolled at Cairo's King Farouk University, where he studied electrical engineering. This was a rare achievement, as anti-Semitic feeling was on the increase everywhere, including the university.

At the same time he took a job as book-keeper in a firm of wood importers. His family, like almost all the Egyptian Jews, were feeling economically the results of the growing anti-Semitism.

Early in 1947 the situation worsened yet again as the British, unable to deal adequately with the Palestinian problem, turned it over for consideration to the United Nations. In May of that year the UN General Assembly convened in a special session to consider the problem, and in November voted to partition Palestine into two states, one for the Palestinians and one for the Jews.

The vote aroused new waves of anti-Semitic feeling. In Egypt as elsewhere there was already talk of a war that would strangle the Jewish state in its infancy. Among the civilian population there was an increase in mob violence directed against Jews. At King Farouk University students and professors alike overtly expressed their anti-Semitism.

Eli's friends begged him to stay away for his own safety, but the idea angered him. He protested that he was "as good an Egyptian as any other. I demonstrated against the British." Eli would not accept that his fellow countrymen were suddenly turning on him. On one occasion his friends had to restrain him physically from facing a group of demonstrating Moslem students. They might have torn him limb from limb. Another time he was not so lucky, and received a bad beating from members of the Moslem Brotherhood, a religious and nationalist group that worked hard to promote anti-Jewish violence.

Even when confronted with such terrifying and widespread violence among his own countrymen, Eli remained as patriotic an Egyptian as he always had been. In the summer of 1947 he tried to prove his patriotism to the authorities in a most unusual way.

At this time, in theory at least, Egypt had compulsory military service for all its young men. Normally when a Jew was called up he would try to bribe an official and get himself an exemption from service. Many conscription officials would call up all the young Jews they could, knowing that a bribe would surely be coming their way.

Eli Cohen beat them to it. He volunteered.

His action caused considerable confusion in the ranks of the military bureaucracy: who had heard of a Jew volunteering for the Army? In the end he was rejected because he would have divided loyalties.

The activities of the Grunberg Travel Agency, which Eli worked so hard for, continued to smuggle hundreds of Jews each day out of Egypt. But Eli himself remained defiant.

He stayed on in Egypt and led as normal and active a life as was possible now for Jews. He continued his studies at the University, even though the threat of physical violence forced him to study at home. In the spring of 1948 he and the few other Jewish students took their exams in a separate room from the rest of the students with armed policemen to guard them.

Eli registered the highest marks in his class.

When David Ben-Gurion stood up in the Tel Aviv Museum and announced the independent statehood of Israel on May 14, 1948, the combined Arab armies launched their promised war on the newborn country.

In Egypt the Jews were subjected to new hardships. Hundreds were arrested without reason. Property was confiscated and special taxes levied. Many jobs were declared open to "Egyptians" only. Eli was forced to leave the university.

Jews were now being openly murdered and robbed in the street while the authorities pretended not to notice. Instead they demanded that the Jewish communities prove their loyalty to Egypt—which was in many cases far stronger than their loyalty to Israel—by contributing heavily to Egyptian war charities.

The war ended in an Israeli victory. Armistice talks began in January 1949, and by July the last agreement was signed.

But ironically, Israel's victory meant further troubles for the Jews in Egypt. Egypt had been the first to sign an armistice agreement, and had been allowed by the Israelis to withdraw her encircled forces—among whom was the young commander Abdul Nasser.

Stung by their humiliation, the Egyptians launched new waves of violence against the Jewish population. Scores of Jews were killed and their homes pillaged.

This in turn brought about an intensification of emigration efforts.

In 1950 Eli's family left for Palestine. He arranged all their travel plans and got them the necessary papers. Refusing to accompany them, he promised to follow shortly.

Eli did not see his family for another six years.

Against the opposition and hostility of the university authorities he enrolled once again at King Farouk University, determined to finish his studies. Eli did not stay enrolled for long. Finally and unequivocally expelled, he worked at a variety of odd jobs and devoted himself to helping his fellow Jews emigrate to Palestine. Of the 300,000 who had been living in Egypt at the beginning of the 1948 war, less than a third were left by 1951.

In that year another top Israeli agent went to Egypt to direct the espionage and emigration effort. His name was Avraham Dar but he worked under the cover of John Darling. One of his first tasks was to recruit idealistic young Egyptian Jews to do serious espionage work.

Naturally, one of his first recruits was Eli Cohen.

Another was a twenty-four-year-old Olympic athlete named Marcelle Ninio. She was on friendly terms with many Egyptian army officers, whom she met at parties given by her wealthy socialite friends. Marcelle and Avraham Dar became lovers, and she helped him find other recruits.

Five of them, including Eli Cohen, were sent to Israel for a crash course in basic intelligence and sabotage techniques. For three months they studied there, seeing no one except their instructors, and then were sent back to Egypt.

When they returned they came under the command of an experienced agent named Captain Max Bennett. Born in Cologne, Bennett had the advantage of looking like an Aryan. He was even uncircumcised. His parents had moved to Palestine when Max was a teenager and he had immediately joined the Haganah. After receiving his spy training he had gone on a major mission to Iraq, where he directed the emigration operations for some time.

When his cover was blown by an Iraqi counter-intelligence agent, Bennett narrowly escaped with his life

After acquiring a new cover in Germany, Bennett was sent to Egypt where everyone knew him as Emil Witbein, a salesman of artificial limbs. He sold large quantities of his wares to the Egyptian Army and became good friends with many of the high-ranking officers, who were touched by his concern for wounded veterans. They didn't realize that their friend was relaying everything they told him directly back to Mossad headquarters.

For some reason Bennett was forced to change jobs, and by the time the young Egyptians returned from their training in Israel he was a consultant for the Egyptian branch of the Ford Motor Company.

At first the hard-nosed Bennett complained bitterly at having to use "amateurs" to carry out complex and dangerous missions. But they did their work well. The stream of military intelligence to Mossad headquarters exceeded all expectation, and Operation Goshen was sending thousands of Jews to Palestine.

Eli Cohen had been trained as the espionage group's radio operator and did his job perfectly. No transmission ever had to be repeated when he was working the radio. Mossad headquarters frequently sent congratulations to him and his co-workers.

At the same time, political changes were going on in Egypt which would, indirectly, bring their successful espionage operations to a dismal end.

In July 1952, General Muhammad Neguib led a military coup that overthrew King Farouk, abolished the monarchy, and established a republican government in Egypt. The new government began almost immediately to step up its anti-Israeli policies. It reinforced its blockade of the Suez Canal against any shipping to or from Israel. Terrorist attacks against the Israeli population increased.

At the same time, developments on the international scene began to worry the Israelis. After the overthrow of General Neguib by Lieutenant-Colonel Gamal Abdul Nasser in the winter of 1954, both the American and British governments became increasingly friendly with Egypt. The British agreed to pull their troops out of the Suez Canal zone, thus ensuring that the blockade of Israeli shipping would become complete and unchallenged, and to equip the Egyptian Air Force with new planes. In the United States, Secretary of State Dulles was urging President Eisenhower to adopt a pro-Arab policy.

The head of Military Intelligence in Israel at the time was Colonel Benyamin Gibli, who had been one of the judges at the informal "court martial" of Meir Tobianski in 1948. Gibli became convinced that the new developments in Egypt's relations with the western powers put Israel in grave danger. He decided that ordinary diplomacy was inadequate in combating the threat, and devised his own plan for direct action.

The plan was simple, ruthless and completely illegal. The Mossad's agents in Egypt would be used to blow up American and British installations in Cairo and Alexandria. These acts of terror would then be blamed on either Communists or extreme Moslem groups, and would create a strong anti-Egyptian sentiment in Washington and London.

The operation was to be directed by two ex-Army men, Mordechai Ben Zur and an agent who went under the name of Paul Frank. Frank had worked in Egypt under the guise of being an ex-SS officer. He was so successful that he had developed a close friendship with men like the Egyptian Navy commander and Interior Minister. The ex-Nazis who were living in Egypt and advising the government trusted him completely.

When Frank told his team of young Egyptian Jews what their assignment was, he met at first with considerable resistance. They were Egyptians as well as Jews. The idea of killing indiscriminately their own countrymen outraged them, and they also feared that such a campaign would have political repercussions for Israel.

But Colonel Gibli in Tel Aviv insisted that his orders be obeyed. And obeyed they were. The young men and women went ahead and planted bombs in the United States Information Service libraries both in Cairo and Alexandria. Other devices exploded in the mailing room of the General Post Office. Centrally located restaurants were also hit.

Whether because they doubted the propriety of their actions or simply because they were inexperienced at sabotage, the team of young Egyptians soon made a mistake that led to their downfall.

One of them, Philip Nathanson, fell into the hands of the Cairo police, whose efforts to identify the bombers had proved fruitless. Nathanson had run from a movie theater with his jacket ablaze. The police grabbed him and put the fire out, and discovered in his jacket pocket an eyeglass case full of explosives.

They took Nathanson into custody and searched his apartment. There they found a vast array of documents and homemade bombs. In a photographic darkroom nearby they discovered prints and negatives of bridges, military installations and other likely targets for sabotage.

For days Philip Nathanson underwent grueling torture at the hands of the Egyptian police and counter-intelligence officers. For days he refused to talk, sticking to his original story that he was a Communist taking orders from a secret cell of Moscow-trained spies. It was only when they told him his mother was in custody and would be shot that he broke down and confessed everything.

The authorities, armed with a full list of Nathanson's accomplices, began rounding up the other members of the group.

Because of her excellent contacts, young Marcelle Ninio evaded capture for a while. But her inexperience enabled Egyptian counter-intelligence men to follow her before they actually took her in. Worried and uncertain of what to do, she went finally to the apartment of Max Bennett, the top agent who had overall responsibility for Israeli intelligence operations in Egypt.

When the Egyptians burst into Bennett's apartment they caught him with his radio transmitter assembled, ready to make a report to Tel Aviv. His fears about working with "amateurs" had been fully justified.

Bennett, like Nathanson, was tortured ceaselessly for days. Unlike Nathanson he refused to crack. Finally, fearful that the torment would break him, he bribed a prison guard to bring him a razor blade. The bribe was half a boiled chicken which his wife had sent him.

In a hastily scrawled note he begged his wife to marry again and asked that a tree be planted in his name in Israel. Then he slashed his wrists and died on the floor of his prison cell.

Like Marcelle Ninio, Eli Cohen managed for a time to evade arrest. Eventually, however, they caught up with him. But he had been arrested once before, in 1952, and was expert at resisting interrogation. So expert, in fact, that he managed to convince his interrogators that he was completely ignorant of the spy ring. Eventually they released him.

Both Avraham Dar (John Darling) and Paul Frank got wind of the roundup before they could be caught and went underground. They managed to escape from Egypt undetected.

The other members of the group, eleven in all, did not fare so well. Throughout the summer of 1954 they were brutally tortured and interrogated. Marcelle Ninio tried twice to take her own life, and succeeded the second time in throwing herself out of a window while her interrogators weren't looking. Doctors saved her, however, and she underwent further torture.

Finally all the ring members were sufficiently broken in body and spirit to confess the truth about all their activities. They told the Egyptians how they had been recruited and trained by Mossad and military intelligence agents; how they had spied on their native country for over two years; and how they had been brought down by the campaign of terror designed to discredit Egypt in the eyes of the western democracies.

At their trial in the autumn of 1954, the group members cooperated fully in the hope that they might be leniently sentenced. They claimed that they were mere pawns in the hands of their Israeli masters. Marcelle Ninio was the only exception: she remained defiant and proud throughout the court proceedings, in spite of the danger she faced.

Marcelle and a student named Robert Dassa received fifteen-year jail sentences. Philip Nathanson and one other youth were sentenced to life. Other group members got lesser terms.

But two of them, Samuel Azzar (a school friend of Eli Cohen's) and Dr. Moshe Marzouk, were condemned to death by hanging. The sentence was carried out on January 1, 1955, outside the Bab-al-Halek prison.

Standing in the crowd of 200 mourners that day was Eli Cohen. He watched silently as Marzouk and Azzar were dressed in the traditional condemned man's uniform of black shirt, red trousers and purple cap. As the caps were placed over his companions' heads he said a prayer.

Then they were dead.

It was the second time he had mourned young Jews who had been hanged for the crime of fighting for Israel.

The sabotage campaign and its ensuing catastrophes created a scandal in Israel known as the Lavon affair, after the Defense Minister Pinchas Lavon, who was subsequently held responsible for it. Careers were ruined, and Ben-Gurion came under severe criticism. The specter of unjustifiable illegality again haunted the Mossad, which was widely blamed for the ill-conceived mission.

To make matters worse, it was discovered that Paul Frank, the crack agent who had helped direct the mission, was a double agent. When he left Egypt he was promoted and sent to Germany. There it came to light that he was secretly in contact with one of his former Cairo friends, Admiral Soleiman, in spite of having been ordered at all costs to avoid seeing anyone he had known in Egypt.

Brought back to Israel ostensibly for a "routine briefing," he was arrested and tried for treason. During the trial he revealed that he had betrayed the mission to the Egyptians and received 40,000 Deutschmarks. It also turned out that during the Lavon affair inquiry in Israel he had given false information; this had led to the blame's being put unfairly on the shoulders of Pinchas Lavon, who was forced to resign as a result.

Paul Frank was sentenced to twelve years in prison. It was one of the Mossad's blackest days.

In Egypt the disastrous sabotage operation resulted in yet another campaign against the Jews, this one more relentless than ever. President Nasser's official newspaper *al-Jumhuriyah* demanded that "World Jewry" be exterminated as the Nazis had so nearly succeeded in doing earlier.

The remaining Jews, who now numbered less than 45,000, fled the country using the Goshen underground network. Other foreigners, including Catholics, Armenians and Copts, sold up their possessions and also left (many by courtesy of Operation Goshen).

In Alexandria, Eli Cohen continued to operate as a spy. He still had his Israeli-supplied radio equipment, and he sent Tel Aviv every bit of information he could collect.

One of the most alarming developments he reported on was the increasing influence in Nasser's government of ex-Nazis who had been given sanctuary in Egypt.

The German presence in Egypt was nothing new. Many men from Rommel's Afrika Corps had stayed there after the end of the war. Thousands more had fled there from Europe, confident that in the anti-British climate there they would be given sanctuary. To hide their true identities these men often took Arab names and sometimes even became Moslems.

Soon they had worked their way into positions of power and influence. Former Gestapo officers took responsibility for reorganizing Nasser's State Security Cadre, the intelligence and internal security service.

Hitler's personal guard commander and Warsaw Gestapo chief Leopold Gleim (now called Ali Nacher) directed the torture of Eli Cohen's friends after their capture in 1954. He was an acknowledged expert on the subject. Bernhard Bender (now Colonel Ibn Salem) was Gleim's boss; earlier he had been a top aide to Heinrich Himmler.

A system of internment centers based on the concentration camp model was set up under the direction of Joachim Daemling, a former SS major and Gestapo chief in Dusseldorf. Eli Cohen had been a guest at one of these camps when being interrogated about the 1954 sabotage attacks.

Little wonder that a West German trade union leader complained: "Nasser's Egypt is a breeding ground for new Nazis."

The situation reached its final crisis after the Suez Campaign of October 1956, when Israel (together with Britain and France) invaded Egypt. Nasser's spirit of vengeance intensified and made life even more miserable for the 45,000 Jews remaining in Egypt.

The Jews were increasingly and forcibly isolated in their ghettoes. Hostages were taken and locked away in prison, and collective fines imposed. Synagogues, as well as Jewish schools and hospitals, were closed down; the use of Hebrew, even in prayer, was prohibited. Jewish doctors and other professionals were not allowed to practice, and often their property was seized. Cafés and restaurants put up signs saying: "No Jews or dogs allowed."

All Jews were required to carry yellow identity cards—a stricture harkening back to the Middle Ages and to Nazi Germany.

In the weeks following the Suez Campaign, Operation Goshen worked at a new frenzy to get Jews to emigrate to Israel. Some 10,000 left the country in that period. Those who resisted emigration were mainly older Jews who couldn't bear to leave the country of their birth.

In November Eli Cohen was once again arrested. As he sat in his prison cell Eli was certain that he would be executed. He had been working actively for the Zionist cause for years; it was inevitable that his activities would come to light.

But throughout his three weeks in prison Eli maintained the same presence of mind that had saved him during his first two periods of interrogation, and somehow he managed to convince his interrogators that he was a Zionist in belief only. They could uncover no evidence of any Zionist activity on his part.

But he would, he was told, be expelled from Egypt nonetheless. And once again he staggered the hostile authorities by defying the example of his fellow Egyptian Jews: he asked for an extension to stay there longer.

The authorities angrily refused: he was to take the next available ship leaving from Egypt.

On December 20, 1956, Eli Cohen found himself aboard the *Msir*, a Red Cross refugee ship docked in Alexandria. He carried one small suitcase and the meager sum of Egyptian pounds allowed him under the currency regulations for expelled persons. His passport had a stamp in it saying "Not valid for return to Egypt."

The ship sailed to Naples, where its passengers disembarked to await the ships being provided for them by the Israeli government. Because there were so many emigrants there was a long wait for ships. Eli spent weeks in a dingy hotel room in Genoa; but in spite of having to wait, he later said, he felt "decidedly lighter in spirit."

Finally a berth became available for him on an Italian freighter called the *Felipe Grimoni*. The ship set sail from Naples at the beginning of February, and on February 12 it arrived at the port of Haifa.

Thousands of Jews had emigrated to Israel through Eli Cohen's activities in Egypt. Now he was joining them.

But his greatest work was yet to come.

2

Like all new immigrants at the port of Haifa, Eli received his papers declaring him an Israeli citizen. Yet citizenship alone did not make his first days there any easier. At the age of thirty-two, he felt himself a stranger in his new land.

In Egypt, writing a letter to Israel was a crime punishable by death. So Eli had not written to his family in the six years they had been there, and he had no idea where they lived.

He did manage to learn his brother Maurice's address in Ramat Gan, a suburb of Tel Aviv, and went there. Maurice wasn't home but a neighbor directed Eli to his parents' apartment in the district of Bat Yam, built on the sand dunes to the south of the city and inhabited largely by North African and Egyptian Jews.

In Bat Yam, Eli paused at the end of the road where his parents lived in a modern white concrete building. It was named "Road of the Martyrs of Cairo"—after Eli's friends who were now dead or locked away in Nasser's prisons. The name would be a constant reminder to Eli of the past he had so recently left behind.

Eli's homecoming was bittersweet. His parents were overjoyed to see him, and asked a multitude of questions about what he had been doing. But his youngest brother Abraham, twenty years his junior, looked up at Eli blankly and asked:

"Who is this man?"

Even to the rest of the family Eli was something of a stranger. He had never been one to show his feelings openly either to friends or family, and long years of working underground in Egypt had reinforced his natural secretiveness. The questions his family asked received curt, uninformative answers. Clearly he did not want to talk about what he had been doing in Egypt.

Maurice Cohen said that "Eli was like a closed book. Never once did he tell us about his work as an espionage agent. We knew nothing from him. . . . He kept his thoughts locked up like a banker keeps his wealth in a strong-box."

Eli went through a long and difficult period of adjusting to his new home. Israel puzzled and disappointed him in a number of ways.

Still a deeply religious man, he was shocked by the irreligious outlook of many Israelis. Eli's Zionism was idealistic at heart, and the revelation of any shortcomings in his fellow Jews came as a trauma to him. It outraged him that there were Jews who committed crimes and deceptions—yet spoke the language of the Bible. So many of them seemed to pay no attention to the Sabbath or to the major holidays—yet they were Jews living in the Jewish homeland. Eli could not understand this.

He also came up against the prejudice which European Jews have for those of Middle Eastern descent. Being a dark-skinned Egyptian he had personal experience of this prejudice, and it alarmed and upset him. The problem still taints Israeli society today, but for an idealist like Eli, devout and dutiful, it was particularly troublesome.

Eli's other problems were more personal ones. At thirty-two he had reached an age when most men have families, or well-launched careers, or both. He had neither.

He shared a room with his eleven-year-old brother, and had to rely on the financial support of his family, who could barely afford it. The heroism of his past exploits meant nothing here, for no one knew about it. His early promise seemed to have come to nothing.

Confused and depressed, Eli found solace in learning. His under-ground work in Egypt had left him with little time for study, and he aimed to make up lost ground. He learned modern Hebrew and Greek, and worked at perfecting his German and Italian. His origi-nal love for mathematics and electronics came back and he worked his way through a number of textbooks in both fields. In a corner of his parents' apartment he set up a darkroom and resumed his photography.

But still he was unsettled. His brothers told him proudly of their experiences as soldiers in the Israeli Defense Force and he listened silently, knowing that he could not share in the triumphs they felt. Having lived so long entirely on his own, he felt himself a foreigner among the intimacies of domestic life.

He spent several months hitchhiking alone around Israel.

It was only at the end of 1957, nearly a year after his arrival in Israel, that he was offered a job. Not surprisingly, the job was in the Ministry of Defense.

This was no accident. Israeli's intelligence forces knew far more about Eli's work in Egypt than his family did, and they had quickly marked him out as a suitable recruit. Even so, they gave him time to adjust.

Eli's job was in counter-intelligence. It consisted of studying Arab newspapers, translating them into Hebrew, and analyzing them for any signs of policy changes. He was also to write analyses of the personalities of Arab policy-makers based on newspaper reports and on his own knowledge of Egyptian psychology. Eli ex-celled at his job but, as might be expected of someone whose training was in undercover work, he was soon bored by it. He couldn't stand the uniformity, the tedium of office life. After a while he began studying marketing and accountancy to occupy himself in his spare time. But after a year or so of the desk job his restlessness caught up with him. He went to his superiors and told them he wanted to see action again.

Their response was typical. Though Eli had all the makings of a first-class agent, the Mossad (and other Israeli intelligence depart-ments) followed a strict policy of not accepting volunteers for field work. The policy had been laid down by Isser Harel, and there was no getting around it. Eli was told firmly, "We don't want any adventurers."

The rejection deeply offended Eli Cohen. It seemed a slap in the face: had he not risked his life in Egypt working for the state of

Israel? Had he not given the years of his youth to intelligence work?

Feeling humiliated and unappreciated, Eli left his job. With new zeal he threw himself into his business studies and gained a diploma in record time. Soon he had a place working as an accountant in a chain of food stores. If he couldn't rise in the intelligence business, then he would simply try something else.

Here too Eli excelled at his work. He was soon made an inspector and toured the country going from store to store and supervising financial operations. Even in this line of work he maintained his secretiveness. He was friendly with everyone but kept his distance: none of the other employees formed a deep relationship with him. Everyone did note his driving ambition, however, and expected him to move up in the company.

Early in 1959 Eli met an Iraqi woman named Nadia at the soldiers club in Tel Aviv. She was a nurse at the Hadassah Hospital—a tall, dark beauty with deep brown eyes. Not one to stand on ceremony, she told him she would like to see him again. Less than two weeks later, while walking together on the beach at Herzliya, the couple decided to marry. They set an August date for the wedding, and celebrated the event with a feast of traditional splendor.

By luck they won a trip for two to Eilat, the resort town at the northern tip of the Red Sea. There they spent their honeymoon, swimming among the lush coral formations for which the Red Sea is famous. Not long afterwards they moved into the apartment their families had helped them to buy.

Eli had settled down and felt that he had started doing something positive with his life in Israel. He was advancing steadily in his work and being paid well. He and his wife were planning a family. He became an enthusiastic football fan and even tried his hand at being a yachtsman. Eli Cohen was a well-adjusted Israeli citizen.

Early in 1960, Eli was walking in a street near his home in Tel Aviv when he ran into a man he had known while working for the Ministry of Defense. The two had never become good friends but they were on amicable terms with one another. Eli's former colleague suggested that they stroll down the beach and have a chat together. Though he still bore a grudge against the Ministry of Defense, Eli accepted the offer.

The conversation soon got around to Eli's departure from the Ministry. The man had never known why Eli had left, and asked him bluntly. His anger resurfaced as he answered the question.

"I was just wasting my time," he said. "What was the point of trying to pick up information from Arab editors when I can do the job a thousand times better and get the real information in person?"

The Defense employee listened sympathetically to Eli's complaints. He understood what moved Eli to leave, he said. The two men talked about other matters like football and the cost of living—ordinary chitchat—and then parted company. Eli was glad for an opportunity to air grievances that still bothered him.

He thought nothing about the incident until a few weeks later, when, while Nadia was out of the house, he had a visit from his former colleague. The man confided that his real name was Isaac Zalman and revealed to Eli his true identity: a senior officer in the Mossad. Would Eli care to go for another stroll on the beach? Eli, perplexed by this mystery, said that of course he would.

As they walked along the beach, Zalman told Eli that the Mossad had watched him ever since his arrival in Israel. They knew of what he had done in Egypt and wanted him to work for them again. But the period following immigration to Israel could be a difficult one, and they decided to make sure Eli found his feet, as it were, before they considered him for any kind of intelligence work. After that they had to test him in a desk job—standard procedure with all prospective agents.

The agent continued: "We turned down your original request to act as an agent for a number of reasons, the most important of which you know. We have been watching you since then, and now we think you are ready for consideration as an agent.

"If you are ready to serve in the intelligence service your application will be considered."

Zalman remembers Eli's response.

"He was so moved that for several seconds he could not reply. Then with total sincerity he told me that he was ready with all his heart to serve his country in any way demanded. He was ready to act as an agent in any Arab country. He was worried, I remember, about becoming an agent in Europe: he felt that as an Arab in Europe he would be out of his depth. Of course, I told him that in the Mossad he would have to do what he was ordered. He understood completely."

There followed long hours of discussion and cross-examination. The agent, whose nickname was the Dervish, took his time in sizing up his new recruit. He was in no hurry. Having worked as an active agent in a terrorist group before 1948, he knew the importance of understanding the men you employed for your most dangerous work.

First the Dervish questioned Eli on his reasons for wanting to join. Was he happy with his wife or did he view the job as an excuse for getting away from home? Did he like the idea of adventure? Did he see the job as a series of exciting spy missions?

Eli responded honestly and frankly to all these questions. He and Nadia were very happy together. They were expecting their first child soon and looked forward to having a large family. He had no desire to get away from home—but would do so gladly if ordered to.

Eli didn't know it, but the Dervish knew his answers before he even spoke them. The Mossad had been making discreet inquiries among Eli's friends and family for months. They knew of his happy marriage and the child he was expecting. They also had a wealth of other details about Eli's personal and professional life, and about his attitudes towards Israel.

Thus, when Eli said that his only motive in getting to join the Mossad was a desire to serve his country, the Dervish could be certain that he was telling the truth.

There followed further questioning about the nature of the job. Did Eli know that he would never be able to tell anyone—not even his wife—what his job was? That the salary, though higher than what he was getting at the moment, would never amount to much? That he would have to accept harsh and total discipline?

Eli was ready for all this. With something of a sly smile he said, "After all, that is what I was doing throughout my youth. *You* know that as well as I do, I should think!"

The Dervish asked in detail just how much the Egyptians had known about Eli's activities as a spy. Whatever the case, said the Dervish, Eli could never return there. But even if he went to some other Arab country they might have received his dossier from the Egyptians—and a step into the country might be his death warrant.

Eli was frank enough at this point to admit that his job in commerce bored him. But boredom alone wouldn't suffice to make him want to risk his life. Again he stated that he wanted only to serve his country.

The Dervish was satisfied. Eli had passed his preliminary test.

Next he underwent a battery of medical and psychological tests, administered by a team of doctors and scientists. Since the early 1950s the intelligence forces had been building up a system of investigation and analysis that would amass all the data needed for knowing how an agent or soldier—enemy or Israeli—would operate. The data was then fed into computers and analyzed. Because of the size of the Mossad, such screening processes were essential: with so few agents they could not afford to take chances on any of them. The tiniest personality flaw would be ample grounds for rejecting an otherwise excellent candidate.

Thus, despite his long record of brilliant service, Eli Cohen had to pass through the most rigorous testing procedures.

At the end of it, the Dervish told him: "You have been given a first-class rating. You may, if you wish, join the Mossad."

Eli Cohen was back at work.

The Dervish explained to Eli the terms of his employment. He would receive full salary from that day, even while he was training. All agents underwent the same training, even those (like Eli) with previous undercover experience. The Dervish continued: "At the end of the training period you will have the right to change your mind about working as an agent. This will always be true: you can quit any time you wish with no hard feelings. Do not regard our relationship as a Roman Catholic marriage. Divorce is allowed— and it is easy. The only condition we insist on is that you do not tell a soul about the true nature of your job. The slightest suspicion that you have broken this pledge of secrecy will mean instant dismissal."

True to his instructions, Eli told Nadia nothing of his new job. He said that he had given up the accountant's job for work in a "commercial branch" of the civil service. Nadia suspected that there was more to the job than that when she asked Eli questions about it and only got the vaguest of replies. But she knew not to press him. Even when he told her he had to leave their home for several months of special duties she did not question him.

Eli now began an intensive six-month course in the techniques of his new trade. Throughout his training he lived in an apartment in Tel Aviv rented by the Mossad as a training center (and used for that purpose to this day). He was not allowed to leave the apartment without permission, and usually went out only for an evening stroll in the company of the Dervish.

Throughout the spring and summer of 1960, Eli studied the entire Mossad curriculum. Experienced sabotage experts taught him how to make explosives and time bombs from the simplest of ingredients. They took Eli to army camps and showed him how to use different explosive devices in blowing up bridges and installations.

Combat instructors showed him the techniques for fighting an opponent unarmed. Others taught him how to use a wide variety of small arms; they were not content until he had passed as a first-class marksman. He learned to identify instantly the various makes of Western and Soviet arms, ships and planes, and was also trained as a burglar. He learned how to pick any kind of lock or safe silently and speedily.

Techniques of gathering and analyzing data formed an important part of the curriculum. Eli became a master at encoding and decoding messages. He had to be able to take to pieces a miniature radio set and repair it; he learned how and where to conceal it when working in a hostile country. The old-fashioned but still highly effective techniques of using invisible inks, and the way they could be used in messages hidden in ordinary-looking letters, were all part of his training. His knowledge of photography was brought up to date by tutelage in the use of microfilm. Again and again he was tested by experts to assess his acquisition of these skills.

Eli constantly amazed his instructors with his sure and quick grasp of all that they taught him. His phenomenal memory—conditioned by memorizing tracts of the Bible and license-plate numbers in his youth—astonished everyone.

At the end of his six isolated months a final report on the new recruit summed him up succinctly: "He has every quality, in abundance, needed by an agent working in the field."

With his basic training done, Eli went on to two weeks playing a peculiar kind of "game" in the streets of Tel Aviv. Eli would be followed by two or more of his fellow recruits (called "shadows") and would move from point to point trying to identify them. Having done that he would then try to give his shadows the slip while not changing perceptibly his behavior pattern. This is an incredibly difficult skill to master, and Eli spent weeks at it.

Finally the roles were reversed, with Eli becoming the tracker while other recruits tried to give him the slip. After that he went through the same exercise with experienced agents. Being in a friendly environment—the broad tree-lined avenues of Tel Aviv—might have led to a certain casualness, but the instructors constantly maintained an alert tension in their recruits. It was hammered home again and again that recruits might one day save their very lives through their mastery of the techniques of spotting a shadow. The ability to track without being noticed might lead them to a man whose assignment it was to kill them.

Perfection in these skills was essential. The new recruits practiced it until it had become an automatic part of their behavior.

The recruits never saw each other except at a distance, when they were playing their tracking games in the crowded streets of Tel Aviv. All of them were kept under the strictest discipline during training. Not only were unaccompanied walks forbidden, but the men could not see or make contact with their families.

In the course of Eli's training, there grew between him and the Dervish—whom Eli now called by his first name, Isaac—a close friendship. This was a heart-felt bond between the two, but it was also a tactical necessity. Senior men knew that the future efficiency and morale of a field agent, living a lonely and dangerous life in a hostile city, could well depend on the trust he had in his links with the "head office." If sympathy and mutual respect had not grown up between the two men, then Eli would have been given a new supervisor.

There was one more important test for Eli to pass before he could be certified as ready for top-priority field work. The test was carried out with the unwitting cooperation of a French businessman named Marcel Cowan. Born in Egypt but now living in Provence, Cowan went for a business trip to Israel in the late summer of 1960. To his consternation, soon after he arrived in Tel Aviv his passport disappeared from his hotel room. Frantic, he informed the police and the French consulate, who issued him with a temporary passport so he could go on a planned trip to North Africa.

But in the crowded streets of Jerusalem, Marcel Cowan spent hours walking like any other tourist. He loved the religious shrines, the historic sites, the clothing and souvenir shops.

Cowan explained to shopkeepers that he lived near Marseilles, but had grown up in Egypt—thus his fluent command of both Arabic and French. His fluency enabled him to talk with anyone and everyone.

Back at his hotel Cowan told the receptionist that he was thinking of emigrating to Israel and was looking for commercial contacts in Jerusalem. Eager to be helpful, the clerk showed the Frenchman those cafés where businessmen normally had their mid-day meals. He even gave him the names of friends in the Civil Service who might be of use to him.

Armed with this information the tourist had lunch that day in the Vienna Restaurant. Being friendly and extroverted, Cowan was soon deep in conversation with a stranger sitting at his table. They got on so well that the Israeli—who turned out to be an official in a government ministry—invited Cowan to dine at his home that night.

Among the other guests that evening was an important banker, to whom the tourist immediately warmed. He explained his thoughts about moving to Israel and asked dozens of questions about regulations concerning the transfer of capital, interest rates, and other business matters. The banker, naturally eager for a new customer, invited Cowan to see him the next morning. They spent hours in discussion, not only about Cowan's personal banking arrangements but about the economic climate of the country in general. They spoke so long that the banker had to let his guest out the back door: it was lunchtime, and all the staff were out of the office. The Frenchman promised to call again soon.

In the days that followed Cowan paid similar visits to dozens of merchants and businessmen, asking their advice about finding an apartment, choosing investments, getting legal and financial advice.

When he finally caught the train back to Tel Aviv, Marcel Cowan knew as much about Jerusalem, and about business affairs in Israel, as any businessman who had lived there for years. Certainly he had established valuable contacts, such as the banker who looked forward to seeing him again.

The banker was to be disappointed. Cowan never returned.

When he got to Tel Aviv Cowan immediately went to a small apartment just off busy Allenby Street in the heart of the city. Inside he was greeted warmly as he threw his passport on a table and resumed his real identity: Eli Cohen, Mossad agent.

The Dervish sat Eli down at the table and opened a large dossier. Inside were dozens of photographs showing "Marcel Cowan" and his new friends in the Holy City. There was also a neatly typed list of all his activities, right down to an account of the money he had spent in cafés and souvenir shops.

For several hours the two men studied Eli's own account of his movements, comparing it with the one in the dossier. Eli noted that the agents who followed him had missed the name of the banker he had met. He added with a faint smile: "Well, I see there's no point in trying to cheat on my expense account!"

When the real Marcel Cowan returned to Tel Aviv, there was a message asking him to pay a call at the local police station. There he was solemnly handed his passport. "Be more careful next time," he was admonished. "Keep your travel documents on your person, and not lying around in your hotel room."

Marcel Cowan still speaks with awe about the efficiency of the Israeli police.

The two recruits whose assignment it was to shadow Eli Cohen and take photographs of him with miniature cameras were congratulated by their instructors. They failed only in one point, when they missed Eli's long talk with the banker. They admitted losing him just that once.

As for Eli himself, he passed this test of his ability to adopt a cover with high marks. The Dervish, in his official report on the exercise, said among other things that "This agent has a multi-sided personality with a quick, intelligent mind. He has the ability to mix with all sections of society and to merge in any environment he finds himself in.

"His facility for speaking easily in several languages is a great asset, and his calm under any pressure and ability to make rapid decisions in the light of changing circumstances indicate that he is likely to be a highly successful agent for the project we have in mind for him."

At this point Eli had no idea what that project was. It was September of 1960, and he had been given his first leave to go home since he started his intensive training. The visit was a joyous one, for it was the first time he had laid eyes on Sophie, his recently-born daughter.

The leave was short, however, and soon the apprentice was back at work—this time in the Arab town of Nazareth. Armed with a false identity, Eli was introduced to Sheikh Mohammed Salmaan as a student at the University of Jerusalem who wanted to study the Moslem religion. He had already learned a great deal in his native Alexandria, but now the trainee spy got down to a serious study of Islam. He not only learned major pieces of the Koran by heart, but knew exactly how to behave when reciting the five daily prayers of Islam.

To perfect his guise, the student visited mosques all over Israel on Fridays when the Muezzein called the faithful to prayer with his traditional words:

"There is no other God but Allah, and Mohamed is his Prophet."

Together with his "co-religionists," Eli bowed and prayed. Soon he felt perfectly confident that no uncertainty or awkwardness would betray his cover as a Moslem even under the greatest strain.

Back in Tel Aviv, Eli's instructor had a surprise for him. "Today we are having a holiday. I am going to drive you to the Syrian frontier." They got into a jeep and headed north toward the Golan heights.

From news reports Eli knew that for several weeks shells from Syrian gun emplacements overlooking the settlements of the upper Galilee had been bombarding the kibbutz of Tel Katzir. Property and crops had been destroyed and several farmers wounded or killed.

Finally the Israeli army had taken action. One night under cover of darkness the crack Golani brigade crossed into Syrian territory and silently made its way toward the artillery posts dug in on the peaks of the Tawafik Hills.

They were not discovered until they were right on top of their target. In a fierce battle that raged until dawn, the Israelis killed dozens of Syrian soldiers and destroyed their gun emplacements. Then they blew up over fifty of the village's stone houses.

Their punitive raid over, the Golani unit brought back large quantities of captured tanks, armored vehicles, and a wide variety of light and heavy guns.

The Dervish showed his pupil these assembled spoils of war and discussed with him some technical features of the Syrian equipment.

"But we have not come for an armaments class. I have brought you here for two reasons. One is to explain how the Golani brigade captured this heavily defended artillery base so successfully despite fierce resistance. They knew the precise position of every single gun. They knew exactly how many men were to be found there, and how they were armed. They knew all possible routes by which reinforcements might arrive, and how long it would take them to reach the area.

"We placed all this information in their hands. Their victory was rooted in our intelligence reports. The second reason for coming here is more to the point as far as you are concerned. There are going to be more battles in this area. We can be certain of this. In the future, the outcome of such battles may depend on you.

"You are going to work in Syria."

Eli could not know it, but the decision to send him to Syria had been made months before. His instructors saw that he was an agent of the highest quality, fit for the most important and exacting assignment. His familiarity with Arab ways made him a perfect candidate for undercover work in one of the Arab countries.

At the time, the two greatest dangers to Israel lay in Egypt and Syria. Since 1958 the two countries had been unified as the United Arab Republic. They had a joint military command, and a large number of Egyptians went to work as "advisers" in Syria (much to the resentment of many Syrians).

Nasser was still smarting from Egypt's defeat in the 1956 Suez Campaign, and felt no urgency about getting into another war with Israel. But the Syrians were eager for battle and had built up a powerful force on their border with Israel. They had two full divisions on the Golan Heights and their Migs frequently crossed into Israeli air space. Eli Cohen had seen the destruction wrought by their bombardment of Israeli settlements and farms.

The Syrians had their own reasons for wanting a war with Israel. For several years their government had been highly unstable, with one military coup following another in rapid succession. The present junta saw Israel as an ideal scapegoat to divert the nation's mind from its economic and political woes. The Russians took advantage of this belligerency by giving Syria massive amounts of weaponry.

Ben-Gurion pressed Isser Harel to strengthen his intelligence-gathering apparatus in Damascus. He stung the Mossad chief with an implied rebuke: "Indifference is the worst enemy of national security."

Isser knew that he had, in Eli Cohen, a solution to the problem.

At an early stage Eli's superiors thought of sending him to Damascus under cover as a South American or Spaniard. But because he looked so much like an Arab and spoke Arabic so well, they chose that as his cover. Syrian society is much more self-enclosed than Egyptian, and it would be difficult enough to get Eli accepted under any pretense.

At the same time it was decided to send Eli to Damascus entirely on his own. There were two reasons for this. One was the smallness of the Mossad. With so few personnel to spare, a large network in any one place was a luxury they could not afford. This was not long after the Eichmann operation, which had tied up many agents for a period of many weeks. It had reminded the Mossad of the limitations on its resources.

The other reason they decided to send Eli on his own was that he seemed to operate best that way. He had shown this throughout his training, and especially in his exercise as Marcel Cowan in Jerusalem. He was used to it from childhood: in Egypt he had worked largely by himself. Most likely Eli would be in least danger that way: he would never fall victim to a partner's indiscretion or mistake, but would stand or fall by himself.

As the Dervish discussed Eli's assignment with him, he learned that Eli agreed with his superiors' decision. Had Eli felt misgivings about it, the plans could have been revised. The Mossad does not expect agents to follow orders blindly but to question, criticize, and make suggestions. Of course, in conditions of battle an order must be followed. But up to that point everything is subject to debate.

Almost immediately after his return from the Syrian frontier to Tel Aviv, Eli began an intensive period of study. He had a crash course in Syrian history, economic development, government, geography and topography. Because the Syrian dialect of Arabic is different from the Egyptian he had learned as a child, a number of teachers (including a Damascus-born professor of linguistics) went to his apartment to coach him. He listened to Syrian radio stations day and night both to soak up the correct pronunciation and to keep himself up to date on current affairs.

A miniature movie theater was installed in the apartment and experts showed him films of Syria, including sequences of Syrian Army units and military installations. Much of this material had been taped from Damascus television broadcasts, part of the Mossad's efforts to monitor every broadcast from every Arab nation.

As if his crash course in Syria and Syrian Arabic weren't enough, Eli also had to learn everything he could about Argentina. He followed a similar course of history, politics, geography; he brushed up his Spanish and learned as well as possible speak it with an Argentine accent.

Puzzled by this extra assignment, Eli asked the Dervish what its purpose was. The Dervish told him that he was going to spend time in the Argentine before going on to Syria. Eli was upset by the news. He wanted to start his real work—in Syria.

The Dervish answered him sharply:

"Consider yourself lucky. Most agents only get their new identity at a hurried conference in an airport toilet and have to learn everything in a few hours. You have two months."

In fact, the Mossad was stalling for time: they didn't want Eli entering Syria while large numbers of Egyptians were still there. But they didn't tell him that.

Eli worked at his lessons from early morning until late at night. Quite deliberately the Mossad instructors kept him totally isolated so they could further assess how he would stand up to the strain. He stood up very well, but at times he looked wistfully out of his window at the crowds filling the streets below.

"I am like a ghost among lost men," he remarked one night. But he made no other complaint. When one of his instructors reminded Eli that he could quit at any time, he showed not the slightest sign of weakening.

Meanwhile, Eli's superiors were biding their time, reviewing in detail every aspect of the cover they had devised for their prize agent. They were also waiting for the moment when it would be safe to send him out into the field.

Finally, at around the New Year, 1961, they gave the go-ahead. The time was right to send Eli into action.

One evening a week or so later some of Isser Harel's agents decided to hold a little dinner party. They were celebrating. These were the men who, some seven months before, had flown out of Buenos Aires with the kidnapped Adolf Eichmann.

The Dervish was invited, and he asked whether he could bring along a trusted pupil he was training at the time. No objections were raised, so Eli Cohen accompanied his teacher.

Throughout the meal Eli sat in respectful silence. He was sitting with the élite of the Mossad, and he listened intently as they told the story of how they had spirited away the infamous Nazi criminal.

The next day Eli told his boss, "I felt inspired by those men I met last night. They have filled me with a great sense of courage. I am reassured by the knowledge that they will support me in the work I must do."

3

It was the first of March, 1961.

The Swissair flight from Zurich arrived exactly on schedule and taxied up to the main terminal of Buenos Aires' Ezeiza Airport. Among the first passengers to get off the plane was a smartly dressed businessman who had sat quietly in the first-class cabin reading newspapers and financial reports in several languages. No one met him at the airport. After going through immigration and customs procedures he went outside and hailed a taxi.

The businessman explained to the driver that he was a stranger in town and asked him to recommend a hotel. The driver took him to a

well-known address in the Avenida Nueve de Julio, in the heart of
the city.

At the hotel the businessman checked in and signed the register:
Kamil Amin Taabes; occupation: exporter. His passport showed
that Taabes was a Syrian. In a few minutes Taabes was out strolling
in the Avenida Nueve de Julio. The receptionist had proudly told
him how President Peron built the Avenida in the style of the
Champs Elysée after visiting Paris with his wife Eva.

Taabes kept himself busy for the first few weeks in Buenos Aires.
He always left his hotel early and stayed out until late. After a few
days there he told the receptionist that he had found other lodgings
and was moving out. He had rented an expensive apartment at 1405
Taquaraa Street, not too far from the hotel. He conducted all his
business from there.

As any traveler might do in a foreign city, Taabes quickly discovered those restaurants and cafés in Buenos Aires where his
countrymen liked to gather. It wasn't difficult. Nearly a half million
Arabs lived in Argentina, many of them in Buenos Aires. To the
irritation of the local population they made little attempt to mix
with non-Arabs, preferring to socialize together as an independent
sub-culture.

Thus the city was full of clubs where Syrians, Lebanese and other
Middle Eastern nationals could gather each evening for conversation and games of backgammon. After making enquiries Taabes
chose what he thought would be a congenial place and, after dining
alone, went there one evening late in March.

Arabs are hospitable and friendly by nature, and Taabes soon
found himself in conversation with a group of men. Being a newcomer, he was asked about himself; and it took little encourage-
ment from his audience to get him telling his life story.

His father Amin and mother Saida had left their native Syria
years before to seek their fortune in the prosperous Lebanese
capital of Beirut. Kamil was born here, as was a sister Aina—but
she had died in infancy.

Things had not worked out the way the family hoped, so they
moved to Egypt, settling finally in Alexandria. It was here that
Kamil had spent most of his childhood. His father had insisted that
the family retain their Syrian nationality, and had instilled in Kamil
a deep love of his country. On his father's death-bed, Kamil told
his friends, he had sworn to visit Syria one day.

Kamil told how he had originally traveled to Buenos Aires in

1947, when he was 17, thanks to the help of a rich uncle. He and his family had started a textile firm in Legazi Street, but, alas, it had gone bankrupt.

Both Taabes' parents were dead and he was running his own highly successful export company. He had spent much of his time in Europe recently but was now settled in Buenos Aires again.

Proudly he showed his listeners snapshots of his family which he carried with him all the time. He had more albums at his apartment, he said, and invited several men to come over later in the week.

Returning to his apartment late that night, Kamil Amin Taabes was justifiably pleased. The evening had been a complete success. His new "friends" had no reason for suspecting that the amiable stranger they chatted with was none other than the Dervish's star pupil, Eli Cohen.

Eli's cover had been prepared with the utmost meticulousness: the Mossad knew that he would be thoroughly investigated, and his background had to be flawless. So they based his cover on a real person, a Lebanese named Kamil Taabes who had emigrated to Argentina. Eli had to know Buenos Aires as if he had lived there half his life, though in fact he had never been there.

He spent his last couple of weeks in Israel studying maps and photographs of the city until he felt he knew the place by heart.

Even more difficult, however, was reconciling himself to many more months of complete isolation from his family. Eli admitted to the Dervish that he hadn't expected isolation to be such a terrible prospect. Already he had found that when he returned home in the evenings he couldn't tell whether it was Kamil Amin Taabes or Eli Cohen who greeted his wife and daughter. In Argentina he would have to immerse himself even more completely in his new identity— and feel increasingly distant from his family.

When the day for leaving came, Eli drove to the airport with a young officer named Gideon, who would later serve as his radio link-operator in Israel. Eli's orders were clear. He was to take a flight to Zurich and disembark there. He would catch the airport bus and get out in a certain street at the side of the main railway station at the end of the Bahnhofstrasse.

Gideon handed Eli a plain white envelope with five hundred dollars in cash. This was his expense money.

Hours later Eli stepped off the Swissair bus in Zurich, exactly where he was told to, and immediately a well-dressed man approached and addressed him in Hebrew.

"I am Israel Salinger. And you are Eli Cohen."

The two men shook hands.

During the next three days, Salinger, a senior Mossad man who operated under cover as a businessman, reviewed with Eli the details of his own cover. As Kamil Amin Taabes he was now the owner of a maritime and air-cargo company involved with importing and exporting between South America and Europe. To avoid being tripped up, Eli had done a crash course in the business methods of such a concern, and in particular learned the technical phrases he would use in the course of his operations. Salinger gave him a checkbook for a Swiss bank account. He explained: "No South American businessman can exist without one."

Salinger took Eli on a tour of the Zurich shops and fitted him out with a complete outfit of the finest clothes, from suits to handkerchiefs. Eli took these in exchange for his own unpretentious wardrobe. He also took the number of a post office box in Zurich where he could contact Salinger and write to Nadia. Not a single letter was to arrive at her apartment with an Argentine stamp on it.

From a suitcase in his apartment Salinger produced a group of photographs that would corroborate Eli's cover from beginning to end. Most of these were brilliantly-executed montages which would stand up to even the most intense scrutiny.

Finally, on the way out to the airport to catch his plane to Buenos Aires, Eli traded his own passport for a perfectly forged document in the name of Kamil Amin Taabes. Now the transformation was complete.

Soon after arriving in the Argentine capital Eli contacted an agent known to him as Abraham. They met, as pre-arranged, in the Cortinas café not far from Eli's hotel. Abraham supplied Eli with rented offices, stationery and equipment, and his new apartment. He also gave him money, as well as a list of influential Arabs living in the city, and advice about where to meet them.

Only one aspect of Eli's training failed to impress Abraham. He told the newcomer that his accent was not quite right and sent him to a trusted local teacher to polish it. Abraham refused to let Eli make contact with anyone else until he had brought his Argentine Spanish to perfection.

After that, the two men met only rarely.

From his first night "on the town," Eli became a popular figure in Buenos Aires' large circle of Syrian emigrés. He frequently invited friends home to his apartment where he served drinks generously and talked passionately of the homeland they all missed. Everyone who went there was treated to a detailed viewing of Eli's scrapbooks of photographs showing him posing with his parents in Alexandria, Beirut and Buenos Aires.

Only Eli knew that these were montages assembled by the Mossad.

Eli had learned that the Club of Islam, a restaurant and social center, was the best place to meet influential figures from the Arab countries. He began to spend much time there reading newspapers from Cairo and Damascus, and one day fell into conversation with a middle-aged balding man who told him he was Abdullah Latif Alheshan, editor of the largest Arab newspaper in Argentina. Alheshan was a dedicated nationalist, and his younger compatriot poured his heart out to him. He confided: "I would love to return to the homeland of my father. I am sure I could help it in some way. But I know no one there, and am helpless because of it."

Alheshan was delighted to find a dedicated patriot in Buenos Aires. Rarely did he meet someone so intelligent who loved his country and took such an interest in its affairs. He introduced Eli not only to leading Arab personalities in Buenos Aires but to wealthy society people and diplomats.

Eli's knowledge of Arab affairs made him a welcome guest at embassy cocktail parties and formal dinners. At one such gathering he met Major Amin Al-Hafez, the military attaché at the Syrian embassy. Hafez, like most other people, was deeply impressed by Eli's nationalist fervor, and soon began to confide in the eager young man.

"I should not talk politics," he said at an embassy dinner, "but you will be well advised to put your faith in the Baath Party. At the end of this year, when my term of duty is over here and I wind up my business affairs, I intend to return to Damascus. Why don't you join me there? We need men of your education and patriotism."

Discreetly and humbly Eli replied, "My general, if I were you I would do the same. Who knows, perhaps I will find the courage to follow your lead."

The Major received his reply gratefully, especially since the clever Eli always addressed him respectfully as "General."

Whenever the two men met after that party, Major Al-Hafez would invariably ask:

"So, my friend—when did you say you were traveling to Damascus to help us?"

The Arab intelligence forces in Buenos Aires were not so speedily convinced of Kamil Taabes' nationalist sentiments.

Ever since the kidnapping of Adolf Eichmann right under their noses they had been extremely wary of anyone who came into contact with important men like Major Hafez. The Deuxième Bureau, as Syrian intelligence was known, began making discreet inquiries into Taabes' background.

They found that everything he told his new friends tallied with the facts. There had indeed been a Syrian Moslem by that name who had been born in the Lebanon and moved afterwards to Alexandria and Buenos Aires. He had worked in all the places that Eli (Kamil) said he worked in, and would be exactly Eli's age.

The enquiries did not stop there.

When Eli went home one day he discovered that his famous album of photographs had been tampered with. Clearly someone had broken in and made copies of them.

Eli had known this would happen. He intentionally made no secret of his address and phone number, giving both to everyone he knew. The album of photographs he casually left lying on a table in his front room.

At the end of their enquiries, the Deuxième Bureau was convinced that Eli was authentic. The superb cover invented for him by his colleagues in Tel Aviv made it impossible to think otherwise.

His genuineness now certified, Eli continued actively to expand his circle of contacts among influential Syrians in Buenos Aires. He entertained lavishly and gave his friends presents. When invited to their homes or embassies he was charming and flattering; with their mistresses he was impeccably discreet. Everyone liked and trusted him, and they deeply respected the nationalist beliefs he was constantly espousing.

Thus it came as no surprise to anyone when, late in May 1961, Eli visited each of his friends to announce with delight that he was getting ready to make his journey to Damascus. He was showered with names and addresses of business people, government people, personal friends. Everyone promised to write to Damascus to insure that the newcomer returning to his homeland would be given every kind of assistance in establishing himself.

In fact, Eli had been ordered to prepare for his departure by Mossad headquarters. Abraham had been keeping them informed of Eli's success in Buenos Aires and by May, only three months after he got there, they decided that he had accomplished his objectives. As soon as he was able to get all his letters of recommendation (without making too much of a fuss about it, of course) he was to come back to Tel Aviv.

The necessary visas were easily obtained for him at both the United Arab Republic and the Lebanese consulates. On the first day of August 1961, the night before his flight, his friends gave a surprise farewell party for him. The next day several of them went to the airport to see him off on his flight to Munich, where he was to stop over en route to Beirut.

Eli got off the plane in Munich and caught the next flight to Zurich. Israel Salinger was waiting for him there.

In the privacy of a hotel room in the heart of town, Kamil Amin Taabes once again became Eli Cohen. He handed over his documents and got back his real ones. He stripped off every bit of Swiss and Argentine clothing and put on his old Israeli garments. Salinger carefully packed everything else in a suitcase.

After Eli had reported fully to Salinger about his stay in Buenos Aires, the two men shook hands and, five minutes apart, left the room. There was just time enough for Eli to buy presents for his wife and children before hurrying back to the airport to catch his plane to Tel Aviv.

On arrival at Lod airport, Eli was quickly reminded, if reminding was ever needed, that the Mossad does all it can to disabuse its agents of the notion that spies live glamorously. He was met at the airport by Gideon, the young radio operator who had driven him there on his trip to Europe. The operator put Eli in his old battered and unmarked van and drove him straight home to Bat Yam, telling him he would have a few days free before the real business of being debriefed got under way at headquarters.

He found that the postcards which Salinger had posted from different parts of Europe had all arrived safely. These had been prewritten by Eli in Zurich when he first flew there early in the year.

From Eli's reports to Mossad headquarters his superiors knew that he was justifying fully the star rating he had been given by the Dervish. But when he told them of the letters of recommendation he had for his mission in Damascus, they were amazed. Eli was too good to be true. The brilliance with which he had carried out his mission in Argentina seemed only to have boosted his self-assurance, and he was now straining at the leash to be off again to Syria.

But once again he would have to wait. He had further specialized training to do.

For several weeks Eli worked closely with the men who would receive his radio transmissions from Damascus. It was essential that they know his individual touch, the nuances and idiosyncracies that characterized his sending of coded messages. Only by this kind of complete familiarity would they work together perfectly: the men in Israel had to be able to tell in an instant whether it was really their agent sending the message or someone impersonating him. They also had to be able to detect any slight changes that would indicate Eli had been found out and was transmitting under duress. They agreed that a slight speeding-up of the rate of transmission would be the signal that Eli had been discovered.

In addition Eli had to learn the latest codes by heart. He also had intensive training in the handling of Schmeisser revolvers and machine-guns, which were the personal armaments most widely used in Syria at the time.

There was further instruction in such espionage skills as the construction of hiding places for microfilm and other equipment. Eli was brought up to date in miniature camera work, learning how to convert a foolscap document to a negative the size of a pinhead. He learned to identify Syrian aircraft and other weapons as well as the different uniforms of the Russian army officers he was sure to see in Damascus.

There was another reason that the Mossad chiefs refused to send Eli to Damascus. The number of Egyptian advisers there still worried them, and they could not take the risk of sending their prize agent to a place where he might easily be recognized. That would be disaster.

It was better to wait for a safe moment and keep Eli busy in the meantime.

As it turned out, they didn't have long to wait. There is a joke in the Middle East that Damascus belongs to the army officer who can get up early enough to seize the radio station and declare himself President while his colleagues are still asleep. On September 28, 1961, there was another coup of this kind. One result of it was the expulsion of all the Egyptian advisers, whom the Syrians accused of dominating their government at every level.

Now the way was clear. The Mossad decided to send Eli Cohen on to Damascus.

To prepare the way for him they arranged to send postcards from all over Europe to the friends that Kamil Amin Taabes had made in Buenos Aires. The postcard to Major Hafez ended with the words: "Long live the Baath Party."

Before his departure, Eli's instructors were astonished by the utter calm with which he faced his mission. As one of them put it, "You would have thought he was a tourist going off for a holiday. We emphasized repeatedly that he was going to a hostile city, where his life would be in constant danger, but he never showed the slightest concern."

At the end of December, Eli Cohen flew to Munich. There he again met Salinger, and the elaborate identity-swap took place. This time, however, Eli took more with him than an expensive Swiss wardrobe.

A powerful miniature radio transmitter, the most advanced of its kind in the world, was hidden in the false bottom of an electric food mixer. The cord of Eli's electric shaver served as a long-range antenna. Cyanide tablets—for use on an enemy or, in dire circumstances, on himself—were disguised as aspirin. Chemicals for making high explosives were stored in toothpaste tubes and cans of shaving cream. His array of the finest Japanese camera equipment included facilities for making microfilm negatives.

Thus equipped, Eli set off for his solitary mission. He and Salinger said little at their parting.

From Munich Eli made his way to Genoa. And from there, on January 1, Kamil Amin Taabes set sail for Beirut in a first-class cabin aboard the Italian liner *Ausonia*.

It was the beginning of an extraordinary espionage mission.

4

Eli began to establish himself as a member in good standing of the Syrian elite even on his boat trip from Genoa.

Soon after the ship set sail he struck up a conversation with Sheikh Magd Al-Ard, a wealthy and influential Syrian. Al-Ard proved an invaluable contact, introducing Eli to a number of powerful Syrians. He also unwittingly helped Eli by driving him from the port where their boat put in to Damascus: riding with such an important person, Eli was able to get past customs without being searched.

In Damascus Eli's first order of business was to find a place to live. He settled on a spacious apartment on the fourth floor of a modern building in the prosperous Abu-Rummanah district. The place was comfortable and luxurious, but to Eli comfort was less important a consideration than the fact that the building stood across the street from the military headquarters of the Syrian Army.

Eli's second order of business was setting up his import-export firm, which he made almost immediately into a great success. He ran the business efficiently and made handsome profits for all those concerned—including the Mossad. However great the quantities of Syrian antique furniture, backgammon tables, jewelry and objets d'art that he shipped off to Europe, his wares always found buyers.

Suppliers liked him because of the promptness with which he paid his bills. They also appreciated his willingness to deposit their checks in numbered Swiss bank accounts—which he had helped them to open. It was always with great pleasure that they joined Kamil Taabes for a cup of strong Turkish coffee in the Hamdia marketplace of old Damascus.

Little did they know that their friendly chats provided Eli Cohen with economic background for his daily reports to Mossad head-quarters in Tel Aviv. Nor could they have suspected that their favorite customer hid microfilm in secret compartments he built into the tables and backgammon boards they sold him.

For when Kamil Amin Taabes went home at night he stopped being a wealthy exporter and became Eli Cohen, spy. After double-locking the doors and drawing the curtains he would take his miniature transmitter—hidden in the decorative copper cup which held in place an enormous crystal chandelier—and take it into his bedroom. There he would write out his messages, translate them into code, and tap them out fast and accurately to Tel Aviv. Among the jumble of innocent television aerials on the roof of his apartment house he had installed his own aerial: he never had to transmit a message twice.

If Eli had taken any photographs during the day he would trans-form his bathroom into a darkroom, process his negatives, and then reduce them to microfilm. The next day he would secrete them in the false bottom or hollowed-out leg of one of his exports.

In Zurich they would be carefully removed and sent through secret channels to Tel Aviv. The man who received Eli's goods—and had Swiss dealers clamoring to buy them—was none other than Mossad agent Israel Salinger.

Eli's reports and microfilm always contained something of interest to his superiors in Tel Aviv. His friends were among the most powerful men in the Syrian military and government. Some of his closest friends were Lieutenant Maazi Zaher El-Din, nephew of the Chief of Staff, Abdul Karim Zaher El-Din; George Seif, the government's Chief Propaganda broadcaster on Radio Damascus; Colonel Salim Hatoum, the leader of Syria's crack parachute regiment.

Hatoum was a particularly fierce anti-Zionist who spent hours at a stretch lecturing his friends on the cowardice of Syrian politicians who were fearful of engaging Israel in battle. Eli listened sympathetically and praised Hatoum for his staunch patriotism.*

Eli had chosen his apartment as carefully as he cultivated his friends. By the number of lights burning in the army headquarters across the street he could judge whether there was some military crisis building up. An unusually heavy traffic of limousines and staff cars going to and from the building could often be a warning of some new offensive being planned against Israel.

Moreover, the neighborhood had about a dozen embassies as well as the headquarters of the United Nations peacekeeping mission. This meant that there was constant radio activity in the area, which provided an excellent cover for the lone operator in his fourth-floor apartment. Eli's short bursts of code were unlikely ever to be noticed.

Two months after Eli's arrival his hunch about being in the right place paid off.

In his first really important message to Tel Aviv he reported:

"For three nights in a row lights blazing until dawn at military HQ. No coups d'etat expected. Likely cause of activity: action against Israeli forces. Press, radio, TV particularly anti-Zionist last few days. Heavy troop movements in streets."

Eli's report was immediately passed on to all command posts on the Sea of Galilee, near the Syrian border, and within twenty-four hours they confirmed it. Columns of heavy armor were approaching from Damascus.

Israel ordered a preventive surprise attack on the Syrian base at Noukeib. Planes and artillery wiped it out.

The Syrian armored units, realizing that the enemy was in high alert, returned to their base.

Eli Cohen had proved the thesis that "a good agent is worth a division of men." In political as well as military intelligence he

---

* Neither Eli nor anyone else knew that Hatoum's brother, Garis, lived in Israel as a strictly orthodox Jew. His family had sprung from the Druze sect and lived in the border area between Syria and Israel; thus one brother was Syrian and another Israeli. When told of his brother's fame in Syria, Garis remarked: "If we ever go to war again, I hope I don't come face to face with my brother."

supplied Tel Aviv with invaluable data. His interpretations of political change in Damascus were so accurate and so well in advance of actual events that the Mossad sent them to the Prime Minister within hours of arrival. Ben-Gurion frequently made important policy decisions—decisions that could mean the choice between war and peace—on the basis of Eli Cohen's trustworthy dispatches.

In July 1962, six months after setting foot in Damascus, Eli was called home to Tel Aviv for a "leave" from his duties. His Mossad superiors wanted him to have a rest from the pressures of working under cover in a hostile city. But they also wanted to question him further about the information he had sent back to them.

So, for a few days they left him in peace with his family. Eli had looked forward to his reunion with Nadia and Sophie; even his demanding bosses would never dream of depriving him of it.

After those few days, however, he was a spy again. A panel of his superiors would question him closely to get more details about the plans and analyses he had microfilmed or written in invisible ink among the welter of business correspondence he sent out from Damascus. Rarely did he fail to satisfy their seemingly insatiable appetite for information. His astounding memory enabled him to recall whole conversations and detailed plans he had looked at for only a few seconds.

Eli made his achievements seem easy to the men who questioned him, but they knew differently. Syria is one of the most fanatically anti-Israeli of all Arab countries; indeed, Syrians tend to be suspicious of any foreigner. Thus it is a nightmare of a place for any foreign agent to operate in. Even the Russian advisers who had flooded the country were kept at a discreet distance from the civilian population, which was urged at all times to "watch out for the enemy within."

Eli's superiors warned him before he returned to Damascus not to take any unnecessary risks. He had total discretion about rejecting any radioed request for particular information if he felt that by getting it he would endanger himself.

Eli responded to the warning with his characteristic self-confidence. "No one will know who I am," he said. His superiors feared that the main trouble with this extraordinary agent would be restraining his enthusiasm. Soon after his return to Syria, Eli justified their fear.

His friend Sheikh Magd Al-Ard took him to the house of an influential ex-Nazi named Franz Radmacher, a man who had been one of Adolf Eichmann's most important aides. Eichmann himself had testified at his trial that Radmacher supervised operations responsible for the extermination of tens of thousands of Jews, particularly in Belgium and Yugoslavia.

Sheikh Al-Ard, only too eager to prove to Eli his important connections among ex-Nazis, had assumed that Eli would count it a great privilege to meet Radmacher. He had heard countless times from Eli how much he admired Hitler.

Thus Eli found himself shaking hands with the murderer of thousands of Jews. He had never forgotten his meeting with the agents who had kidnapped Eichmann, and had even driven discreetly past Eichmann's house on Garibaldi Street during his months in Buenos Aires.

Now he was in a position to enjoy personal revenge on one of Eichmann's foremost aides. He decided to kill Radmacher. That night he radioed Tel Aviv: "Met former Nazi Franz Radmacher now working as adviser for Deuxiéme Bureau, Damascus. Lives Shahabander Street. Propose to liquidate him."

The discovery threw Mossad headquarters into an uproar. Radmacher had managed to escape at the end of the war despite efforts by the Allied powers and their own secret agents to track him down. Now they knew exactly where he was. But Eli's plans to kill Radmacher caused his superiors to panic. He was far too valuable supplying military and political information to take unnecessary risks killing off aging Nazis.

Eli did not give up so easily. He suggested to Tel Aviv that it would be simple to send Radmacher a homemade letter bomb. Again he was told unequivocally to leave Radmacher alone and concentrate on gathering intelligence.

Israeli diplomats passed on the information about Eichmann's old colleague to German authorities, who eventually extradited him to stand trial.

Eli's enthusiasm had its non-professional side as well. He remained a great football fan and loved to listen to the Arab service of Israel radio on the receiver in his apartment. On the day after a visiting team beat the Israelis in Tel Aviv, he decided to break the strict "business only" rule for transmission. His radio contact in Tel Aviv was startled to receive the message: "It is about time we learned to be victorious on the football field. Tell the losing team that they have shamed us!"

On other occasions Eli sent short messages like "Please send my wife anniversary greetings" or "Happy birthday to my daughter." These exasperated the Mossad only slightly: the value of Eli's information entitled him to break the rules.

In Damascus, Eli had his own personal problems with Magd Al-Ard who was outraged by his friend's refusal to marry. The wealthy Sheikh introduced Eli to dozens of eligible young women and made strenuous efforts to marry him off to Saliah, the daughter of a landowner named Abu Mahmud. Saliah even fell in love with Eli, but he tried—as politely as possible—to discourage her.

So much pressure was exerted on him that he had to plead with his Mossad bosses for advice. All they could tell him was, "Stall as long as you can." In the end he caused deep offense to Saliah and her family.

Eli's other friends took little interest in his marital status. In fact, they probably preferred that he remain a bachelor: a wife might put an end to the lavish generosity he always showed them at his apartment.

Eli's influential friends probably got to know his apartment as well as he did. There were frequent parties there, always well supplied with liquor, expensive food and the finest hashish. Eli would pretend to join in the festivities and get drunk while listening intently to everything his powerful friends were saying. When his guests included such illustrious figures as Colonel Sallah Dalli, one of the brightest stars in the Syrian Army, Eli would make a point of staying within earshot of him the entire evening.

In addition to his hospitality, Eli exercised much-appreciated tolerance of his friends' extramarital affairs. Syria was run on strictly orthodox religious lines. A married man who had other affairs would be guilty of a serious social crime, and was certain to lose his job and be cast off in total disgrace.

Eli not only welcomed and discreetly acknowledged his friends' mistresses at his parties, but even tactfully left his front door key in the letter box downstairs when any of them had a particularly delicate rendezvous and needed privacy. He encouraged his friends to consider his apartment always open for the intimate orgies they were so fond of. Frequently they brought along an attractive woman for their kind host, but Eli never seemed to hit it off with any of the women. He preferred to remain discreetly in the background, waiting to pick up any tidbits of information dropped by his friends in their unguarded moments.

Once when he was going off on a "business trip" to Europe, Eli was asked by Colonel Sallah Dalli whether he might possibly leave behind the keys to his apartment. He promptly agreed. The decision alarmed his superiors in Tel Aviv but Eli felt it was a risk worth taking. For his Syrian friends repaid his favors amply with the information they gave him. His espionage equipment was so cleverly concealed that there was hardly a danger of its being discovered while he was away.

One friend who particularly appreciated the use of Eli's apartment was George Seif, who spent many afternoons there with his secretary Reita Al-Huli. In return, Seif made his office a second home for Eli and he would often drop by in the afternoon for a friendly chat and a cup of coffee. It didn't take long before the guards, used to seeing Eli there, stopped asking him for his identity papers.

Seif's job was to collect government documents to be used for propaganda, and he often had confidential papers lying around on his desk. He showed them to Eli, who of course memorized their contents while pretending to casually scan them. Only one time did he get a fright, when a senior official came to see Seif and was shocked to find a stranger reading a top-secret report. The official openly criticized Seif for this laxity.

"Oh, he is my friend, my brother," replied Seif. "It is as though I myself am reading the document."

Several other times the Mossad agent visited Seif when he wasn't there. While waiting for his friend to return Eli would calmly photograph whatever documents were sitting on the desk. He always carried his camera with him in the event that just such an opportunity should arise.

It was through another of his dear friends, Lieutenant Maazi, the nephew of the Chief of Staff, that Eli scored one of his greatest espionage coups. Eli and Maazi liked to discuss military affairs, in which Eli displayed a keen but ostensibly amateurish interest. Naturally the subject of Syria's border relations with Israel often came up in their conversation. Eli asked how the Syrians could fortify the frontier so effectively and make their glorious attacks on Israeli settlements with so few casualties to themselves. (Eli cunningly pretended not to know about Israel's retaliatory missions against Syria.)

Eventually Lieutenant Maazi, eager to satisfy his friend's curiosity, offered to drive him up to the Golan Heights and show him around personally. No other civilian was allowed to enter the area—anyone who went there without authorization would be shot on sight.

Eli, however, was treated as an honored guest. Knowing him to be a close friend of General (formerly Major) Al-Hafez, commanding officers showed him everything he wanted to see. He toured extensively around the deep concrete bunkers being built by the Syrians to house the long-range artillery that the Russians sent them from the Black Sea port of Odessa. On one trip he counted 80 of the latest Russian 122-millimeter mortars dug in place on the Western slope of the Golan Heights. He saw exactly where they were aimed, ready to fire their shells at ranges of up to twelve miles into the farms and villages of the Jordan valley.

The Mossad had asked Eli to make the gathering of information about Syria's emplacements on the Golan Heights one of his top priorities. Thus they were understandably delighted when he started sending them the information, and pressed him continually for more. From the autumn of 1962, when he made his first visit to the Golan, through the spring and summer of 1963, he returned with Lieutenant Maazi as often as possible.

The Syrians trusted Eli completely, even to the point of allowing him to photograph their top-secret installations. With telephoto lenses attached to his camera he took seemingly innocent views of the "hated Zionists" in the valley below. These photographs enabled the Israeli military to see exactly where the cannon were located and exactly where they were aimed.

Noticing on one trip how Lieutenant Maazi was admiring his photographic equipment, Eli casually handed him the camera and told him to take some pictures himself. "I will be happy to process the film for you," he told his friend. Maazi happily clicked away, unaware that his snapshots would form part of Eli Cohen's next shipment to Tel Aviv.

Several times Eli contrived to get Syrian officers to show him drawings and plans of the entire defense scheme. The proud officers boasted that their scheme was the most complex system of underground artillery anywhere in the world outside the Soviet Union. They would explain it to Eli at length, point by point. To make sure that he had understood it all, he would plead a layman's ignorance and ask them to go through it again.

"I am just a businessman," he apologized. "It is difficult for me to grasp abstract plans like these." The officers, flattered by his boyish enthusiasm, would gladly comply.

Though Eli, with his acute intelligence and his extraordinary memory, understood far more than he let on, the plan was indeed a complex one. The Golan Heights had been converted into a thirteen-mile-wide military outpost. With strong points built on ridges and mountain peaks, the area was criss-crossed with deep communication trenches screened from the view of local villages, many of which were suspected to conceal Israeli spies. Anti-tank bunkers, concrete observation sites and heavy machine-gun posts were mingled with tanks and cannon dug into the black earth. Ammunition dumps were hidden deep underground. The whole area was protected by mine fields and zones of barbed wire.

Several times Eli stayed overnight in the town of Kuneitra, the nerve center of the whole Syrian southern command. There he saw maps and scale models of the area and was taken to radar stations. Russian officers patiently allowed themselves to be photographed by the important visitor from Damascus.

Eli took in everything he saw and heard and faithfully reported it back to Tel Aviv. He operated with the highest standard of cool professionalism. But at times even he could not help feeling the unnatural solitude of his situation. On one of his tours of the Golan, he looked down into Israel—at the settlements stretched out below the Sea of Galilee and the hills of Canaan—and had an almost irresistible urge to return home to his family.

"I felt despair," he said later. "I wanted to seize a boat, cross Galilee below, and come home. The lake was like a vast and terrible ocean separating me from my friends and family. I felt like an isolated lighthouse, desperately passing its warning signal through the night to save the ship of Israel from the dangers threatening it."

In Tel Aviv, Eli's superiors sensed his growing loneliness and decided that he was due for another trip home to Israel. It was June 1963, nearly a year since his previous visit. Separation from his family might depress him to the point of causing errors of judgment. At the conclusion of one of their radio "conversations," Gideon told Eli that he was ordered to come as soon as possible to Tel Aviv.

This order went unchallenged.

Before Eli left, however, he attended one very special gathering. In another bloodless coup the Baath Party had seized power with Eli's friend General Al-Hafez as President. Early in July 1963 Al-Hafez gave a banquet at the Mohajerine Palace, his official residence, and of course he invited Eli.

When Eli arrived with Samy Al-Goundi, the new Minister of Information, President Al-Hafez greeted him warmly. Al-Hafez had a special affection for his patriotic young friend who had given up a prosperous business in South America to help his country through a period of economic and political uncertainty. The President insisted that an official photographer take their picture together. As he drew Eli to him with both arms he whispered:

"My wife thanks you for the fur coat you were kind enough to send her."

The young patriot bowed modestly. He knew that the thousand dollars the Mossad spent on that coat would prove a valuable investment.

When the photographer finished, Eli asked him for a copy of the photograph he had taken. Turning to President Al-Hafez he said, humbly, "It is something I will treasure all my life."

In the year Eli had been away his family had grown: when he arrived in Tel Aviv he laid eyes for the first time on his new daughter, Irit, then three months old.

This was a joyous period for Eli. He spent hours every day with Nadia and his two little girls, walking on the seafront or going to the beach. The family even took a short vacation together. Eli boasted to his friends at Mossad headquarters of "the three women in his life," and carried around a wallet full of photographs of them. Anyone who displayed the slightest interest—and some who didn't —got a complete picture show.

Yet even in his interlude of domestic happiness Eli was troubled. From his first days of immersion in the character of Kamil Amin Taabes he had experienced occasional difficulty in changing back to his original identity. Having lived as Taabes now for eighteen months, he found the instant switch even more difficult to make. "I have to concentrate very hard on remembering what my real name is," Eli confided to the Dervish.

Nonetheless, after about a month in Israel Eli was in better spirits and ready to return to his assignment.

Not long after his return to Syria in August 1963, Eli found that his name was being bandied about in conversation as one of the brightest hopes for the leadership of Syria. He had the trust and friendship of many of the most powerful figures in both the political and military spheres, and was well respected in the business community. He seemed a natural candidate for government office.

Already his name had been put forward as the next Minister of Information and Propaganda. The President, to whom he was becoming steadily closer, suggested an even better idea: why not groom Taabes for the Ministry of Defense by appointing him the present Minister's deputy.

Eli played his hand coolly. He had to exploit his prospects but could not move too fast. Humbly he suggested to Al-Hafez that he was not yet ready for such an honor. He had only joined the Baath Party recently and, though active, could not hope to be equal to the responsibility of government office.

Eli had another suggestion. Perhaps he should make a propaganda trip to Buenos Aires. He could be useful in drumming up support for Al-Hafez and the Baathists among the wealthy Syrian community there. And, the journey, he hastened to add, would be done at his own expense.

Al-Hafez, touched by his friend's sincerity, gladly agreed.

Eli not only made the trip a great propaganda success, but even managed to raise $9,000 for the Baath Party's coffers. To round out the figure he added his own check for a thousand dollars and handed it all to President Al-Hafez personally. It was not a large amount, but more than anything it demonstrated good will and patriotism.

Eli was now a leading figure in the highest echelons of the Syrian ruling class. He visited President Al-Hafez frequently and even carried out a personal secret mission for him, going to Jordan to persuade one of the President's political opponents to return. He was invited by Syrian overseas radio to broadcast appeals to fellow Syrians living in South America to come home and support the Baath Party. (These broadcasts were monitored by the Mossad. They had arranged with Eli a series of key phrases through which he could communicate with them in case of an emergency.)

Because of his new importance in military affairs Eli was able to arrange for several more trips to the most secret parts of the Syrian frontier throughout 1964. As a prospective Minister of Defense, he had to be kept up to date. It was natural that he should spend the night at Army headquarters on the southern front of the Golan Heights and be briefed extensively on the weapons buildup.

Eli was taken on tours of the vast complex where the Russians had installed their latest surface-to-air missiles and anti-tank weapons. He saw how the vast stockpile was processed, and where it was either stored in secret dumps or distributed to different bases around the country.

And of course the well-known amateur photographer always took his cameras with him.

This was one of Eli's most fruitful periods as a spy. In one particularly impressive shipment to Tel Aviv he sent detailed plans of the entire fortification system defending the key town of Kuneitra. They included the size, position and depth of the concrete gun emplacements and the precise siting of the deep trenches in which tanks and other armored vehicles were to be hidden from air attack.

Another report contained news of the arrival in Syria of over 200 T54 tanks, the first of these advanced weapons to be sent from Russia to the Middle East. Later still he sent copies of the complete set of Soviet-devised plans for how the Syrians could cut off the northern part of Israel in a surprise attack.

There followed a series of closeup photographs of the Mig 21, Russia's most recent fighter. These were the first such pictures to arrive on the desks of Israel's military High Command. Eli had to work long hours hollowing out the legs of his antique tables and constructing false bottoms for backgammon sets to accommodate the huge quantities of material he was sending to Zurich. Someone at Mossad headquarters joked that when Eli retired he could earn his living as a cabinet-maker.

In the summer of 1964 Eli received one of the most urgent requests yet sent him from Tel Aviv.

Israel depends for its water on an elaborate system of pipelines that distribute water to the entire country from the sea of Galilee. Galilee is fed by the Jordan River, which is fed in turn by the Baniyas and Hatzbani Rivers. The sources of these two rivers are imbedded in the Golan Heights.

Now Syria was moving ahead with a plan to divert the Baniyas and Hatzbani, thus cutting off Israel's water supply.

The plan had been approved at an Arab summit conference held in Alexandria early in the summer of 1964. President Nasser was a particularly vehement supporter of the plan. He was pressing the Syrians to move ahead with it as rapidly as possible. The contract for the immensely costly project went to a Yugoslavian firm called "Energo-Projekt," which was now in the process of building a series of channels that would divert the two rivers and prevent them from flowing into the Jordan. The threat to Israel was as great as an all-out attack.

From Tel Aviv, Eli Cohen received his orders: "We need full details of the project—plans, diagrams, the type of equipment being used and precisely where it is located.

"This is absolutely top-priority."

Eli did not let them down. By a lucky coincidence his friend Colonel Hatoum had been appointed commander of the military units responsible for protecting the project. Hatoum happily showed Eli full plans and blueprints of the scheme, declaring gleefully that "We don't care what happens to the water . . . as long as the Israelis don't get it."

Hatoum also introduced his friend to the men in charge of the project. One of these was Michel Saab, a Lebanese engineer who had drawn up the work program. Another was Muhammad Ben Landan, owner of the fleet of bulldozers which would be doing much of the excavation work. Ben Landan readily agreed to show Eli complete details of when and how he was to operate. The spy had casually dropped a hint that he was going to buy land in the area so "I can make a little money for all of us."

With this incentive Ben Landan allowed his distinguished visitor to take the plans home so he could study them at leisure and determine the most profitable areas for investment.

Eli photographed every last piece of paper that came into his hands. Within three months he had sent Mossad headquarters plans for the entire scheme: where the canal was to run, its defense arrangements, exact dates for completion of the project in its various stages. He even threw in details of something the Mossad didn't know about —giant pumping stations to speed up the work.

Thus, when Eli went to Israel for his third visit in November 1964, his superiors knew he richly deserved a holiday. It had been over a year since his previous visit.

This time Eli joined in the family celebration over the birth of his third child—the son he had so eagerly hoped for. The proud father could not contain the happiness which Shaul his son gave him. He wanted to invite everyone he knew in the Mossad to the boy's circumcision—but had to be delicately persuaded that the sight of mysterious strangers gathering at a small ceremony in a gossipy neighborhood would surely be imprudent.

In spite of his paternal pride, Eli showed unmistakable signs of strain. It must be remembered that he ran a business full-time in Damascus in addition to his espionage duties. After a hard day's work he had to gather whatever information he had amassed and spent hours making and condensing reports, then translating them into code and transmitting them to Tel Aviv. Often he would work till dawn in his darkroom making microfilm copies. In addition to this he had to keep up all his contacts with his friends, giving and going to parties and arranging for the small favors which helped him keep their good will. There was nothing glamorous about Eli's life in Damascus: often he ended up working a twenty-hour day. Exhaustion combined with the intense psychological strain of working alone in a hostile country to produce a definite change in his character.

Everyone in his family noticed the change. One day Eli's mother asked if he would like her to cook him one of his favorite dishes—a Syrian specialty she knew from her childhood in Aleppo. Eli snapped back: "I eat that food all the time!" This bad humor was completely out of character for him, for he had always been calm and even-tempered. His answer was also a bad slip, since he could hardly have been eating Syrian food if he was living, as he told his family, in Europe. A slip like that in the wrong company could have cost him his life.

Another time when he visited his brother Maurice he gave one of his nieces a doll from the Galeries Lafayette in Paris. Maurice innocently asked: "Oh, have you been in Paris recently?"

Eli, forgetting himself, said that he hadn't been there in months. This answer aroused Maurice's curiosity.

"Well," he asked, "how come you have this gift from Paris?"

"Are you calling me a liar?" Eli shouted. "Are you testing me or something? Mind your own business!"

Such an uncharacteristic display of anger might have hurt a brother's feelings, but in fact Maurice already had his suspicions about what Eli was really doing. By a pure coincidence Maurice was working as a radio operator for the Mossad. Naturally he knew of the top agent in Damascus who sent such valuable reports back to headquarters, but he, like all but a few Mossad staff members, had never been told the agent's identity.

After a while he became struck by some odd coincidences. Whenever the man in Damascus sent a personal message—for instance, wishing his daughter a happy birthday—Maurice noticed that the date coincided with the birthday of one of Eli's daughters. These coincidences added up, and now they were confirmed by the complete silence from Damascus during Eli's weeks in Israel. Maurice knew for certain that his brother was Israel's top spy.

The realization moved Maurice beyond expression. He had always admired and respected his brother, and now he admired him even more. He was dying to tell Eli that he knew his secret. But

Maurice held his tongue. He would do nothing that might endanger Eli's self-confidence.

Another of his brothers, Ephraim, also guessed the truth. Eli had brought him a pair of expensive shoes as a present, and Ephraim noticed that the size was written in Arabic numerals. Eli's explanation that they had been bought in Turkey did not convince him . . . but he too said nothing.

One day at a family gathering Eli gave himself away in a completely unexpected manner. The family often spoke Arabic together, since that was their first language. Arabic speakers are highly sensitive to different accents in the language, and as Eli spoke everyone noticed that he now had a Syrian accent rather than the Egyptian one they had all developed as children. Eli's mother was the first to notice this. Like her two sons, she said nothing of it to anyone.

More than anyone else, Eli's wife Nadia noticed the change in him. He was tired and often melancholy. When they were together he seemed distant, isolated. Nadia had long before guessed generally what Eli's work was, but she, like his brothers, never let on. This time, however, desperate to show Eli that she believed in him, she shared her secret.

"I knew even before you went off to Buenos Aires," she said, "but didn't want to trouble you with the thought that I would be worrying about you." She added with a smile, "See, I am a good Israeli too."

Eli's superiors in the Mossad saw the strain he was under and granted him extra leave. They told him that there would be no objections if he requested another assignment and chose not to go back to Damascus—he had already done more than anyone could reasonably expect.

But Eli felt that duty outweighed all other considerations. "I must go back one more time," he told his bosses. "I still have work to do in Damascus. When I have done it I will come back."

At the end of Eli's leave, he and Nadia went on holiday together to the seaside town of Caesaria. On their last night together they dined at the Straton restaurant overlooking the Mediterranean. There Eli told Nadia of his decision. "I am tired of always being away from you and the children. But I must go abroad again. When I get back, I promise that I will never leave you—not for a single day."

After they parted the next day, Nadia wept bitterly.

5

There was a light rain falling as dawn drove back the darkness of a January night in 1965. Eli Cohen lay back in bed next to his radio transmitter. He was waiting for Tel Aviv to respond to the long message he had just sent.

From his good friend Salim Hatoum, with whom he dined the previous evening, he had learned of a new strategic decision taken by President Al-Hafez and the chiefs of the Syrian secret service. They had evolved a project to unite the splintered groups of Palestinian refugee activists and create a single, coordinated terrorist organization. The men would be trained secretly at army bases and then sent out to wage guerrilla war against Israel.

"We will emulate the struggle in Algeria," said Hatoum, "and throw out the Jews as did our brothers against the French colonists in North Africa."

Within twenty-four hours of this decision being taken, the details were rushed by special courier to the Israeli Prime Minister.

Eli glanced at his watch. It was eight o'clock. Gently he turned the knob of his receiver to the precise point where he knew the all-clear signal would be made, as usual, from Mossad headquarters.

Suddenly there was a violent knocking at the entrance to his apartment.

Before he had time to react, the solid wood of the door disintegrated as a squad of eight armed men burst in with pistols drawn. They were dressed in civilian clothes. As Kamil instinctively covered the transmitter with one hand two pistols were pressed against his head.

"Don't move," the men screamed at him.

Thrusting his way to the bedside came a uniformed figure. Eli recognized him immediately. It was Colonel Ahmed Souweidani, Chief of Counter-intelligence.

The game was up.

Later, in interviews given to Lebanese newspapers, Colonel Souweidani claimed that he had been suspicious of Kamil Amin Taabes for some time.

"I had him followed and kept close watch on the people who came and went from his apartment. I personally found his radio antenna on the roof of the building. I knew from his lists of very important friends and contacts that he was a dangerous spy. His telephone was tapped and his letters intercepted."

The Colonel was lying.

He had good cause to do so. At no time throughout the three years that Kamil had carried out his espionage mission in Damascus was there the faintest suspicion that the man was not what he pretended to be. None of his friends had been either followed or arrested. There was no surveillance whatsoever.

Eli's capture had nothing to do with the Colonel's vigilance or any known mistakes committed by the spy, but was related to complaints lodged over a period of months by the radio operators at the nearby Indian Embassy. They had told the Syrians about disturbances which distorted their own radio messages to Delhi. The authorities had tried to trace the source of the trouble, but did not have equipment sophisticated enough.

What happened then is still not known in all its details to this day. What is certain is that the Soviet "advisers" who had worked in Syria for over two years were asked to help solve the mystery. They quickly realized that somebody was sending unauthorized radio messages in the neighborhood of the Indian Embassy.

One of the most advanced mobile detection units in the world— already in use by the Russians or perhaps specially sent from Moscow—began patrolling the streets around the army head-quarters. The trackers quickly picked up Eli Cohen's transmission, but he did not broadcast long enough for the technicians to pick out immediately his precise location. Thus on the night before Eli was arrested, the building next door, which seemed the likely source, had been surrounded and searched from top to bottom.

Eli Cohen knew nothing of this. Perhaps he should have been more on his guard. The warning signs, in hindsight, were clearly there. Two nights before his capture he had complained in his message to Tel Aviv that he had transmitting problems resulting from an unusual blackout of electricity. He was able to transmit during the blackout by using batteries.

On the morning of his arrest there was yet another electricity blackout in the district. Eli was again using battery power to trans-mit, and had no idea of the fresh interruption to electricity supplies. Locating him was easy: his transmitter was virtually the only radio still in operation.

Having positive identification of Eli's building as the source of the transmissions, the Russians advised the Syrian counter-intelligence men to search the rooftop. It was then that they stumbled on the radio aerial leading directly to Eli Cohen's apartment.

Colonel Souweidani immediately passed the news on to President Al-Hafez. He was bewildered and embarrassed. Kamil, a trusted friend, had betrayed him.

Souweidani proposed that they keep the spy under surveillance for a few days. He wanted to have time to trap him with his ring of operators, as well as find out the names of traitors who were helping him. The Colonel, who had political ambitions of his own, was eager to make the most of this triumph.

Al-Hafez was quick to see the political dangers to himself if Souweidani was given full control. He ordered the immediate arrest of Taabes. News of the arrest, however, was not to be revealed to the public for the time being.

"This would not be in the national interest," warned Al-Hafez.

Thus when Colonel Souweidani burst into Kamil Amin Taabes' apartment he had not the faintest idea of the spy's real identity or for whom he was operating, although it was not difficult to guess that he was in the pay of Tel Aviv.

As he stood over his captive on his bed, Souweidani's voice was filled with anger and self-satisfaction. He literally shouted:

"We've caught you, you swine. Who are you? What is your real name? Who are you spying for?"

Calmly came the reply: "I am Kamil Amin Taabes, an Arab from the Argentine."

"We will see about that," said the menacing voice of the security chief.

"Just wait. You will die. But before you do, by Allah, you will talk. You will tell us all your secrets, and the names of your accomplices. You will wish you had never been born."

While the Colonel shouted, his men searched all five rooms of Eli's apartment.

With a cry of triumph, they found the second transmitter. They slit open the cakes of Yardley's bath soap and in the cavities thus exposed saw powdered explosive material, miniature detonators and poison tablets. Several dynamite sticks and other espionage material were also discovered.

The only explanation the Colonel got from Kamil at this stage was: "The explosives were not for sabotage purposes. They were meant to blow up the two radio transmitters—if I had time to do so."

For the next seventy-two hours the security men literally tore the apartment to pieces. Dozens of men cut up clothing, smashed furniture, and tore down the ceiling as well as the walls. They wanted to find the list of fellow spies which Kamil was certain to have hidden somewhere.

The trapped agent suffered no torture during this period, but was grilled for hour after hour by the Colonel himself and his deputy Adnan Tebara.

"Where are your other transmitters?" they asked him.

"I only had two. They served my purpose adequately," replied Kamil Amin Taabes.

With a pistol thrust in his neck, and with a team of technicians alongside to see that he obeyed instructions, the spy was ordered to broadcast to Tel Aviv on the evening of his capture. In his hand was a message dictated by Colonel Souweidani, who had the idea of feeding false information to Tel Aviv either to mislead the Israelis, or else to try and trick them into revealing details of other spy networks in Syria.

In any case, Kamil did what he was told.

As he tapped out the message Syrian radio experts watched his every move, just to make sure he followed Colonel Souweidani's text exactly. He did. Moments later from Mossad headquarters came the reply that the message had been received. The Syrians were pleased with the success of their ruse.

What they had failed to notice was the subtle change of speed and rhythm that Eli introduced into his tapping. To the Syrians this meant nothing. To the Israelis it could mean only one thing. Their man was telling them: "I am captured."

Again and again the operators in the Mossad communications department played and replayed the tape-recorded message from their master-spy. "Perhaps you are mistaken," begged the Dervish. He had been summoned from his home as soon as the transmission came through.

But the verdict of the experts was adamant. Eli Cohen was prisoner in the hands of the Syrians. His change of tapping rhythm was clearly deliberate. He was warning his headquarters that he was now a doomed man.

The chief of the Mossad was alerted and a message sent immediately to the villa of Levi Eshkol, who had succeeded Ben-Gurion as Prime Minister. Although he was in bed, Eshkol's wife Miriam immediately took him the news of Cohen's capture.

Next morning Souweidani again made Eli send a coded message to Tel Aviv. The reply convinced him that the Israelis had fallen into his trap.

"Your message of last night and this morning garbled. Please try and repeat them this evening."

Eli Cohen knew otherwise. Tel Aviv was telling him that they had understood his warning. They were playing for time. His signals had never been garbled before. Certainly not to the extent that he was asked to repeat whole transmissions.

The Colonel was delighted with his project of keeping the subterfuge going for weeks. But the President of Syria wanted the spy dealt with quickly—and kept under his personal control. Souweidani was a dangerous potential rival who was sure to try and exploit Kamil's friendship with the ruling circle to lever himself into the President's shoes. The Colonel was told to stop playing games.

On the morning of January 24 he ordered Eli Cohen to send the following message:

"To the Prime Minister of Israel and the chief of the Secret Service in Tel Aviv. Kamil and his friends are our guests in Damascus. You will hear of their fate very soon. Signed: the counterespionage service of Syria."

Within minutes the communication was placed on the desk of Levi Eshkol. An hour later Damascus radio announced that a "spy from Israel" had been captured.

Naturally, the news brought anguish to Mossad chiefs. But it also made several very important Syrians tremble for their own lives. To protect himself and his friends the President sent Salim Hatoum and Sallah Dalli to Kamil's apartment to help with the interrogation. As Al-Hafez drily told the colonels:

"You two probably know the apartment better than anybody else in Damascus."

The President was well aware of the "orgies" his trusted officers liked to conduct in the apartment of Kamil Amin Taabes.

Colonel Souweidani was less than pleased about the "help" he was sent. His triumphal boasting about his great coup turned to angry silence as the two colonels decided to transport the prisoner, on the night of the 24th, to the military headquarters of the 70th armored brigade just outside the city.

A few hours later Al-Hafez himself drove to the military base. When he arrived, Colonel Souweidani ordered the prisoner to be brought to him.

The Syrian leader had no need for an introduction. Standing before him was the Argentinian Arab he had befriended in Buenos Aires and whom he had so trusted in Damascus.

His wife still wore the coat Kamil had brought back from a trip to Europe. This traitor had been a guest at his Presidential Palace on a number of occasions and was treated like a brother. He had risen so high that he was on the verge of becoming a Minister of State and joining the government. Al-Hafez was even thinking of grooming him as his own successor one day.

The two men looked at each other in silence.

It was the spy who spoke first.

"I am Eli Cohen. From Tel Aviv.

"A soldier in the Israeli Army."

As Colonel Souweidani was trying to bring down his political enemies in Damascus with his revealing and self-praising interviews to a Lebanese newspaper, so President Al-Hafez used the same method of diverting any guilt from himself and his friends.

Granting an exclusive interview to another newspaper, he declared: "I personally interviewed the prisoner. At first my security service believed him to be a genuine Arab by the name of Kamil Amin Taabes who had been recruited to spy on us by Israeli agents in the Argentine. But the minute I looked into his eyes I knew that he was a Jew."

The General explained how he had trapped the spy by asking him to repeat the most important Moslem prayer.

"He hesitated, and I knew that he was no Arab. I then handed him over to my security officers, showing them which line of enquiries to take."

The President added, "I personally spoke to Cohen several times after that. He refused my cigarette, nor did he drink. He was always under perfect control. He conducted himself at all times in a courageous manner and with dignity during his difficult hours."

The "difficult hours" referred to the four weeks that Eli Cohen spent in the military camp. During those weeks he was systematically tortured. Electrodes were placed in his genital organs, his nostrils and other sensitive parts of his body, and he was given repeated electric shocks. His nails were pulled out one by one. He underwent other refined cruelties taught to the Syrian interrogators by ex-Gestapo and SS men who had sought refuge in the country.

At no stage did the Syrians succeed in breaking Eli Cohen.

When the torture was over he was transferred to a civilian prison. Although he was harshly treated, the wardens developed a grudging respect for the man called the "Israeli Devil." They nicknamed him the "brave one."

As a result of Eli's capture, over 500 Syrian men and women were arrested during this period. They included Government secretaries, air-hostesses and the other women who had taken part in the orgies at Eli's apartment. Men like Maazi Zaher El-Din, George Seif and the Sheikh Al-Ard were all thrown into prison.

The counter-espionage service, playing up their role of vigilant patriots, circulated the wildest stories about the man they had captured. Their magnificent triumph, as they termed it themselves, only served to underline the extent of Eli Cohen's success as a spy.

It was the *El Hayat* newspaper of Beirut which summed up the feeling prevalent in the Arab world at the time:

"Damascus took decisions at cabinet meetings in the morning. Eli Cohen transmitted them to Tel Aviv the same evening."

Only one Arab journalist, also from the Lebanon, was allowed to interview the spy. He reported him as saying: "I went to Syria to work for my country—for the future of my people, of my wife and three children. I want it known that I never betrayed Israel."

To try and save the life of Eli Cohen, the Prime Minister of Israel personally asked newspaper editors in his country to play down at first the importance of the incident.

"Modern civilized countries no longer execute spies," he explained. "They are generally either exchanged for other spies, or else kept in prison for a while and then quietly released."

A vast political and diplomatic campaign was launched to save the life of the agent. Israel's envoys asked ambassadors, high-level government contacts, businessmen and heads of state to try and influence the Syrians.

As the day approached for the convening of a special military tribunal that would hear Eli's case, the pressure increased. Leading lawyers from several countries offered their services to the Syrian government to act as Eli's counsel. Two French lawyers flew to Damascus to attend the trial as observers. One of them, Jacques Mercier, had defended many nationalist Algerians in France when Algeria was fighting its war of independence. He was a man the Syrians could never accuse of anti-Arab sentiment.

But when the tribunal was convened, the Israelis saw that their agent was doomed. The court refused him legal counsel. Mercier and his colleagues were barred from attending the trial in spite of requests from several European governments.

Worse still, it was announced that Colonel Dalli would preside over the court and that Colonel Hatoum was to be one of the five judges. These two men knew that their own reputations would depend on the outcome of the trial; so would the President's. They could hardly show leniency to a man who, having deceived them completely, had gained access through them to top-secret information.

It was clear that Eli Cohen was going to die.

The proceedings were heard behind closed doors. Carefully selected portions of the trial were shown on television.

Eli Cohen demonstrated that despite the torture he had suffered, he was in full control of himself. He spoke calmly and lucidly at all times.

Strangely enough, when asked if he knew the identities of Colonel Dalli and Colonel Hatoum he replied in the negative. Yet he did mention the names of large numbers of other Syrians whom he admitted were his friends.

A spasm of hope was felt in Tel Aviv. Mossad officers knew of Eli's connection with the two colonels. Had he done a deal with them? His silence over their identities in return for his life? It was a theory quickly backed by the French lawyers who had traveled to Damascus in the hope of helping Cohen. Syrian officials had led them to believe that Eli would not be executed even if a death sentence was passed.

How dangerously the colonels on the judge's panel were living became apparent when George Seif was interrogated about his frequent visits to Cohen's apartment. "I did borrow his key to take girls there. But I was not spying for him," he said. Then looking straight at Dalli, he added: "I was not the only one to use the apartment in that way."

On May 8 it was announced that the death sentence had been passed on Eli Cohen. He was to die on the gallows. His "accomplices" like El-Din were given five years of hard labor.

The efforts to save Eli were now intensified. Nadia Cohen traveled to Paris to plead personally with the Syrian Ambassador. He refused to see her. Pope Paul VI, Queen Elizabeth the Queen Mother of Belgium, Canadian Prime Minister John Diefenbacker, the International Red Cross—and scores of other individuals and organizations—appealed to the Syrian authorities for mercy to be shown. Cardinal Alfredo Felcius of Buenos Aires on his death bed sent a personal letter to General Al-Hafez asking him to regard his plea for the life of Eli Cohen as being the last wish of a dying man.

Israeli Radio announced the names of a number of arrested Syrian spies. They were prepared to swap all of them for Cohen.

Dr. Maurice Kuss, a French doctor who had saved General Al-Hafez only a few months previously by carrying out a delicate kidney operation on him at the American Hospital of Neuilly, wrote to the Syrian President: "In the name of the life I have given you, I ask you to spare Eli Cohen."

There was even a muted appeal from Communist capitals to Damascus "to be reasonable."

Damascus, however, was deaf to the rest of the world.

There is evidence that General Al-Hafez hesitated about giving final orders for the execution to take place. He was well aware of the damage he was doing to his country's reputation in the eyes of the civilized world. But he was pushed and pulled in the political intrigues going on around him. Souweidani was clearly just waiting to seize on any signs of "weakness" on the part of the President to precipitate yet another coup d'etat.

A powerful spirit of revenge against the spy was also an important factor in Syrian thinking. This was understandable. Eli Cohen had done fearful damage to the country and had massively sabotaged the Government's plans for destroying Israel. For instance, in November 1964, six months previously, Israeli heavy artillery and mortars had suddenly let fly in the direction of the Jordan water diversion scheme. They fired a few rounds and then stopped. The specifications supplied by "Kamil Amin Taabes" were so precise that the entire bulldozer fleet, the pumping stations and other installations were completely wiped out in minutes. The project was abandoned and the Yugoslavs went home.

It was now clear to Damascus that Cohen had been responsible for this disaster.

Yet Israel made one last attempt to save the life of their spy. A French army officer, a personal friend of President Al-Hafez and married to a Syrian woman, flew to Damascus. He was ready to buy the life of Eli Cohen. In his pocket was a check for a million dollars and a letter promising to deliver tractors, bulldozers, medical equipment and ambulances to the Syrians. If necessary he would increase the quantities of the non-military material which would benefit ordinary Syrian people.

The hand of the Mossad was clearly behind this offer. The secret service organization was living up to its belief that its agents were never expendable. President Al-Hafez refused to see the French army officer.

When this failed, strong voices in Israel suggested taking direct action. The "hawks" said that all diplomatic efforts would end in failure. A military blow should and could be delivered against Syrian positions. Leading personalities could be kidnapped—to be exchanged against the life of the spy. This plan was rejected.

At 10 PM on the 17th of May, Radio Damascus announced that the condemned man would die shortly in El Marga Square—the Square of Martyrs, the traditional place for hangings. Frantic last-minute efforts were made in Paris. The Vatican was telephoned and a cardinal promised to get the Pope out of bed to make yet another appeal to Damascus. Prime Minister Georges Pompidou did not hesitate to awaken President de Gaulle.

All their efforts were in vain.

At shortly after 2 AM on May 18, the heavy doors of Damascus' El-Maza prison were flung open and the headlights of military vehicles in the courtyard picked out the figures of four armed guards surrounding a lone prisoner. Walking toward the van that was waiting for him, Eli Cohen stumbled and fell. His guards had to push and drag him to the van.

Incessant torture had left Eli weak and unsteady.

To comfort the condemned man during the last minutes of his life came the eighty-year-old chief Rabbi of Syria, Missim Andabo. Unable to control his emotions, the white-bearded rabbi wept openly. Eli spoke to him softly to calm his grief.

A few minutes earlier the prisoner had recited the Vidui, the prayer of a man about to face death: "Almighty God forgive me for all my sins and transgressions." Now he and the old Rabbi prayed together. The van, guarded by a convoy under the personal command of Colonel Souweidani, sped toward El Marga Square.

Eli knew where the convoy was heading. He knew that his execution would be witnessed by hundreds of Syrians, and his body left to dangle for all passersby to see.

He did not know of the international campaign that had been launched to save his life. No one had been allowed to tell him. As Jacques Mercier later said: "He went to the gallows feeling he had been abandoned."

But as Eli rode toward his death, he showed no sign of bitterness. He told the Rabbi: "I owe no man anything. I have no debts." Earlier that evening he had been granted his last request: he would be allowed to write a letter of farewell to Nadia.

At the grim police station facing onto El Marga square, Eli was led to a tiny room with a bare wooden table. There he wrote his letter. The officials stipulated that he could not write it in Hebrew, so he wrote in Arabic.

> *To my dear wife Nadia and my dear family. I ask you to remain united. I beg you Nadia to forgive me. I ask you to take care of yourself and the children, and to make sure that they are brought up correctly. Look after yourself and see that the children lack for nothing. Stay on good terms with my family. I want you to remarry so the children will not grow up fatherless. I give you total liberty to do so. I beg of you not to waste time crying for me. Always think of the future. I send my last kisses to you, to Sophie, Iris and Shaul, as well as the rest of the family.*
>
> *Don't forget to pray for the memory of my father and for my own soul.*
>
> *To all of you, my last kisses and Shalom.*
>
>

Eli Cohen
18.5.1965

As the Syrians watched him in stony silence, the prisoner carefully read through his letter and showed it to his captors. Then taking another sheet of paper he rewrote the same message, this time in French. He could not bear the thought that his final words should be read by his wife in the Arabic tongue.

As they began to slowly walk out into the square, Rabbi Andabo recited the final prayers: "Sh'ma Yisrael," Hear O Israel. . . .

His voice failed and slowly died away. Impatiently the Syrians pushed Eli outside.

The center of the square was illuminated by giant floodlamps. Thousands of men, women and children had gathered to witness the hanging.

Alerted by Damascus radio for the past few hours they had come streaming from all over the city. Poor folk from the old city were joined by the smartly-dressed citizens from the more modern residential quarters. Many of the women wore their jewelry and expensive fur coats.

Other than the shuffling of feet, there was now total silence. The vast crowd was confronted by hundreds of police and army guards, who stood to attention behind rows of barbed wire. Scores more security officers and plain clothes men surrounded the area. There were soldiers on guard everywhere, on rooftops, in hotel entrances, even in the underground sewers. The Syrians feared a lightning Israeli revenge attack.

Refusing the aid of accompanying officers Eli Cohen climbed the wooden steps of the platform where he was to meet his death. The gathered ranks of journalists and TV men who were given a grandstand view described the prisoner as looking pale, but totally calm.

Abbu-Salim, the executioner of Damascus, a giant of a man with an enormous belly and heavy moustache, flung the traditional coarse white sack around the prisoner. He did not free the condemned man's hands, which had been retied before leaving the police station.

The hangman, whose official title is Mualem (Master Artist) offered his victim a mask to cover his eyes. With a shake of his head the prisoner refused, like the two assassins of Lord Moyne whose hanging he had witnessed twenty-one years before. The journalists heard him repeat a Hebrew prayer.

The trap door swung open. Eli Cohen was dead.

It was 3:35 in the morning.

A large sheet of paper with the details of the death sentence printed in Arabic was pinned to the white garment covering his body.

For the next six hours, thousands upon thousands of Syrians marched past the dangling body. Damascus TV ran and re-ran the film of the execution to the background of military marches. Loudspeakers all over the country broadcast dramatic descriptions of the event.

Then the authorities cut the rope and quietly took the body away for burial in the Jewish cemetery of Damascus.

In Israel, prayers of mourning were said in every synagogue. The chief Army Rabbi conducted a service in Nadia Cohen's apartment. David Ben-Gurion led a protest march through Tel Aviv. In every city and major community, streets were renamed after Eli Cohen. Forests and parks were dedicated to him.

Nadia Cohen had watched on television how the hangman placed the noose under her husband's neck. Then she tried to kill herself. She was taken to the hospital and her life saved.

When Nadia was later asked by foreign journalists whether it had all been worthwhile she defiantly answered: "My government did more than any other government in the world would have done for one of its agents." Nadia had received Eli's last letter to her, and did everything he asked of her—except remarry. She has the letter to this day.

In a small private ceremony to which Mossad agents came to mourn their dead colleague, a short speech was given by Meir Amit, the man who had recently replaced Isser Harel as chief of the Secret Service. He said:

"In our job there are moments when we all have to remind ourselves of our own human limitations. Eli never accepted that he had any limitations. He was a pure idealist. He always tried to do more. He went further than anybody else.

"He was the greatest one, the best among us."

Wolfgang Lotz

WHEN THE LEADERS OF the Mossad were deliberating on where to send their prize agent Eli Cohen, they knew that he would be most valuable in one of the two most anti-Israeli Arab states, Syria or Egypt. They had to rule out Egypt, Eli's native land, because of the danger that he would be recognized there; Syria was therefore the logical choice.

Eli did not know it, but there was another reason his superiors in the Mossad chose not to send him to Egypt. They already had a man there, a high-living German-born Jew named Wolfgang Lotz.

Lotz was born in Mannheim in 1921. His parents were both in the theater, his father Hans being a director and his mother Helene an actress. Though Helene was Jewish neither she nor Hans had any religious conviction. They raised Wolfgang as a German, rather than a Jew, even neglecting to have him circumcised.

Wolfgang's parents drifted apart there and in 1931 they were divorced. Two years later Helene, frightened by the growing anti-Semitism of her native land, took Wolfgang and emigrated to Palestine. Helene found work there with the country's leading theater group, the Habimah. Life was hard in those days, especially for new immigrants who knew no one and arrived speaking no Hebrew whatsoever.

Wolfgang attended the Ben-Shemen agricultural school not far south of Tel Aviv, where he became an expert equestrian and horse-trainer. After a few years in Palestine he joined the underground army of the Haganah. His duties included guarding the armored bus that provided the only means of getting to Ben-Shemen, which was surrounded by increasingly hostile Arab villages and towns. He also had to do horse-back guard patrol around the school itself.

At the beginning of the Second World War, Wolfgang, who looked older than his years, lied about his age and joined the British Army. Being fluent in German, Arabic, Hebrew and English, he was immensely useful for interrogation of German prisoners and was stationed in Egypt. He remained there throughout the war and rose to the rank of Quartermaster Sergeant.

After the war Wolfgang returned to Palestine and took an administrative job in the Haifa oil refinery complex. But he wanted more interesting action than that and soon became involved in smuggling arms for the Haganah. When statehood was declared and the Arab invasion began, Wolfgang took part in some of the fiercest fighting in the Latrun area. He stayed in the Army after the war, and as a Major in the Suez campaign commanded an infantry brigade.

It was not long after Suez that the Mossad approached Wolfgang and asked whether he would like to join. It is one of the Mossad's greatest strengths that it can draw on the ethnic and cultural diversity of the state of Israel to collect agents of nearly every background. Thus the agency never needs to force an agent to take a cover which he or she doesn't know intimately either by upbringing or family connections.

Wolfgang Lotz was approached because he was blond and blue-eyed, and spoke German. He was also known to be courageous, and ready to risk his life in action. He had an extrovert nature and a superb acting ability inherited from his mother. And because he was not circumcised, he would find it easier than most to pass, if necessary, as a non-Jew.

As for Wolfgang, he saw himself approaching a dead end. His thirty-fifth birthday had passed, and he did not want to spend the rest of his life training young Israeli soldiers. Though fully aware of the rigors of life as a Mossad agent, he happily accepted the offer.

Like Eli Cohen, Wolfgang Lotz found that his previous experience counted for nothing among the Mossad instructors who trained him. He went through the same tough, concentrated program that all recruits must pass before they can be certified ready for field work. For several months he worked many hours a day at mastering the various aspects of the art of espionage.

After basic training Wolfgang received an intensive course in Egyptian history, politics and culture. As early as 1957 the decision had been made to send him there so he could collect information on the Soviet arms being supplied to Nasser's government.

There was another important reason that the Mossad wanted a top agent in Egypt. An increasing number of reports was coming in about the growing influence of German advisers who had been invited to the country by Nasser. Many of them were former Nazis. Scientists, engineers, doctors, police experts—they had come to occupy a central place in the running of the country. Especially worrisome to the Mossad were the aircraft and aerospace engineers. What were they doing in Egypt?

This was what the Israelis wanted Wolfgang Lotz to find out. As a German himself he would have an easy time getting friendly with his countrymen who were serving Nasser so faithfully.

But before Lotz could go off he had to have a foolproof cover. It was decided at the outset that he should keep his real name rather than try and adopt a completely new identity. Even though much of the cover would have to be invented, some of it, at least, would be completely true. The divergence from truth would come in the explanation of what Lotz had done from the age of thirteen onward. Instead of emigrating to Israel, he would claim that he had stayed in Germany and, when the war preparations began, had joined Rommel's Afrika Corps. (Wolfgang already knew a great deal about the Afrika Corps from his interrogation of German prisoners, and with extra study could learn enough to convince anyone he was telling the truth.)

After the war, so his cover went, he had moved to Australia and lived there for eleven years breeding and running race horses. He had returned home to Germany and from there traveled to Egypt. His occupation in Egypt—breeding horses, of course. Wolfgang's training at the Ben-Shemen agricultural school was producing an unexpected dividend.

In November 1959 Lotz went to Germany to prepare his cover. He explained to the authorities there that he had had enough of Israel and wanted to return to the country of his birth. They gave him every assistance in acquiring the necessary papers. He lived first in Berlin and then in Munich, moving from one address to another in order to make his trail more difficult to trace. He knew that if anyone in Egypt probed far enough they would be able to uncover the truth about his identity.

After a year in Germany Wolfgang and his Mossad superiors decided the time was right for him to make his move to Egypt. He drove by himself to Genoa and from there boarded a boat that took him to Egypt, where he arrived in January 1961.

The rich German tourist immediately set out to make contacts among the sort of people who could be useful to him. One of the goals he set himself was to get an introduction at local riding clubs. By a stroke of good fortune, the first club he went to was the fashionable Cavalry Club on Gezira. Egyptian army officers regarded the Cavalry Club as a kind of second home, and the very first man Lotz met there was Youssef Ali Gahourab, Chief of the Egyptian police. Lotz introduced himself as a horse-breeder, and the two quickly became friends.

News of the latest arrival did not take long to spread among the Egyptian élite. Within days Lotz was being deluged with invitations to dinner parties, cocktail parties, swimming parties. Wealthy horse-fanciers were asking his advice. Police chief Gahourab made arrangements with him to go riding daily.

Lotz amply repaid the generosity showed him by his numerous hosts. He entertained often and lavishly, carefully noting the titles and military ranks of the acquaintances he made. Lotz was a charming and handsome man, and he showered the women he met with gifts and discreet compliments. Guided by Gahourab, he bought several horses of his own and stabled them at the Cavalry Club.

After six months in Cairo, Lotz returned to Europe for a debriefing session with his superiors. They were delighted with the progress he had made: clearly he was going to fulfill the expectations of the Mossad instructor who had dubbed him "The Eye of Tel Aviv in Cairo."

Armed with a large sum of money and a radio transmitter, which he was to smuggle through customs in the hollowed-out heel of one of the pairs of riding boots he bought in Germany, Lotz prepared to go back to Egypt. But before he returned, an unexpected complication arose. On a train journey he met a beautiful blonde named Waltraud Martha Neumann, an East German refugee who lived in America and was visiting her parents in Germany. The couple quickly fell in love, and after spending a few weeks together they married.

Lotz's superiors in the Mossad knew nothing of this until the agent told them he was already married. To their consternation, he informed them that he would not return to Egypt without his wife. This was most unusual—and worrying. On a dangerous mission like the one Lotz had been given, a wife would almost certainly be a handicap. To make matters worse, Lotz told her at the outset that he was a spy for Israel. If he should be captured in Egypt, her complicity would weaken his ability to resist the brutal torture which he was certain to undergo.

On the other hand, the Mossad could not afford to lose his services. Already he had proved himself a spy of immense value. His reports on military and political events in Egypt were precise and accurate. He had created his cover with assurance and skill, and promised to make brilliant use of it in the future.

Isser Harel, still commanding the Mossad at this time, had no choice but to give Lotz the go-ahead to return to Egypt with Waltraud.

Lotz returned to Egypt in the summer of 1961 aboard the Italian liner *Ausonia* (which, some seven months later, would bring Eli Cohen from Italy to Beirut). Waltraud was to follow a few weeks later. In his suitcases, aside from his spy equipment, were dozens of presents that he and the Mossad had bought in Europe.

When the boat docked at Alexandria harbor, Lotz received a royal welcome. Police chief Gahourab was there to meet him personally and drive with him to Cairo, where a lavish party was thrown in his honor. Even a party couldn't keep him from making his first transmission to Tel Aviv.

Lotz received a salary of only $850 a month from the Mossad, but his expense account was virtually limitless: as a wealthy, free-spending tourist, he had to have large financial resources at his disposal. One of the first things he did in Cairo was to buy—with Mossad blessings and money—a string of Arab thoroughbred horses. Lotz was going to start a riding school.

He entered the spirit of his new role with joyful abandon. Before Waltraud arrived he rented a spacious apartment at 16 Sharia Ismail Mohammad Street in the wealthy suburb of Zamalek. Conveniently sited only a few minutes away was the island of Gezira and the fashionable Cavalry Club. In Giza, almost within the shadow of the pyramids, he rented stables and other buildings for his school.

By the time Waltraud arrived he had everything set. His friends were so delighted by the news of his marriage that they literally covered the apartment with flowers for her arrival.

The carefree couple proceeded to lead a gay and active social life. They rode with friends during the day and partied with them at night. Their ever-widening circle of military and political acquaintances included invaluable contacts like Brigadier General Fouad Osman and Colonel Mohsen Said, both key figures in military intelligence.

Osman in particular was worth cultivating. As head of security for rocket bases and military factories, he had the responsibility for protecting exactly those installations that Lotz wanted to find out about. Hussein El Shafei, vice-president of the Council of Ministers and one of Nasser's closest advisers, was also a frequent guest at Lotz dinner parties. He often told Wolfgang of important state decisions before most government officials knew about them.

In addition to his Egyptian friends, Lotz became very friendly with the many Germans who lived in Cairo. Particularly—and genuinely—close were a couple named Franz and Nadia Kiesow, who were working in Cairo for an industrial firm. Another friend was Gerhard Bauch, who claimed, like Wolfgang, to be a former Nazi officer. Some of Lotz's friends, however, had their doubts about Gerhard Bauch. One day General Fouad Osman drew Lotz aside and confided: "Listen, Wolfgang. That man Bauch is always hanging around listening to every word you say. Be careful. Officially he is here as an industrialist, but we know he is a spy for the Bonn government. We allow him to operate freely, as President Nasser wants good relations with the Germans.

"We also know that the information Bauch gets here is passed on to the CIA. As you are a German he may try and exploit your position here. Forgive me for saying so, but you are a little naive about the dirty business of espionage. I thought I had better warn you."

Lotz solemnly thanked his solicitous friend and promised that he would be careful of Bauch.

But most of Lotz's German acquaintances were the ex-Nazis whose activities he had been sent to investigate. He was a regular guest at the home of one of the most "distinguished" of them all, a man named Johann Von Leers who had been a top aide to Goebbels. It was at Von Leers' house that Lotz met the notorious Dr. Eisele, who had conducted hideous pseudo-medical experiments on thousands of men, women and children in Nazi concentration camps. Eisele was believed to be in Egypt for research in biochemical warfare.

Lotz found the pretense of having to make friends with men like Eisele one of the toughest tasks in his mission in Egypt. The pretense proved invaluable in establishing his cover—he got himself a reputation as a rabid anti-Semite—but also caused some moments of embarrassment and misunderstanding. The Kiesows, whom he genuinely *did* like, would often try and persuade him to avoid the company of ex-Nazis. Smoothly Lotz would explain: "I am not interested in politics. Anyway, as a true son of Germany I am not going to desert these men now just because it is fashionable to criticize Hitler." But inwardly he cringed at having to lie this way about his beliefs.

Lotz's pro-Nazi reputation had its more amusing side as well. Another Mossad agent had been sent to Egypt as a tourist in preparation for going there on a full-scale mission. When he returned to Tel Aviv he discussed with his superiors the cover he should use. To their alarm and amusement he said:

"Why not let me open a horse farm like that fascist swine Wolfgang Lotz? I paid one visit to the place, and it's crawling with Egyptian army men who have nothing better to do than ride that Nazi's horses. They like him because he was in the SS.

"Listen, when I go there I'll set up another riding school. When I get friendly with Lotz I'll bump him off! What do you think?"

It was with the greatest difficulty that the Mossad men kept a straight face. One of them told the eager recruit: "We really could not afford such a luxury as a horse-breeding establishment. We will have to find something simpler for you."

There was a certain amount of truth to the Mossad man's statement about their limited funds. The Mossad is not vastly wealthy like the CIA or KGB, and Wolfgang Lotz was costing a fortune. The accountant who went through his lists of expenses nicknamed him "The Champagne Spy" in tribute to the vast quantities of the beverage that he and his friends consumed—at the Mossad's expense. Eli Cohen also had a large budget, but he made every effort to skimp on it. While Lotz could never be accused of abusing his expense account neither can he be charged with penny-pinching.

His superiors in Tel Aviv became accustomed to receipts for the cameras, watches, and tape recorders he bought in Europe for his Egyptian cronies. They had a slightly harder time understanding a mammoth bill from a leading plastic surgeon in Germany. It turned out that Lotz had retained the man to straighten the hooked nose of Hannah Gahourab, the teenage daughter of his valuable friend Youssef Gahourab. He gave Hannah her new nose as a birthday present on her eighteenth birthday.

In return for their generosity the Mossad got a wealth of information. Lotz's riding partner General Abdel Salaam provided a complete picture of how the army was being reorganized by Soviet advisers. General Fouad Osman sought Lotz's views on the training maneuvers his troops engaged in, and invited him out several times to inspect the troops personally. Lotz had cleverly managed to conceal his fluency in Arabic, and overheard valuable conversations that no one believed he could understand.

His intimacy with military men enabled Lotz to visit even the closely guarded, top-secret bases near the Suez Canal. He and Waltraud were allowed access to airports where the Egyptians stationed their newly arrived Migs, and took photographs of the aircraft at close range with their pilots standing proudly by. Armaments storage buildings and hangars were all open to him. The Egyptians even boasted about the clever way they kept real planes on airfields intermingled with dummy planes, thinking that if the Israeli Air Force bombed the place they would waste bombs on elaborate wood-and-aluminum fakes. Lotz admiringly complimented his hosts on their ingenuity while making notes on the location of the dummy planes.

One time Lotz received an urgent message from Tel Aviv asking him to confirm a report that a Russian SAM missile base was being built near Ismailia. Lotz knew that this base was absolutely off-limits to any civilian. But he and Waltraud risked their lives anyway by driving straight past the armed guards on duty along roads that were clearly marked: "No Entry. Forbidden Military Zone." When finally stopped by Egyptian soldiers, who could barely believe the intruders' audacity, they were taken directly to the base commander. Lotz, his acting abilities inspired to their highest achievement by the danger he and Waltraud were in, protested loudly and vigorously that it had all been a mistake. They had no idea, he said, that they were doing anything wrong. If the commander had any doubts about his integrity, he should telephone Lotz's friends like Youssef Gahourab and Fouad Osman; they would back him up, he claimed. In the end, Lotz's high-ranking friends got him off the hook —with the base commander apologizing humbly and inviting Wolfgang and Waltraud for lunch.

And, of course, being arrested enabled Lotz to get a close-up look at the missile launching pads that Tel Aviv had asked him about.

Through his numerous contacts Lotz was able to keep a constant flow of information to his Mossad bosses. At times he was so overburdened with details that he had to make special trips to Europe, usually Paris, for full debriefing sessions with Mossad agents.

In August of 1962 Lotz received another urgent message ordering him to Paris for one of these meetings. To ensure that he wasn't being followed he flew first to Vienna and then to Munich before finally making his way to France. There several of his Mossad contacts were waiting for him, and their welcome was not particularly warm.

Unknown to Lotz, Isser Harel was desperately trying to convince Ben-Gurion of the danger posed by the German scientists working in Egypt. Isser was certain that a major effort was in progress to build an arsenal of surface-to-surface missiles which could be used in an attack on Israeli cities. The danger, he believed, placed the survival of Israel in jeopardy.

Lotz was rebuked for not being aware that the Egyptians had made a successful test firing of a prototype surface-to-surface missile, the flight of which had been monitored by the CIA. The Israelis had heard about the firing from the Americans, and they were furious. With such an expensive agent working out of Cairo they should not have to learn of such a development from second-hand sources. The Mossad agents in Paris told Lotz:

"We appreciate that it is necessary to pour limitless quantities of alcohol down the throats of Egyptians and ex-Nazis, and you need the delicacies you are forever ordering in Cairo to satisfy their appetites. We are not complaining about the expense. But we want more information from you, particularly about the German rockets. We must have more details—and soon. You have established yourself, now let us have faster, more complete and more detailed results."

Lotz returned to Cairo a chastened and worried man.

Not only did he want to fulfil the trust and confidence placed in him, but he was deeply dedicated to his country. He had taken on the dangerous job of being a spy for more idealistic reasons than his enjoyment of the life of a rich horseman.

And this time he did come up with the goods. Within six weeks he was back in Paris with a full list of every single German scientist living in Cairo. He had their Cairo addresses and the locations of their families in Germany and Austria. Through high-placed sources he had gained details of the exact role which each man played in the Egyptian armaments factories.

Lotz also gave his Mossad colleagues a microfilm of the blueprints of the top-secret 333 project, which was the program for designing the electronic control systems for their missiles. To their immense satisfaction the Israelis learned just how much trouble the

Egyptians were having in finding a reliable guidance system. When he left Paris this time, Lotz got hearty congratulations and thanks.

For some time Lotz had been stabling his horses at a new location in Heliopolis. Not coincidentally, the new site was right next door to the Egyptian Army's main training ground and storage base for armored vehicles. If there was any kind of military buildup going on, this base would buzz with activity for days before.

Lotz spent day after day here, watching his horses work out from a ten-foot-high wooden tower. No one noticed the way he combined his horse-watching with curious observation of the goings-on next door. But Tel Aviv appreciated the advance news he gave them of any large-scale armor movement.

Early in 1964, Lotz bought more horses. Feeling that his present stable was too small to house and train them properly, he began scouting around for new accommodations. His problems were solved by the generosity of his good friend Colonel Omar El Hadary, who suggested that Lotz stable his new mounts at the stables inside the giant Abassia military compound. El Hadary provided Lotz and Waltraud with passes enabling them to travel in and out of the base at will.

But even this wasn't good enough for Lotz. He moved his horses to a site on the Nile delta, about ten miles south of Cairo. There he set up a full-scale riding establishment of his own, complete with miniature race track, stables, paddocks and a training ring. All of Lotz's friends admired his enterprising spirit, and they came in droves to ride and watch races there. This was just as Lotz had planned: he knew that his new establishment would attract more officers, whom liberal doses of champagne would turn into excellent sources of information.

There was another reason for choosing this location. It lay close to the missile range where the German scientists were now carrying out advanced tests on the rockets they had designed for Nasser. Army officers took great delight in telling their German friend how these rockets would annihilate Israel in the war to come. From his stables Lotz could watch the experiments himself.

By now Lotz knew advance details of every important movement of troops and armor that went on in Egypt. He was given written permission by General Salaam to visit the most secret zones along the Suez Canal—zones where, he explained, the best fishing was to be had. So well known and trusted was he that no one ever dared question him or even stop him from taking photographs.

In addition to living up to his nickname of "The Eye of Tel Aviv in Cairo," Lotz also ran his business on sound commercial lines. His reputation as a breeder was such that he even exported some of the animals he raised to Italy, earning valuable foreign exchange for the Egyptian treasury.

Another of his imports would have been welcomed with considerably less enthusiasm by Egyptian officials. This was a packet of high explosive which he smuggled past customs in a hollowed-out bottom of a case of French cheese, bought on one of his many trips to Europe. He carried the deadly parcel in the back seat of a new Volkswagen the Mossad purchased for him on the same trip.

The explosives were to be used in a ruthless campaign of dissuasion. Isser Harel had decided that the only way of stopping the German scientists from developing their rocket program was through violence and threats of violence. Wolfgang Lotz was to participate in the campaign along with other Mossad agents planted in Egypt. He turned over some of his explosives to a contact he met in a Cairo restaurant. Some of it he kept himself. What he gave to his Mossad contact was used in letter and parcel bombs to German scientists.

Lotz's role in the campaign was limited primarily to sending warning letters to some of those scientists. Their names had been supplied by Lotz himself but the letters were all typed out for him in Europe. One of them, addressed to a man named Heinrich Braun, read:

We are writing to tell you that your name now appears on our black list of German scientists employed in Egypt. We would like to think that you care for the safety of your wife, Elizabeth, and your two children Niels and Trudi. It would be in your interest to cease working for the Egyptian military.

The letter was signed: "The Gideonites." Gideon was the Old Testament hero who repulsed the invasion of Israel by nomadic tribes spearheaded by the Midianites.

In the autumn of 1964, changes took place in Egypt's foreign policy that would lead, virtually by accident, to the downfall of Wolfgang Lotz.

For some time Egypt had been almost totally dependent on Russian military and economic aid. Exploiting its power over Nasser, the Soviet Union began to insist that he invite East German President Walter Ulbricht to pay a visit to Cairo. This would be tantamount to official diplomatic recognition, and would be considered a major political victory for Moscow. The Bonn government reacted swiftly and energetically, threatening to break off its own relations with Nasser if he welcomed Ulbricht to Egypt. But Nasser had no choice. He ordered Ulbricht's visit to go ahead as planned for February 24, 1965.

The West Germans now threatened to cut off all economic aid to Egypt.

Nasser needed to demonstrate that such threats—even from the powerful Bonn government—could not push him around. He also needed to smooth over relations with the Soviet Union on one particular grievance of theirs. The Russians working in Cairo repeatedly complained that the Gehlen, the West German intelligence organization, was working closely with the CIA to spy on them. Soviet counter-intelligence demanded that Nasser do something to stop their spying.

Nasser hit on a plan that would deal with the Moscow and Bonn governments in one neat move. He ordered the arrest of some thirty West Germans living in Cairo. This would satisfy the Russians and prove to the Bonn government that they couldn't threaten Nasser with economic bullying.

Any West German who had even remote connections with the Gehlen was to be included in the mass arrests. But the Russians also claimed that West German tourists also posed a potential threat. Bonn might be organizing an assassination plot against Walter Ulbricht when he made his visit, and would certainly make use of German nationals already in the country.

As a prominent member of the German community in Cairo, Wolfgang Lotz was perfect material for arrest. He was frequently seen in the company of Gerhard Bauch, who was widely believed to be chief of West German espionage operations in Egypt. And by chance, Waltraud's parents arrived for a long-overdue visit in mid-February. Eager to please their Russian advisers, the Egyptian secret police ordered the arrest of Wolfgang, Waltraud, and Waltraud's parents.

Thus on February 22, just two days before Herr Ulbricht was due to arrive in Cairo, four carloads of police drove to the Lotzes' residence. The four Germans were not at home, having gone to pay a visit to General Gahourab at Mersa Matrouh, where he occupied the Governor's seat. When they returned they were seized and tied up.

The arrest of Wolfgang and his family was one of about thirty such arrests, a token diplomatic gesture. When the West German Ambassador complained about it he was assured that those arrested had been taken in for "preventive custody" during Ulbricht's visit.

The Minister of the Interior assured the ambassador that "all will be released immediately after the departure of our honored guest." He had no reason to think differently: the arrests had been purely a matter of form.

But Wolfgang Lotz had no way of knowing that his arrest was a coincidence, timed with the visit of Herr Ulbricht. Nor was he aware that dozens of his friends, including the completely innocent Franz and Nadia Kiesow, were also in custody. By a stroke of bad luck, Lotz had been away at his friend Gahourab's house for the few days before his arrest. Had he been in Cairo he probably would have heard of the impending arrests and would have known the danger.

As it was, however, Lotz could only assume that somehow or other the Egyptians had learned about his spying operation. He had to think fast.

As it turned out, he completely justified the misgivings at Mossad headquarters about allowing him to operate under cover while living with his wife. In figuring out his best course of action, Lotz placed the highest importance on saving Waltraud and her parents. The best way to do this, he decided, was to cooperate fully with the Egyptians right from the start.

When they began to interrogate him, as a matter of routine, he confessed all.

"What do you want to know? My wife and in-laws are completely innocent in all this."

The security officer in charge of the routine questioning was astonished: he hadn't the faintest idea of what Lotz was talking about. But he was a well-trained, professional officer. Unfortunately for Lotz and the Mossad, he kept his head.

"I want to know where you hide your espionage equipment," he replied. He still had no expectation of finding anything, but he continued with the standard interrogation line. "We know everything. So as to avoid wasting time—mine and yours—it would be best if you confessed fully right here and now."

To the security officer's amazement, Lotz replied coolly:

"You will find the radio transmitter in the bathroom scales." Indeed, this was where Lotz kept it hidden. The officer sent a man to dismantle the scales and was soon holding in his hands one of the most advanced pieces of radio equipment in the world.

Lotz went on to tell the Egyptian where the rest of his apparatus was. In bars of soap they found explosives and microfilm. Hidden away in other caches was over $75,000 in small bills.

Still barely able to believe what he was seeing, the security man ordered Lotz and his family to be taken immediately to a detention and interrogation center. When his intensive interrogation began, Lotz had to walk a fine line between truth and deception. He had two goals: to save the lives of Waltraud and her parents and to give up as little information as possible. With his superb acting ability he was able to find just the right balance—and to achieve both his goals.

From the very beginning he stuck to the cover story he and his Mossad bosses had invented for him in Tel Aviv. He was a German, born in Mannheim and educated in Germany. When the war broke out he had joined the army and served in Rommel's Afrika Corps. It was in Africa, he said, that he had learned to ride and train horses.

After the war he had moved to Australia and spent eleven years there. When he moved back to Germany his experience with horses got him a job as an instructor at a riding club in Berlin. Here he worked for several months.

It was at the riding club that Lotz received an attractive offer. A wealthy club member named Elias Gordon approached him and asked whether he would like to have his own establishment for breeding Arab thoroughbreds. This was a dream that Lotz had cherished, he told his interrogators, since his days in Africa when he had ridden some of these magnificent animals. He eagerly accepted the offer.

Gordon had then taken him to meet another horse-loving business-man, a friend named Ruby Bernstein. Together Bernstein and Gordon explained that the location they had in mind for the riding establishment was Egypt. They told Lotz that they would pay his way there for a visit to explore the possibilities. Lotz, who confessed to his interrogators a weakness for the easy life, had enjoyed his visit immensely. His expense account and the luxury it bought him were much to his taste. Also, he hastened to add, the prospects for opening a horse-breeding farm seemed excellent.

"I did not know then that I was being led into a trap," he complained to the Egyptians. He explained how, not long after his return to Germany, his two "partners" had introduced him to a third friend named Joseph. "This Joseph was tall and thin and spoke atrocious German," said Lotz. "He told me bluntly that he was head of the Israeli intelligence network in Europe. Elias and Ruby were his agents. Clearly they hadn't given me their real names. I was shocked—I thought they were my friends.

"I was in a fix. Here I was—an officer of the German army being asked to work for Jews in Egypt. They were going to set me up to breed horses on my own farm—I had always dreamt of this. But there was a price to pay. I had to transmit information for them to Israel.

"I am a weak man. I agreed right away. I did not even hesitate. I feared, at the time, that if I backed out my life would be in danger. The Israelis were ruthless and arrogant like all Jews. I thought it safest to follow their suggestions."

Only later, Lotz told them, did he find out what harsh taskmasters the Israelis could be. All the time they wanted more and more information. They trained him to photograph army installations, he said, and ordered him to send letter bombs to German scientists. And all of this in addition to his regular radio reports to Tel Aviv.

"They were like Shylock in the Shakespeare play we had to read in our English class at school," he complained. "They demanded their pound of flesh a hundred times over. Never have anything to do with them," he earnestly warned.

Lotz was so convincing in his role of a gullible, dim-witted ex-soldier that his astute interrogators were inclined to believe him. They had good reasons for doing so which had nothing to do with the intrinsic merits of his plea, however. For one thing, it was in Cairo's interests at the time to believe him. They were trying to mend their relations with West Germany, and knew that lenient treatment of this German spy would help them in this effort.

Moreover, at exactly that time the Arab press was full of the story of how Eli Cohen, the Israeli spy, had infiltrated the highest levels of Syrian government. Mocking voices throughout the Arab world were still talking loudly about "The Mossad agent who nearly became the Syrian Minister of Defense."

Relations between Syria and Egypt had been shaky since they dissolved their United Arab Republic in 1961, and the two countries maintained a mild but insistent rivalry. The last thing Nasser wanted was to be told by the Syrians, "You are no better than us! You have your own Israeli spy!" If Lotz was just a German who had been used by the Mossad, then the damage to Egypt would be minimal. Thus the Egyptians bent over backwards to believe his story.

But his interrogators did insist on one crude and humiliating test of Lotz's story. If he was a German and not a Jew, then they would examine him to see whether he was circumcised.

A doctor was brought in for the examination, and had Lotz stripped stark naked. Standing the prisoner before a large polished-metal table, he bent down and minutely examined his genitals.

The examination lasted several minutes. In those minutes Lotz thanked his parents for their irreligious ways. Had he been circumcised he would now be destined for the gallows, and he knew it. He tried to keep his head upright and his eyes wide open, in spite of the two powerful lights that seemed to be burning their way into the back of his skull.

At last the doctor was satisfied. With a gentle tap on Lotz's shoulder—as if to say, "You need not worry, you are not a fake"—he walked over to the officers who were seated at the table. Bending over he whispered something to one of them, a balding, middle-aged officer. Lotz had recognized the man immediately as Salah Nasr, head of Egyptian intelligence and security. Nasr had decided to take part in the spy's interrogation himself. He addressed Lotz directly in fluent English spoken with a soft, easy-going tone of voice. "You may get dressed now, Mr. Lotz."

The projectors were turned off, and when he was fully clothed again the prisoner was invited to sit down. "Have a cigarette, Mr. Lotz. Perhaps a cup of coffee? Now, let us not waste time.

"You will forgive us for putting you through the indignity of the medical examination. But it was important for us to establish whether or not you are in fact a Jew. We could not take it on trust, you understand, when you said you were uncircumcised and a 100 percent pure Aryan German."

A faint smile crossed Salah Nasr's face as he glanced at the glowering Abdul Hakim, one of his senior intelligence officers. This soft approach toward the spy did not meet with Hakim's approval. Bluntly he told his chief in Arabic: "German or Jew I don't give a damn! Give me two hours with him and he will sing like a bird!"

Salah Nasr retorted harshly:

"You have the brains of a donkey. You understand nothing about political considerations." Turning to the prisoner, who pretended not to understand what had just been said, he continued smoothly:

"Mr. Lotz, we are not anxious to hang you. This will not serve any purpose. Your career as a spy is over anyway. I am going to ask you to trust me. You have my personal word for it that I will look after you if you cooperate.

"I want the truth about your contacts here in Egypt. I want the names of all your fellow spies. I want to know how you were trained, and who trained you. I will require precise details about the men who sent you on your espionage mission to our country. Details which Mr. Hakim here will carefully analyze and check.

"And remember Mr. Lotz, it is not only *your* life at risk if you try to deceive us. . . ."

The Egyptian had no need to spell out how he held an invisible knife at the prisoner's throat. Earlier that day Lotz had heard the screams of a woman being tortured in a neighboring cell. The agonized cries still rang in his ears.

His jailers were not being very subtle, but the pressure they were exerting on their captive had to be underlined with the harsh alternatives to full cooperation—torture and death for himself, Waltraud, and his wife's parents.

Lotz knew that he had to keep walking his tightrope. After days of interrogation he succeeded in convincing his captors that Waltraud's parents were completely innocent. They were released. He wasn't so successful with Waltraud herself. The Egyptians would not believe—quite rightly—that a woman could watch her husband transmitting messages on a miniature radio and be completely ignorant of what he was up to.

Both Wolfgang and Waltraud, as well as their friend Franz Kiesow, were committed for trial on ten charges of crimes against the Egyptian nation.

These were black days indeed for the Mossad. Two of their top agents had been imprisoned in enemy countries; both faced harsh treatment and penalties of death. At that very moment Eli Cohen was being tortured in a Damascus prison. To make matters worse, the Mossad had no idea of how Wolfgang Lotz had been captured. If he had been betrayed, then whoever betrayed him would have evidence that was certain to get him hanged.

But Lotz had luck on his side. The Egyptians were eager not to execute him: they did not have to contend with the kind of internal power struggles that made Eli Cohen's death a political necessity. Moreover, Lotz managed to cooperate with them in a way that served both his interests and Israel's. From the beginning his logic had been that by pretending to cooperate fully he would be able to control in some degree the amount of information he gave out. Were he to remain silent and submit to torture, there was no telling what he would say. In the end, by cleverly using the truth he managed to conceal everything important—and he didn't incriminate anyone else.

Even before the trial began, Lotz agreed to make a television broadcast to his fellow Germans. With Waltraud sitting nearby he spoke clearly and earnestly into the camera:

"I have been spying in Egypt for the Israelis since 1961. I sent them details of Soviet missiles which are based in the Suez Canal region, and I carried out other espionage tasks." As he spoke the cameras panned over to Waltraud, who had begun weeping piteously. Lotz continued:

"I regret my actions very much. Only now do I realize the harm I have done out of greed for money. I am being treated very well by the Egyptians in prison." This last statement happened to be perfectly true.

"If the Israelis must send spies to Egypt, let them in future use their own people and not recruit honest Germans for the job. I strongly advise anyone in Germany who considers taking on such a job to resist."

The Egyptians were, needless to say, delighted by the way their repentant prisoner acted as a propagandist for them. They didn't realize that his television message was being received with equal delight at Mossad headquarters. It proved conclusively that the Egyptians still believed his cover—and that Lotz was still safe.

The trial opened in July 1965, and was broadcast during prime time on Egyptian TV. This was a deliberate insult to the Syrians, who had conducted their trial of Eli Cohen in secret and broadcast only selections. Lotz and Waltraud were also provided with defense lawyers and an observer from Germany was allowed to be present. In comparison with the Syrians' treatment of Eli Cohen, the trial was conducted fairly and courteously.

Throughout the proceedings it became obvious that the Egyptians were still determined not only to show the world how civilized they were but to maintain their belief in Lotz's story about his German background. And Lotz continued to play along perfectly with his expert combination of truth and deception.

For example, he wasted vast amounts of time by going into the most ridiculously intricate detail about how he had disposed of his first transmitter, which had proved too difficult for him to repair.

He described how he had broken the apparatus into small pieces and then gone for a picnic at a certain place on the Nile. Renting a boat he had rowed out into the river and dumped the smashed-up radio into the water. He was ready to take the authorities to the precise spot, he claimed. "It is opposite a clump of five palm trees just down river from. . . ." and then he went into another hopelessly detailed description. His television audience—and those in the court—swallowed every bit of it.

Again and again the prisoner insisted that his wife had played no part in his espionage work.

"I met her purely by chance on a train," explained Lotz. "She knew I was sending messages from the radio transmitter in our bedroom. She watched me at work. But she believed that I was doing it for NATO, in connection with my job."

In court, looking elegant in a simple white dress, Waltraud won the sympathy of the judge as well as Egyptian television viewers as she told them:

"I was shocked when I heard about the true nature of my husband's activities. But it is my duty to stand by him in times of misfortune. As strange as it may seem to you I love my husband more than ever now. His fate is in your hands and I appeal to you not to be too severe on him."

Pleading Waltraud's cause, her defense lawyer said: "It is clearly the love of a wife for a husband which has brought Mrs. Lotz before us. She knew that he was spying—but thought it was on behalf of NATO. He could never tell her the true nature of his work. For she is anti-Semitic and hates Israel."

As the trial progressed it became apparent that the Lotzes were convincing everyone they were telling the truth. Of course Lotz had been a spy, the authorities were saying. But at least he and his charming wife were Germans and not Jews. They would be punished, but not unfairly.

If the Egyptian public hung on to every word spoken in the courtroom, at Tel Aviv headquarters the Mossad was even more attentive. Every scrap of information, every bit of testimony, was studied minutely again and again. Just how much did the Egyptians *really* know about "The Eye of Tel Aviv in Cairo"?

The Lotzes' only frightening moment came late in the trial when a letter arrived from Germany. It was sent by a Munich lawyer named Alfred Seidl, who was representing the families of some of the victims of the letter-bomb campaign. Seidl, thirsty for revenge on behalf of his clients, informed the court that Lotz was in fact an Israeli citizen. He accurately reported the year in which Lotz had emigrated, and pointed out that his mother was Jewish.

The letter also truthfully revealed that Lotz had served in the Israeli army as an officer and that the Mossad had sent agents to Germany following his arrest to prevent this news from being published there. When the incriminating letter was shown to Lotz in court, his courage momentarily failed him.

But he quickly gathered his wits and explained: "It is an effort on the part of the men representing the German scientists making rockets for the Egyptians to get me hanged."

In closed sessions with the judges Lotz swore blind that the information was inaccurate, and that his mother was a Protestant who had died in the Allied air raids on Berlin in 1944.

"It is true that I visited Israel once. It was in 1964, and I was there only for six days. My superiors in Europe who hired me insisted that I go there for a meeting with Israeli intelligence officers. I met a man called Meyer or something like that. The only truth in that letter is that they have my birthplace, Mannheim, correct."

The damaging information was rejected by the court.

On August 21, 1965, the court in Cairo passed its judgment on Wolfgang and Waltraud Lotz.

Wolfgang was sentenced to life imprisonment with forced labor, and a fine of 32,539.50 Egyptian pounds. Waltraud received three years, and was fined one thousand Egyptian pounds. Franz Kiesow was freed. The only Egyptian who suffered as a result of Lotz's spying activities was General Gahourab, who was stripped of his rank and jailed.

The "forced labor" was never applied to model prisoner Wolfgang Lotz. Not only was he allowed unusual privileges, but he was able to see his wife from time to time. He ordered meals from a Cairo restaurant. Another prisoner cleaned out his cell.

At the infamous Tura prison Lotz met a number of other jailed Jews. They included Victor Levi, the friend of Eli Cohen who had been sentenced to life for planting bombs in Egypt. Although still a young man, Levi was turning gray. He had served eleven miserable years in Egyptian custody.

With him were others caught at the same time: Phillip Nathanson and Robert Dassa. Their companion Marcelle Ninio was sitting out her fifteen-year sentence in a woman's jail, the same where Waltraud had been sent.

Lotz was warmly greeted by his fellow "agents," although at first they believed him to be a German. Finally Wolfgang came clean and to the astonishment of Victor spoke to him in Hebrew. After that the group were even more tightly knit.

The men were kept with other prisoners considered "political" on the top floor of the Tura jail. Although life had been tough at first for Victor Levi and the other spies, for they had been compelled to work in a stone quarry for the first three years of their sentence, they were now well organized. Using supplies of cigarettes to bribe their jailers they were able to prepare their own meals in their cells and even had electricity from an outside cable so that they could read at night.

For over two years Lotz remained in Tura while his wife served her sentence in another jail. Then came the Six-Day War of 1967, which was to change not only his life but that of the other imprisoned spies as well. They were moved to top-security cells and feared for a time that they would be killed either by their own airplanes or by angry Egyptians.

But nothing happened. The war ended and they were moved back to their regular cells.

Christmas, 1967. Eight months after the war's end.

The years stretched ahead as far as Wolfgang Lotz was concerned: a life sentence meant twenty-five years in Egypt—and he still had twenty-three to go.

His morale was sustained by the knowledge that it was a basic principle of the Mossad to try and bring about the release of all captured agents—and even recover the bodies of dead spies. But he also knew that the Mossad had only limited powers. They had failed, for instance, to save Eli Cohen from being hanged. And right there in Tura was the visible proof in the shape of Victor Levi and his friends that it was not that easy to save their men despite noble intentions.

Unknown to Lotz, however, incredibly tortuous negotiations were going on at the time between Israel and Egypt through the offices of the United Nations Secretary General U Thant and his Middle East representative Gunnar Jaring. The first deal had already been agreed upon.

In exchange for the 5,000 Egyptian soldiers captured during the

1967 war, Israel demanded the release of a group of naval frogmen and some pilots who were in Cairo.

The Israelis, however, had another offer to make. They held nine Egyptian generals and scores of senior officers in their POW camps. They would only release them if Cairo would agree to send home the ten Israeli spies they held.

At the top of the list appeared the name of Wolfgang and Waltraud Lotz. For Tel Aviv had come right out into the open and for the first time admitted that the "German" in Tura was in fact an Israeli.

It took eight months of delicate negotiations with a touchy President Nasser. On no account were the Egyptians to appear to lose face. Everything had to be done in the greatest secrecy. No news of the release of the Israeli spies was to appear in the newspapers. Finally, a letter had to be written to Nasser praising his humanitarian motives, and declaring that the Israelis were prepared to accept his word of honor that he would stick to his side of the bargain. As a token of good faith, the Israelis released several Egyptian generals before a single spy was freed.

Nasser kept his word. The spies were all found to be suffering from "incurable disease, cancer or heart ailments," and all were given medical certification to this effect. Quietly they were released and simply turned up unannounced in Israel. The Lotz family were taken to Cairo airport on February 4, 1968. Here they were put on Lufthansa flight 674 heading for Munich via Athens. But they never made it to Germany. They were taken off the plane in Greece, and sent on another flight to London in the care of "friends" who looked suspiciously like Mossad agents. Forty-eight hours later they arrived in Tel Aviv, wearing brand-new clothes they bought in London at the Marble Arch Branch of Marks and Spencers. There they mingled with scores of Arab customers from the Middle East.

For a while Wolfgang and Waltraud lived in a modest home outside Tel Aviv. They were visited from time to time by Herr Otto and Frau Klara Neumann, Waltraud's parents, who flew from their German home town of Heilbron.

Wolfgang, nicknamed "Sus" (Hebrew for horse) by his neighbors, started a small riding school. Waltraud learned Hebrew and became fanatically pro-Israeli in outlook.

A few years later, misfortune overtook them. Waltraud suddenly became ill and died. Fellow ex-convicts from their days in prison like Marcello Ninio, Victor Levi and Philip Nathanson called frequently to try and console the broken-hearted Wolfgang. To this day he wonders whether his wife's health was broken by her two years in an Egyptian prison.

Since Waltraud's death Lotz has been restless. His riding school in Israel failed and in 1974 he set out for the United States "to make some money," as he put it. "There were not as many rich customers in Israel as I used to find among rich Germans and Egyptians," he said.

Lotz settled first in Los Angeles and then in Seattle, where he lived in a nine-room apartment with his new wife, an Israeli woman named Naomi. With a partner, Wolfgang Lotz opened a private detective agency. As he said: "I know a thing or two about security."

The business collapsed when the wife of his partner ran away with the company's funds.

In January 1978, with a mere thousand dollars in his pocket, Lotz went to Germany. He found a job in a Munich department store selling fishing tackle. Money problems worry him. He says: "I used all my back salary and compensation paid to me by the Mossad to set up my riding school in Israel, but lost it all. Now all I get is a pension of $200 a month from them. I don't think it's very generous."

After the visit of President Sadat to Jerusalem when peace between Israel and Egypt seemed a real possibility Lotz was debating a "brainwave," as he calls it.

"Maybe they will allow me back into Egypt," he says. "I would love to set up a horse-riding school along the Nile."

Then he reconsiders: "Maybe not. . . . I made such fools of them, I doubt if they will ever forgive me."

Confrontation

EARLY IN THE MORNING OF June 1, 1967, the telephone rang at the home of CIA Director Richard Helms. Helms was surprised: the call had come through on his personal, unlisted line. Picking up the phone, he recognized the voice at the other end immediately. It was Meir Amit, his old friend from the days when both had been students at Columbia University. Since 1962 Amit had been head of the Mossad. Helms knew from his tone of voice that he was not calling for a friendly chat.

"Dick, I have to see you," said Amit. "I am calling from a phone booth at the airport. No one knows I am here. I just flew in.

"It is very, very urgent."

Though taken aback, Helms recovered his composure quickly.

"I am busy with meetings during the morning," he replied. "But I will meet you some time later in the day. In the meantime, if you go out to our headquarters at Langley I will arrange for you to see some of my men. If you tell them what's on your mind I will be briefed by the time I arrive."

"I will be there," Amit replied.

Meir Amit's unconventional visit to Washington was the culmination of weeks of turmoil in Tel Aviv.

Throughout the spring and early summer the Soviet Union had been waging a war of nerves. As the major supplier of arms and intelligence advice to Syria and Egypt they had been trying to convince their Arab clients that Israel was planning an all-out attack. On May 13 the Russian ambassador had called President Nasser to warn him of an imminent attack on Syria. For days afterward they fed both Syria and Egypt with information about the supposed Israeli armor buildup on the Golan Heights.

Egypt responded to the warnings by ordering immediate mobilization of the Egyptian army. Chief of Staff Mohamed Fawzi flew to Syria to plan joint action. Soon both countries were on full alert, with over 100,000 Egyptians ready for battle in the Sinai.

The question facing Israeli leadership was brutally simple: were Egypt and Syria playing along with the Russians' policy of "controlled tension," or did they want an all-out war? Mossad agents throughout the Middle East and Europe were pressed for every scrap of information that might answer the question.

On May 20 the Mossad, using an emergency communication channel, relayed a brief message from Prime Minister Levi Eshkol direct to President Nasser: "We don't want war. We will withdraw all our units now stationed on our frontiers if you withdraw your armies from Sinai to previous positions."

The reply from Cairo was terse: "You will get our answer in time."

The Israelis did not have long to wait. Forty-eight hours later President Nasser ordered the closing of the Straits of Tiran, thus shutting off Israel's route through the Red Sea to Africa and Asia.

Among the leaders of Israel's military and intelligence forces this move had a single, unanimous interpretation: war was imminent; Israel's only chance to overcome vast superiority of men and equipment was to attack.

As forcefully as he could, Meir Amit presented this point of view to Prime Minister Levi Eshkol. But the cautious Eshkol, under pressure from the United States to cooperate in trying to ease tensions through diplomacy, hesitated and played for time. He appealed to the Russian Ambassador Zoubakhine to tour the country's frontier regions so he could see that Israel was not preparing for war.

The appeal was rejected out of hand. Zoubakhine, an urbane and charming man most of the time, suddenly became rude and strident, Eshkol found himself being hectored savagely about Israeli aggression. The attacks grew so intolerable that even the mild-mannered Eshkol nearly lost his temper.

In Israel this period of waiting created immense strains. Popular morale was low, and Eshkol came under heavy criticism from the press and from his more militant advisers.

An index of the frustration among Eshkol's advisers came dramatically at a conference held toward the end of May in the Prime

Minister's office. General Ariel (Arik) Sharon arrived for the conference with a revolver strapped at his side. When the cabinet chief politely reminded him that government ministers did not normally carry weapons into meetings, Sharon angrily flung the pistol onto a desk and, in a shout loud enough to be heard by Levi Eshkol, declared:

"If you think anybody needs a pistol to arrest this Prime Minister, you are crazy. All you have to do is shout and he will run away!"

This outburst deeply distressed Levi Eshkol, who was after all an honorable man and as patriotic as any general. He simply wanted to follow the path of negotiation as long as he could.

But the situation had worsened. To add to Israel's woes, President de Gaulle warned them not to attack the Arabs. Coming from Israel's greatest friend during the previous decade, and from their sole supplier of arms, this was a cause for grave concern.

It was against this background that Meir Amit decided to make his secret trip to Washington. He was certain that the key to victory in the coming war lay in the United States, and equally certain that Foreign Minister Abba Eban was failing to impress President Johnson with the gravity of the situation. As he said later, he believed that the survival of Israel depended on the outcome of his talks with CIA officials at their Langley, Virginia headquarters.

In a briefing room at Langley, Amit faced a group of top CIA experts on the Middle East. These were imposing and dispassionate men whose job it was to analyze data without emotion; Amit knew that they were going to be a tough audience. Pulling out his maps, charts and data sheets, he began abruptly.

"There is going to be a war," he said. "Our army is now fully mobilized.

"But we cannot remain in that condition for long. Because we have a civilian army our economy is shuddering to a stop. We don't have the manpower right now even to bring in the crops. Sugar beets are rotting in the earth.

"We have to make quick decisions. If we do not move against the Egyptians they will destroy us."

Amit then proceeded to lay out in detail the Mossad's analysis of the military situation. At every turn he was questioned and cross-examined by the Americans facing him. Showing as much calm as if they were asking politely after his family's health, they demanded to know how many dead Israel would suffer if they attacked first, and how many if Egypt fired the first shots.

"If we can get the first blow in," Amit answered, "our casualties will be comparatively light. Hundreds of dead—but no more. If we have to sit and wait for them to attack, we will still win—but our dead will be closer to ten thousand."

The CIA men could not help being impressed by Amit's cool, logical analysis. They did not need to be told what a national disaster it would be for Israel to lose 10,000 men. But they continued to press him. When Amit was finished with his presentation they pulled out their own maps and the information that had reached them from their own network of agents and diplomats.

To Amit's relief, every bit of CIA data corroborated his own. They knew he was not bluffing. Indeed, he found that they accepted all of his arguments except one.

Their principal spokesman said to Amit, "Our belief is that the Egyptians are deployed in the desert in a defensive role. Our military experts agree with this interpretation after studying all the aerial pictures of their troops and other military forces. We do not believe that they are going to strike."

Amit argued back fiercely.

"I tell you, *our* experts say the Egyptians are in an *offensive* position. Why should they suddenly march into the desert to defend themselves?"

The CIA men responded calmly and reasonably: "Because they are convinced that *you* are going to attack *them!*"

The debate became acrimonious at times, but Meir Amit finally swung opinion his way.

"Look," he pleaded. "It makes no difference whether they are in what the textbooks say is 'defensive' or 'offensive' positions. We have to mobilize whatever their intentions. We cannot allow the Egyptian army to be poised on our frontier in the hope that they are just playing games. We had to call up our reserves *after* they marched into the Sinai. You know that is correct from your own sources: they acted first and we responded.

"For us the problem is the same whatever maneuvers the Egyptians indulge in. Our economy will be destroyed if the entire country is on war footing for any length of time.

"And in any event, you know without my having to spell it out that troops in defensive positions can swing into the offensive literally in a few minutes' time. Whatever the Egyptians' original plan was, they believe now that they can beat us. The Russians have been telling them this for weeks. They will not suddenly change their minds and tell Damascus and Cairo that they should withdraw their troops. Moscow wants a war and they have convinced the Arabs that this is the time for it."

It was now mid-afternoon. The grueling session had been going on since 9:00 AM, and they decided to take a break for coffee and sandwiches.

When they resumed the discussions, Meir Amit sensed that the CIA analysts had come around to agreeing with him. He was professional enough to know that if they did see things his way it was because they considered it in the best interests of the United States to do so. These were not men to be swayed by arguments about the safety of Israel.

Nonetheless, by the time Richard Helms arrived, Amit could no longer control his emotions.

"Look, Dick—we cannot stand it any longer. Israel is a small country. We are discussing our survival. I am talking about my own family, my wife and three daughters, and about the families of all the other men putting on uniforms right now."

But Helms needed no convincing. In the brief time that passed between his arrival at headquarters and his meeting with Meir Amit, one of his aides had briefed him. And Helms agreed with his old school friend.

"I want you to meet McNamara," he said.

At 6:00 PM that evening, Meir Amit was shown into the office of Secretary of Defense Robert McNamara. For the third time that day he stated his case. Though he ran through the facts with outward calm, he knew the importance of the impression he made on McNamara. At times he could not help conveying the tension he felt.

As Amit reached the end of his plea, a cold fear gripped him. McNamara had sat through the whole thing without saying a word. Not once did he indicate, even by a twitch of his eyebrows, that he was moved or convinced by his visitor.

At that moment an apologetic aide opened the door and handed McNamara an urgent cable. The Secretary opened it and read it carefully. Then he looked up at Meir Amit and announced quietly:

"Moshe Dayan has been made Defense Minister of Israel."

The Mossad chief understood immediately the implications of that decision. Dayan had been advocating attack all along. His inclusion in the Cabinet meant that he would throw his full weight behind this course of action. Israel's weeks of hesitation were about to end.

Hardly had these thoughts flashed through Meir Amit's mind when McNamara spoke.

"I know Moshe Dayan very well. I met him when he was in Washington. I am very glad he has been appointed. Please wish him good luck from me."

Then McNamara looked hard at his visitor. Carefully choosing each word, he added:

"Whatever decision he takes, I wish him good luck."

McNamara's words of support were subtle and oblique, but Amit knew exactly what they meant: the US government would support Israel if it made a preemptive strike against Syria and Egypt.

From the Pentagon, Meir Amit went hastily to the Israeli Embassy. With military attache General Joseph Geva he wrote out a long protocol about his day's activities. Then he sent a coded cable to Tel Aviv saying: "The Americans consider us to be a sovereign state and believe that we have the right to take whatever decision we think necessary for our survival. There will be no rebuke from them if we attack first. They will understand our motives. And I am certain that they will positively deter the Russians in case they are thinking of direct intervention."

Eager to get back to Israel, Amit went to the airport and managed to get squeezed on to an El Al cargo plane. The plane was carrying a shipment of gas masks, urgently requested by military leaders who feared that the Egyptians would use the gas warfare equipment that the Russians had supplied to them. The only other passenger was Abe Harman, Israeli ambassador to Washington. Thousands of Americans were clamoring to fly to Israel to help the beleaguered state, but only these two men were able to board the cargo flight.

When the Israeli Air Force launched the war in the early hours of June 5, their first targets were the airfields where the Egyptian air force had its warplanes stationed. The Israeli pilots had a complete breakdown of where the Egyptian radar installations were, as well as an analysis of their radar "blank" or blind spots. They flew right through, undetected until the last moment. The pilots also had precise information about what time the Egyptian pilots liked to have their breakfast. This was exactly the time that the attack was launched.

During those vital minutes the Israelis destroyed most of the Egyptian air power. Squadron after squadron was bombed on the ground. To the Egyptians' horror, the Israeli Mirages even knew which grounded planes were real and which were dummies. Not a bomb was wasted on the dummies: Israeli armored units found them intact amidst the wreckage when they advanced through the Sinai a few days later.

In the following days Israeli planes knocked out Egypt's entire network of surface-to-air missiles. The vital armaments factory at Helwan, its location believed to be a well-kept secret, was completely destroyed.

Much of the information that insured the success of these lightning attacks had come into Israeli hands from Wolfgang Lotz, the horse-loving spy who still languished in a Cairo prison, believing himself to be at the beginning of a twenty-five-year sentence.

For the first few days of war the mighty network built by the Syrians into the Golan Heights went unattacked; it contented itself with bombarding Israeli settlements. On June 9, however, the tables turned. A wave of Mirage fighter-bombers pounded the Heights and knocked out many of the emplacements there. Then tanks stormed the hills and mountains that had once been considered impregnable. They knew the location of every gun site, every land mine, every fortified communications trench. After a fierce battle they drove the Syrians out of the area and captured thousands of their soldiers. Their vast complex of tanks, mortars, and computer-controlled artillery was a shambles.

The devastating victory on the Golan Heights was made possible by Eli Cohen's dispatches from Damascus. He had pin-pointed every important site so precisely that the Israeli tanks, fighters and infantrymen knew exactly where they were.

When Syrian and Egyptian pilots did manage to take to the skies, they discovered that their Migs were no match for the Israelis in their French Mirages. The Israeli Air Force is acknowledged by military experts to be superbly trained; its pilots are of a uniformly high standard. But the Arab pilots realized that the Israelis also knew far more about Migs than they had expected them to. The Israelis took advantage of the slightly sluggish performance of the Mig, and of its lower speed capability. They also knew that the Mig, unlike the Mirage with its 360° visibility, had definite blind spots: directions from which the pilot would be unable to spot an attacker. Knowledge of these weaknesses molded Israeli tactics in the air war and gave them a strategic advantage in any dogfight with a Mig.

Of no less importance was the knowledge that the Migs used ordinary gasoline to give an independent boost to their ignition systems. This provided great speed leaving the ground, but it also meant that the extra fuel tank—built on at the point where the wings meet the fuselage—was incredibly inflammable. The Israeli pilots had only to score a direct hit on that fuel tank to see their adversary's aircraft burst into flames. One pilot, Yehuda S., described seeing this happen: "I felt sorry for the pilot. He didn't have a chance."

The complete knowledge of the Mig, its faults and strengths, came to the Israeli air force because of the woman Mossad agent who convinced Munir Redfa, the ace Iraqi pilot, to fly his plane to Israel. Months of testing under combat conditions gave the Israeli pilots an insuperable advantage.

These three stories—of Wolfgang Lotz, Eli Cohen, and Munir Redfa—document only a portion of what the Mossad contributed to Israel's victory in the Six-Day War. Many other agents—and their colleagues in Israel—made smaller but no less vital contributions. Some day their stories will be told.

Above: David Ben-Gurion and Isser Harel. Their trust in each other was without limit.
Opposite: Isser Harel (Isser the Little). He made the Mossad what it is today.

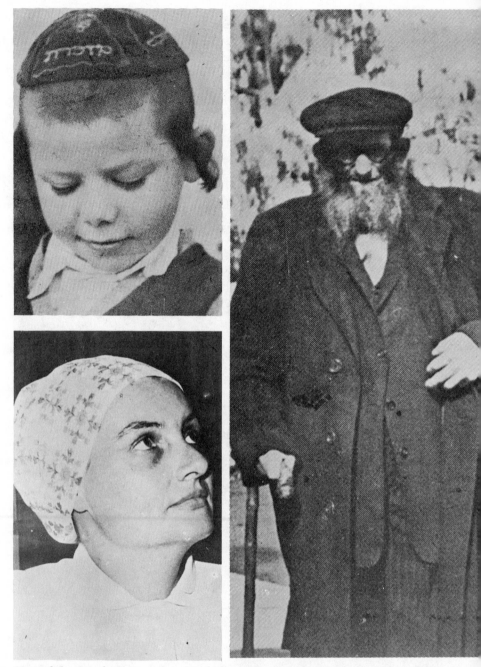

*Upper left: Jossele Schumacher. His kidnapping touched off a worldwide manhunt.
Right: Nahman Shtarkes. Jossele's grandfather—the "kidnapper."
Lower left: Madeleine Frei, now Ruth Ben-David. One of the few to get the better of Isser Harel's Mossad.*

Top: Munir Redfa's Mig 21, the first to come into the hands of the West.
Bottom: The Cohen family. Eli is second from the right, first row.

Eli Cohen. Probably the most remarkable spy of our century.

Top: A snapshot, taken in early 1960 by a Soviet advisor, of Eli Cohen (alias Kamil Amin Taabes) inspecting Syrian military fortifications in the Golan Heights.
Bottom: The Syrian military tribunal that sat in judgment on Eli Cohen. They had all known him as a friend—now they condemned him to hang.

170

الى زوجتي ناديا والمعاني بأولادنا امرغم بيده الكفاءات ي
اضطرت للقيام بهذا العمل الجاسوسي تحت الضغط الشديد
اسرائيل وذلك بعد ان قطع عني كل مورد للعيش واني الآن
وبعد ما صارت الحقيقة جلية ونهاية كل باغي وقعتها اقول لكم
انتبهوا من اسرائيل وعيشوا خارجاً وضعوا بالحرية كما
نحيا الشعوب لا كما نحيا اسرائيل . احذروا من تكرار
ما جرى؟ لأمه العائلة مية . والسلام عليكم
ايلي كوهين
١٩٦٥/٥/١٨

171

A microfilm photograph of an Egyptian memo concerning Nasser's armaments program—one of many obtained by the Mossad during Wolfgang Lotz's spying days in Cairo.

Opposite above: Eli's last letter to his wife Nadia, written in Arabic minutes before his execution. She shares it with her children to this day.
Direct opposite: The end: Eli Cohen on the scaffold (he refused to be blindfolded) . . . and hanging on public view in Damascus' Square of the Martyrs.

172

One of the most remarkable spy photographs ever taken. Just hours before the now-famous missile boats left Cherbourg harbor, author Uri Dan was allowed to observe the final plans being made. Admiral Mordechai Limon (center) worked non-stop

with fellow Israelis to perfect the daring Mossad scheme that fooled the entire French security organization.

Above: A Mossad coup: the French missile boats safe in Haifa after the perilous 3,000-mile journey from Cherbourg.

Opposite: The famous missile boats—equipped and ready for action.

176

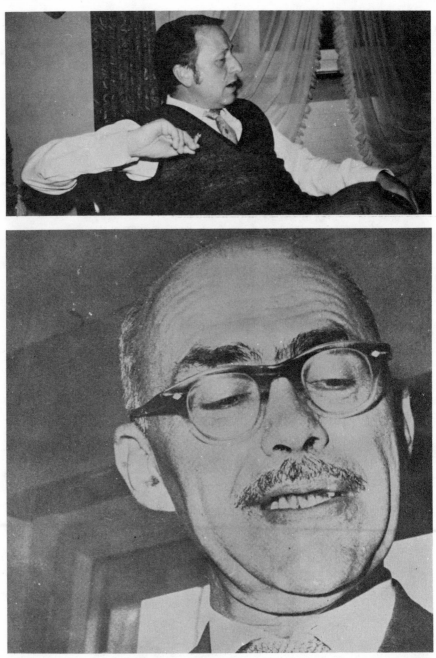

Top: Alfred Frauenknecht. This mild-mannered Swiss engineer worked with the Mossad in devising and executing one of history's most daring espionage coups.

Bottom: The mysterious Israel Beer. He had access to Israel's most guarded secrets—some of them learned directly from Ben-Gurion's diary.

Meir Amit, former Mossad chief.

Aharon Yariv, chief of Military Intelligence at the time of the Yom Kippur War.

Top: With Shaul Cohen, Eli Cohen's son, at the bar mitzvah for the sons of men killed in battle: Ezer Weizman, Minister of Defense; Prime Minister Menachem Begin; Chief of Staff Mordechai (Motta) Gur, among others.
Bottom: Prime Minister Begin leads the bar mitzvah congratulations for Shaul Cohen—the son that Eli Cohen saw only once, thirteen years before, as an infant.

The Downfall of
Isser Harel

REPORTS THAT GERMAN scientists who had formerly worked for Hitler were being employed in large numbers by Nasser began to reach Mossad headquarters as early as 1956, when Eli Cohen sent radio messages to that effect from Cairo. At the time the Mossad was more worried about the military aid being provided to Egypt by the Soviet Union, which sought to increase its influence in the Middle East. Vast quantities of armaments arrived almost daily at the port of Alexandria.

But Egypt was short of foreign currency, and by 1958 found itself unable to pay for the Soviet shipments. Angrily the Russians cut off their aid.

Worried by this threat to his plans to build up a military force strong enough to match that of Israel, Nasser turned increasingly to ex-Nazis who had sought refuge in Egypt. He wanted them to assist in the recruitment of German scientists who could help set up a self-sufficient Egyptian armaments industry. Offering large, tax-free salaries he was able before long to lure a number of leading scientists into his scheme.

Willi Messerschmidt, the preeminent German aircraft designer, had been working since the war in Spain, for the Hispano-Switza company. When approached by fellow Germans acting as agents for Nasser, he willingly accepted their lucrative offer. As his chief aide Messerschmidt chose Professor Alexander Brandner, top designer at the Junkers arms factory during World War Two. Brandner had been captured by the Russians at the end of the war, together with hundreds of other aeronautical experts. Not relishing the prospect of living in a labor camp, he offered his services as an engineer. Eventually he designed the engine that was used in the Soviet jet airplane Tupolev-11.

A pair of factories were built for Brandner and Messerschmidt at Helwan, fifteen miles south of Cairo. Aided by dozens of skilled German technicians and engineers—and a budget of something like $500,000,000—they set about the design and construction of two supersonic aircraft for Nasser.

Even more disturbing to Tel Aviv was the recruitment by Egypt of hundreds of German missile experts. Most of these were men who had worked at the rocket research center at Peenemünde, where the deadly V-1 and V-2 rockets were designed and built. They were recruited by Nasser for the same kind of research. This time, however, their long-range weapons were to be directed against Israel.

A Swiss-Egyptian businessman named Hassan Said Kamil directed the operations. Among the scientists employed was Dr. Eugen Saenger, who in 1935 had set up the first German rocket research unit on Luneberg Heath. Another was Wolfgang Pilz, who, with Saenger, had worked on the V-1 and V-2 rockets. After 1945 Pilz had worked for the French before being recruited by Egypt.

Unable to find trained Egyptian personnel, the Germans bought modern technological expertise through consultant firms in Germany and Switzerland. They also went abroad to purchase parts for their rockets. The MECO Corporation and MTP Company (both of Zurich) and the Stuttgart INTRA company became major suppliers.

Like ghosts arising from the roll call of Hitler's leading scientists, Pilz, Saenger and their colleagues got to work producing rockets like Al Zafar (The Victor), with a half-ton warhead and range of 375 miles; Al Ared (The Explorer), range 600 miles; and, most deadly of all, the Al Kahir (Conqueror), which carried a warhead of one ton of explosives.

The specter of ex-Nazis working in Egypt for the annihilation of Israel haunted the sleep of men like Isser Harel. For them the memory of the Holocaust—in which one third of the Jewish population of the world was destroyed—was a living reality. Few agents in the Mossad did not have friends or family who had perished in Hitler's "Final Solution of the Jewish Question."

To Isser Harel, the threat posed by the German scientists became an obsession, and he ordered a campaign to put an end to their activities. As part of this campaign the Mossad leaked to German and Israeli newspapers the names of many of the scientists. The precise nature of their activities was spelt out, and one of the most alarming revelations was that a former SS Colonel who had conducted nerve gas experiments on prisoners at the Dachau and Ravensbruck concentration camps was currently in charge of the Egyptian chemical warfare research. Documents were produced showing that Wolfgang Pilz had sent out agents to Europe and North America to buy cobalt 60 and other radioactive materials. Clearly the Egyptians were planning to produce atomic weapons.

To emphasize Israel's seriousness, Isser Harel paid a personal visit to Rheinhardt Gehlen, head of Germany's intelligence service. He accused Gehlen of turning a blind eye to the activities of his fellow countrymen.

Gehlen suggested to Isser that he leave the problem to German intelligence.

"We are using some of them to obtain information vital to the Western community," he maintained. Gehlen implied that he could put a stop to the German scientist's activities by his own discreet methods.

Isser was not convinced. "I want them stopped, and stopped now," he demanded. "I am not interested in long-term efforts. For us there is only the short term. The long term can mean after their rockets have fallen on our heads. In the long term we are dead men."

Isser made it plain that unless the German government took immediate action to bring its scientists home from Egypt he would be forced to take his own steps.

Early in 1962 the Mossad's propaganda war finally persuaded Chancellor Konrad Adenauer to order pressure to be exerted on the German scientists. Leading German firms were approached and they promised to provide more peaceful employment for the men working in Egypt.

The success of this ploy was minimal. Few of the scientists returned to Germany: they were under no legal compulsion to do so, and they enjoyed the luxuries of life in Egypt. Those who did return

On July 22, 1962, Egypt put on display two medium-range missiles. Nasser proudly proclaimed: "We are now capable of hitting any target south of Beirut." It required little imagination to know that Nasser was referring to targets in Israel. Nor was it difficult to see the destruction that would ensue if a full-scale rocket attack were launched. Israel's population and industry, which are concentrated into a few major areas, could easily be devastated by intensive rocket attacks.

To make matters worse, not long after Egypt announced her new rocket capabilities, the Mossad received detailed reports of an Egyptian plan for a coordinated all-out attack on Israel. Rockets would hit selected major cities and military bases, and a concerted artillery and air attack would follow. The German advisers had also devised a plan for using poison gas and chemical warfare against Israel.

Isser Harel decided that he could no longer stand idly by while Egypt mounted this deadly arsenal. Stretching his immense powers as chief of all of Israel's intelligence agencies to their limit, he ordered a terror campaign against Nasser's rocket experts.

In September, a German named Heinz Krug was reported missing. His car was found abandoned a few days later and he was never heard from again. Krug had been manager of the Munich offices of INTRA, one of the main supply companies for rocket parts.

In November, Wolfgang Pilz received a letter at his Cairo office. When his secretary Hannelora opened the letter it exploded in her face, injuring her seriously and leaving her blind. A few days later five Egyptian engineers were killed when a parcel addressed to their boss, General Kamal Azzaz, exploded while being opened. General Azzaz had responsibility for working with the German rocket scientists.

In the next few weeks, several other similar packages were opened and examined by bomb experts in Cairo. The message was clear: stop working on Egyptian rockets or your life is in danger. It was reiterated in February 1963, when a certain Hans Kleinwachter— who headed an Egyptian research center for developing rocket guidance systems—was visiting the German town of Lorrach. Kleinwachter was driving along a narrow lane when another car pulled up abruptly in the middle of the road and forced him to stop. A man jumped out and shot Kleinwachter several times with a silenced revolver. Kleinwachter narrowly escaped death by grappling with his assailant even while he was being fired at.

In Switzerland at around the same time, Heidi Gorck, the daughter of an Austrian scientist named Paul Gorck, was approached by a man who claimed to be a "friend of your father." The man asked

Heidi to travel to Egypt—where her father was employed at the rocket factory—and tell him that his life would be in danger if he didn't stop his work there. Frightened by the threats, Heidi went straight to the police, who persuaded her to arrange another meeting with the man. When they met again their conversation was taped and listened to by Swiss intelligence officers, and the stranger—along with a companion he had brought with him—was promptly arrested.

The first man turned out to be an Austrian named Otto Joklick, a physicist who had served with the German army during the war and later went on to become director of Italy's Institute of Atomic Physics and Nuclear Technology. The other was an Israeli named Joseph Ben Gal.

Joklick had been offered a job with the Egyptian rocket team by program director Colonel el-Din. It was only when he arrived in Cairo that he realized what the object of the experiments was: Israel's annihilation. Horrified by the plan, he decided to cooperate with the Israelis.

At their trial in Switzerland, Joklick and Ben Gal won sympathy for themselves and for their cause by producing masses of documentary evidence concerning the Egyptian plans for the destruction of Israel. Joklick told how he had spent millions of dollars buying radioactive materials for use in rocket warheads. Other plans included biological and chemical warheads. He caused considerable embarrassment by revealing the extent of Swiss cooperation with the Egyptians' program of destruction.

In the end, the court was so moved by the defendants' concern for Israel that even the prosecutor, Hans Wieland, suggested only token punishment. He said: "The activities of the German scientists have created the greatest concern to the whole world."

The trial proved a great moral victory for the Mossad. Upset by the worldwide publicity which painted the work of the German scientsts in "an evil light," as it was expressed in the Swiss court, the German government passed a law forbidding its citizens to work for Nasser's rocket and armament factories. One by one they returned to their homeland.

In any case, the Mossad had drastically overestimated the real danger to Israel posed by Nasser's German friends. They had never perfected a guidance system for their rockets, which were thus useless as weapons. When Marshal Abdel Hakim Amer went to view the launching of one of the advanced models—which he had been assured was "in perfect operational condition"—he was almost killed by the rocket: it rose a few yards and then crashed back to the earth in flames. A Mossad report on the incident solemnly stated:

"The rocket turned around in mid-air and nearly landed on the head of Marshal Amer, who was seen running for his life."

The Mach 2 aircraft promised by Willi Messerschmidt similarly failed to live up to its expectations. In anger President Nasser turned on his friend Hassan Kamil and demanded that he return the money he had received as middleman in the scheme. But Kamil gave them nothing: he had declared his bankruptcy in a Swiss court. Nasser's arms program ground to a halt through the incompetence of the men who ran it.

But the furor caused by the arms program did take one unexpected victim in Israel. It brought about a head-on confrontation between Isser Harel and his boss, Ben-Gurion.

Unknown to Isser, Ben-Gurion had previously made a secret agreement with Chancellor Adenauer of Germany. In meetings at New York's Waldorf Astoria they agreed that Germany would make major financial reparations to Israel in atonement for Nazi crimes, and would supply Israel with large quantities of arms.

Thus, while the Mossad's terror campaign against the German scientists was in full swing, Germany was acting as the main supplier of arms to Israel. This troubled Ben-Gurion deeply. He was convinced that the real danger to Israel was not nearly so great as Isser had supposed it to be. And even if it was, sending letter bombs to German citizens could only endanger the good relations he had established through painstaking negotiations with Adenauer. He was looking toward the future, toward the eventual normalizing of relations between Israel and Germany in spite of what the Nazis had done to the Jews some twenty years before. He knew that it was in Israel's best interests now to cultivate the Germans, not antagonize them.

In late March, 1963, the two men discussed the problem at a hotel near Lake Tiberias where Ben-Gurion was resting. The Prime Minister put the matter bluntly:

"Isser, Bonn is helping us with tanks, helicopters, ships and other weapons. A German mission has already been here, as you know, to discuss the further supply of armaments. Your campaign of letter bombs is upsetting the Germans in Bonn. It is causing antagonism. You must stop it right away."

Isser had always worshiped Ben-Gurion, the man who had led Israel through its most difficult years of birth and infancy. But he had a blind spot when it came to the question of the German scientists. He was convinced that "appeasement," as he put it, would lead to disaster.

Moreover, Isser was now at the height of his power and the Mossad at the height of its prestige. The Eichmann capture was still fresh in his countrymen's minds. Isser knew that Ben-Gurion was growing old and tired, and saw himself as the right man to follow in his path. As his critics said at the time, the Mossad chief really viewed himself as Vice-Premier of Israel even if he had no legal claim to any such title. He had exercised so much authority over the years that he now felt it his duty to come out and openly challenge the old man he had served unquestioningly for over a decade.

Despite Ben-Gurion's wishes, Isser Harel ordered that the pressure against the German scientists be stepped up vigorously. It was the first and only time that he had overstepped the authority vested in him by Ben-Gurion.

A week after their meeting at Lake Tiberias the two men confronted each other again in Ben-Gurion's office.

An observer would have commented on the physical similarities between the two men, both short and fierce-looking. They even walked with the same kind of fast, abrupt step. For over a decade they had worked together in total and unquestioned trust, but in a relationship that was unmistakably defined: Isser was the servant, Ben-Gurion the boss.

Now that relationship had been broken, the trust undermined.

Two pairs of eyes met each other as the Prime Minister spoke.

"I want to see the documents for myself," he said coldly. "I want to make up my own mind about the reliability of the reports on the German scientists and their rockets. I will judge."

This was the first time that Ben-Gurion had ever questioned Isser's interpretation of data, and the sting hurt. It was the first time he had ever wanted to see for himself, the first time he ever doubted his lieutenant's wisdom and integrity. Isser felt deeply insulted.

"If you don't trust me," he announced, "I am resigning."

Without saying another word he rose from his seat, turned his back and walked with short quick steps to the door. Only once did he turn around to speak:

"My successor will give you the answers!"

Later that day the Prime Minister realized that Isser had no intention of backing down. He told an aide: "The son of a gun is going to do it—he really *is* going to quit."

Ben-Gurion was a big enough man to offer the olive branch. That afternoon he put through a telephone call to Isser. It was one of the few occasions on which he used this method of communication which he called simply "The American Way."

The call went unanswered.

The next day an official letter of resignation arrived on Ben-Gurion's desk. The newspapers got hold of the story and it staggered the country. The Mossad itself felt the blow keenly. One of Isser's right-hand men described it as "an earthquake."

"Harel had concentrated so much power in his hands," he said, "and so many top decisions were made by him—personally and alone—that for a time we were like a ship without a rudder. He had created the Mossad and made it what it was. None of us even began to realize just how much we had grown to depend on him always being there at the head.

". . . it was clearly an error to have so much authority vested in one individual."

A secret committee was set up to investigate the reasons for Isser's resignation. Ben-Gurion was fiercely cross-examined, and became outraged by what he considered to be manipulations on Isser's part to influence the press and present his own version of events. The Prime Minister had felt increasingly isolated in the preceding months, and increasingly weary. The furor over Isser's departure from government was one of the final setbacks that led him to resign several months later, and turn over the reins of government to Levi Eshkol.

Nonetheless, he wrote to Isser: "Even after what has happened since your resignation my opinion about your talent, loyalty and patriotism has not changed one iota. Against my wishes you resigned. You did not accept my plea to withdraw your resignation.

That was your business and I am not going to be your judge."

Meir Amit, the man who replaced Isser as head of the Mossad, made a striking contrast to his predecessor. Formerly head of military intelligence, he was a cultured and sophisticated soldier who spoke several languages and had studied at Columbia University. Soon after his confirmation as head of the Mossad he set about reorganizing the agency along modern, more democratic lines.

Knowing that he could never make himself the charismatic

leader that Isser had been, he refused to concentrate so much power in his own hands. He decided that intuition and daring would play a less important role in the formulation of policy than science and careful analysis. He gave his lieutenants much more scope for decision-making than they had ever enjoyed during Isser's reign. Slowly and carefully he worked to win the confidence of agents accustomed to Isser's style of leadership.

It took time, but eventually Amit did gain his men's confidence. They were particularly impressed by his efforts to save the life of Eli Cohen, and to free the spies being held in Egyptian prisons. They saw that cautious but decisive leadership was as effective as Isser's more unorthodox and flamboyant methods.

Isser spent two years in uneasy, restless retirement. He returned to the intelligence scene briefly in 1965, when a number of coincidences conspired to undermine confidence in the direction of intelligence affairs. First the Bonn government broke its agreement with Israel to supply arms, setting off a flurry of recrimination and leading Isser to claim triumphantly: "I told you the Germans would betray us. I had to stop blowing up their scientists in Egypt because they were supplying arms. Now look: no more arms!"

This coincided with the arrest of Wolfgang Lotz and the visit by East German President Ulbricht to Cairo. Everything seemed to be going wrong.

Pressured constantly by the aggressive Isser, Levi Eshkol finally gave in and agreed to bring him back into intelligence affairs by appointing him "special adviser for intelligence matters in the Prime Minister's office." Eshkol probably thought of the appointment as the best way of keeping Isser quiet, but Meir Amit rightly viewed it as an implicit challenge to his own authority. Isser would not be content until he was running the whole show again. As a result of the appointment, the Mossad leadership was involved in a time-consuming internal power struggle. Finally, Levi Eshkol had to choose between the old boss and the new.

He decided that the days when the Mossad could be run as a one-man operation must be well and truly ended. Isser was relieved of his special appointment, and Meir Amit was retained as head of the Mossad. Rejected once and for all, Isser Harel retired permanently from public life. Today he lives quietly with Rivkah at their home near Tel Aviv, where he works on writing about his experiences in the Mossad. If you go down to the beach early in the morning, you can usually see him—a tiny, solitary figure taking his daily run.

Proudly displayed at Isser's home is a photograph he will always treasure. In June 1966, Paula Ben-Gurion, wife of the ex-Prime Minister, brought the two old associates together for a conciliatory meeting. At a party held at Ben-Gurion's home the two men met for the first time in three years. It was a dramatic moment when they came face-to-face—these two giants who had played such an important role in the building of the Israeli state. As they embraced, Isser wept openly. Ben-Gurion presented him with a photograph of himself, inscribed on the back with the words:

"To Isser, a guarantor of the honor, the security, and the secrets of state. David Ben-Gurion."

Fighting the Embargo

ON JUNE 2, 1967, Charles de Gaulle declared that France was ending immediately all shipments of "aggressive weapons" to the Middle East. The announcement meant that Israel would get no more arms from the country which had been for several years her primary supplier. Had the 1967 war lasted much longer than it did, Israel's French-built Mirages would have been grounded for lack of spare parts. The air force would have been impotent.

France's embargo continued and intensified after the war had ended, thus leaving Israel in a more vulnerable military position than its leaders thought the country could afford. The situation required extraordinary measures, and as usual the Mossad was called into action more than once.

The following two stories tell of just a small part of what they did to combat the French arms embargo.

The Missile Boats of Cherbourg

IN 1962, EGYPTIAN-BASED Mossad agents like Wolfgang Lotz reported to headquarters that the Soviet Union was planning to strengthen Egypt's navy by adding to it a number of fast Komar and Osa missile boats. Each of these small but speedy boats was to be armed with surface-to-surface missiles with a range of up to twenty-five miles. The potential danger to Israeli coastal cities—including major population centers like Haifa and Tel Aviv—was obvious.

At that time Israel's navy consisted of nothing more than two antiquated British-built submarines, a dozen torpedo boats and a couple of slow and cumbersome destroyers. Egypt already had twelve modern submarines, ten frigates, six destroyers and over fifty torpedo boats. With the addition of the missile boats her naval superiority would be overwhelming.

Israeli military experts decided that the best defense against the new threat would be small, fast missile ships similar to the ones being supplied to Egypt by the Soviets. The day of the great warship was over, they said: modern long-range rockets made them too vulnerable to attack. The Israelis knew that Germany's armed forces had already reached the same decision and were building the "Jaguar," the most advanced missile craft then in existence. The superbly maneuverable Jaguar could reach speeds of up to forty-five miles an hour at full stretch.

The Jaguar seemed to meet Israel's needs exactly. Armed with the Israeli-built "Gabriel" missile it would be a formidable opponent indeed for Egypt's new weapons. The Gabriel missile had an advantage over its Soviet counterparts in its ability to fly low over the sea after launching, and thus avoid detection by radar.

Later in 1962, Prime Minister Ben-Gurion sent Deputy Defense Minister Shimon Peres to Bonn, where he met Chancellor Adenauer. Adenauer had agreed to supply Israel with arms as part of an attempt to make reparations for Germany's crimes against world Jewry, and now he signed an agreement as requested to supply Israel with twelve of the Jaguar vessels. They would be built at the naval yards in Kiel and delivered in stages over the coming years. The only condition of the sale was the same that Adenauer had insisted upon from the beginning: because of the potential displeasure of the Arab countries with which Germany did big business, the arms deal was to remain secret.

By December 1964, within two years of the agreements being made, the first three missile boats were delivered to Israel. It was then that the details of the pact were leaked to the *New York Times* by a member of the German administration who—like many of his colleagues—found it difficult to forget his former Nazi sympathies. He disagreed violently with Bonn's policy of trying "to be nice to the Jews."

When the story appeared on the front page of the *Times*, it aroused anger in every Arab capital. Considerable pressure was applied to the Bonn government with warnings that a continuation of the sales to Israel would result in economic sanctions, possibly a complete trade boycott. The pressure was too much for the Germans: they agreed that no more Jaguars would be built in Kiel for Israel.

But the Germans also agreed, bending over backwards not to offend the Israelis too much, that the boats could be constructed elsewhere. After much deliberation, the Israelis decided to give the work to the shipyards at Cherbourg, France. It was a logical enough step, since the French at that time were supplying Israel with 75 percent of its military hardware.

The move satisfied the Israelis and also pleased Felix Amiot, Director General of the Cherbourg shipyards. He was only too delighted to secure jobs for his work force.

Within a couple of months, over 200 Israelis were living and working in the port town of Cherbourg. The place began to resemble a tiny outpost of the Israeli marine headquarters, as technicians and engineers from Haifa took up residence in houses and apartments near the dock area. They worked closely with their French counterparts, for they had designed some of their own ingenious features for inclusion in the boats. These features, some of them quite novel in western naval design, were later incorporated into the construction of French warcraft.

The Tel Aviv authorities made every effort to send to Cherbourg military personnel who had moved to Israel from the North African nations, like Algeria and Morocco, which had once been under French colonial domination. When this was impossible, it was still a top priority to send men who spoke French fluently. With no language differences and little cultural barrier, the newcomers in Cherbourg fitted in happily with the permanent residents of their temporary home. Their wives shopped locally and their children went to local schools.

Still, there were some restrictions on the Israelis, who were all under military control. Even the bachelor sailors who took their evening meal in local establishments like the Restaurant de Tourville rarely drank alcohol—not even the occasional demi-carafe of wine with meals. When they wanted to join the young people of Cherbourg in the bars along the rue Gambetta for a social evening they always had to have permission from their officers. Madame Giot, an elderly concierge of the local hotel where they were quartered, spoke admiringly of their impeccable behavior. "They called me 'Madam,' " she said, "and only now and then did I have to tell them not to make so much noise when they came back late in the evening."

Of course, there were occasional problems. One Israeli sailor was arrested when he became drunk and made a public nuisance of himself. He declined to be taken into custody and it took a carload of gendarmes to bring him under control. As if that weren't enough, the sailor was accompanied by a prostitute, who was also arrested. This caused a number of red faces the next day as both Israeli and French officials tried to play down the incident.

On another occasion a young boy somehow managed to slip past the security men guarding the shipyard and was discovered happily taking photographs of missile boats. An overly zealous Israeli grabbed his camera and hustled the boy out of the area. When he arrived home without the camera his father, an important businessman, complained vehemently to the local authorities. It took enormous tact on all sides to smooth things over, and the Israelis bought the young boy a fresh roll of film when they returned his camera. Needless to say, he never recovered his "scoop" snapshots of the boats.

The Cherbourg boat-building operation was supervised by a tall man named Brigadier General Mordechai Limon, whose responsibility it was to oversee the purchase of European arms for Israel.

Though only in his early 40s, Limon had over two decades of first-hand experience of the sea and ships. He first saw the sea when, as a boy of eight, he emigrated from Poland to Palestine with his parents. As soon as he was old enough he joined the Pal-Yam, the naval division of the underground Jewish armed forces in Palestine. When World War Two came he volunteered, like many Jewish youngsters, for the British Merchant Marine: not only would he assist in the fight against Hitler but he would gain valuable experience and serve his country well after the war.

During Limon's training period under the British, it was written of him that "He is a typical English gentleman type, but one who would always react quickly and positively in an emergency." During the war he served on the hazardous convoys which brought American supplies through the Murmansk Sea on British ships to Russia. Several times he fought for survival alongside his fellow seamen; their ships were often torpedoed beneath them.

At the end of the war, still only twenty-one years old, Limon was chosen to command some of the rickety refugee ships which tried to penetrate the British blockade of Palestine. This was a job fraught with constant danger. On one trip Limon's boat developed engine trouble; a storm arose and its propellers were fouled. And, as if that weren't enough, they were spotted by a British patrol vessel. In a desperate bid to clear the propellers, Limon dived into the water and tried to do the job by hand. Again and again he dove alone, until he finally succeeded. The engines were started and the boat hastily tried to take evasive action. But the British overtook them. After a hand-to-hand battle in which several refugees were killed, the British boarded Limon's ship. He had hidden in a secret compartment and evaded capture despite thorough searches for him. When the boat was brought to Cyprus, Limon dove overboard and once again managed to escape. Within a few days he was back in Palestine preparing to set sail again for Marseilles, where he took command of yet another refugee ship.

Another time, in 1948, Limon undertook a seemingly suicidal mission against Egyptian warships docked at Port Said. He traveled to the port alone in a small speedboat—virtually all the navy that Israel could boast at the time—and then, swimming in darkness, planted a mine on the keel of an Egyptian ship. To insure that nothing went wrong, he stayed in the water nearby—his only protection from the blast was an old mattress that he had brought to wrap around himself. When the bomb went off he was lifted right out of the water, mattress and all. By a miracle, he survived. But the warship went down.

His extraordinary exploits made Mordechai Limon a national hero, and it was scarcely a surprise when in 1950, at the tender age of 26, he was made commander-in-chief of Israel's tiny navy.

Four years later, thinking he was getting a little old for the job, Limon retired from military service and went to New York, where he took a business degree at Columbia. Thus, when he was appointed several years later to supervise Israeli arms purchases abroad, he was well equipped to spend the millions of dollars that were placed at his disposal. He played a vital role in Israel's attempts to modernize its armed forces in the late 50s and early 60s.

Working closely with Director General Felix Amiot and the technical people responsible for the Cherbourg missile boats, he followed the operation from preliminary planning through every stage of construction.

Thus, the day in April 1967 when they launched the first boat—named *Mivtash*—was a happy one for Mordechai Limon. With a small group of associates, French and Israeli, he gathered at Cherbourg's Sofitel Hotel to celebrate with wine and champagne. While corks were popping he introduced Felix Amiot, with whom he had become good friends, to the boat's commander, Lt. Colonel Ezra Kedem. Ezra, a shaggy-haired blonde giant of a man, had such a fierce expression that the Frenchman promptly nicknamed him "Ezra the Shark." A few days after the boat was finished he took command and sailed it to Haifa. The second was ready about a month later, and it too sailed uneventfully for Israel.

To the Israelis' regret, the boats arrived too late to be of use in the Six-Day War, since there was no time to arm them.

But by then the Israelis had other worries to keep them occupied. General de Gaulle had stopped all supplies of "offensive weapons" to Israel, which meant that their air force was unable to collect vast quantities of planes, spare parts and other essential equipment.

In Paris, Mordechai Limon headed an Israeli delegation which argued furiously with the government in an effort to get them to honor their commitments. The French, however, were firmly sticking to a pro-Arab policy.

But in Cherbourg, for some reason, no one seemed to have heard of the embargo. Two more completed vessels sailed out in the autumn, and the Israelis continued to work with their French colleagues on the remaining boats.

In December, however, things took a drastic turn for the worse. On the 28th, a team of Israeli commandos staged a retaliatory raid on Beirut airport. Without harming a soul, they blew up thirteen aircraft and then returned to Tel Aviv without sustaining a single casualty.

De Gaulle seemed determined to use this latest example of "arrogance on the part of Jerusalem" to teach the Israelis a lesson. Without even informing his deputies he issued instructions to customs officials to forbid the departure of any French military cargo to Israel.

The embargo was now to be total. Crates containing spare parts for Mirage planes were held up in Marseilles. An Israeli transport plane on the runway at Le Bourget airport was forbidden to take on board a shipment of electronic equipment. The boats at Cherbourg were also "frozen." Earlier Limon had been led to believe that these items would be excluded from the list of banned items, and would be delivered as "exceptions." He was surprised and outraged when a friendly whisper (the decision had not been made official) informed him of the new order.

Immediately Limon sent off a telegram to Defense Minister Moshe Dayan. Within hours it was being rushed to his home in the Tel Aviv suburb of Tzahala, where most of the senior Israeli army officers live. When he read the telegram he passed his hand pensively over his black eye-patch—a sure sign, as his colleagues well knew, of intense concern and concentration.

"It's curious," said Dayan, "that General de Gaulle always manages to drop us his bombshells on Fridays, just before the Sabbath." He could not help remembering a similar telegram sent on June 2, 1967, announcing de Gaulle's ban on the further shipment of "offensive weapons" to Israel. That telegram had been an incentive to go ahead with a preemptive strike against the Egyptians, in order to get the war over with quickly before the Israeli stock of spare parts could be depleted.

Dayan had long been an admirer of the French president. He had lost his eye in Syria while fighting the forces of the Vichy regime—de Gaulle's hated enemies—during World War Two. When links between Israel and France began to strengthen in the late 50s, he had agreed completely with David Ben-Gurion, who called de Gaulle "a true friend, a true ally." De Gaulle had sent Dayan a personal letter of congratulations on his book *The Sinai Campaign 1956.*

Now the same de Gaulle was imposing a total embargo on the dispatch of arms—already paid for—to Israel; the same man was being hailed as a hero by the Arab press. The "true ally" was refusing to hand back the money paid in advance for a shipment of Mirage fighters that were not going to be delivered.

When Dayan broke the news at a Cabinet meeting held the following Sunday, Minister of the Interior Shapira, who was also head of the Religious Party, commented by quoting from the Book of Kings:

"Hast thou killed, and also taken possession?"

In Cherbourg harbor, three more of the missile boats were almost complete. Their decks were littered with oxygen cylinders and tools, thermos flasks of coffee and bottles of wine left by the French construction crew.

At 5 PM on January 4, 1969, a week after de Gaulle's dramatic announcement, the skeleton crew of the three vessels casually made their way one by one into the deserted yard. The work force had already knocked off for the weekend. Without showing any undue haste the Israeli crew members spent three hours of intense effort trying to get the boats ready for a sea voyage. When all was ready and the motors were warmed up, they boldly raised the Israeli flag and set off. No one challenged them. They simply sailed into the English channel and never returned.

When news of the daring move reached Paris, the Minister of Defense asked Mordechai Limon where the ships had gone. The reply he received was simple and uncompromising: "They were given orders to sail for Haifa. They belong to us."

President de Gaulle was furious at the bold move. Michel Debre, the grandson of a rabbi who had been converted to Christianity, was among those in the French cabinet who wanted to impose stringent sanctions on Israel. He urged that diplomatic relations between France and Israel be severed immediately. More moderate colleagues called for restraint, but an inquiry was launched anyway.

In Cherbourg, naval authorities and customs men simply shrugged their shoulders. By an extraordinary coincidence, no one seemed to have read a newspaper, watched television or listened to a radio during the preceding days. Said one of the local people: "We did not know anything of the embargo."

Officials claimed that they first heard of the embargo in a letter of instructions received from Paris on the 6th—2 days after the boats had left. They produced documents and a statement from the post office supporting their claim. The whole incident must, they agreed, be terribly embarrassing for the government: frequently they had complained of how slow the postal service was between the capital and their own city. Perhaps the President would have a word with the Minister of Communications about improving it. . . .

A battle raged for weeks between Paris and Cherbourg. Long reports were compiled, accusations bounced back and forth between one department and another. Meanwhile work continued on the last five missile boats as if nothing had happened.

Messages from Tel Aviv began bombarding Mordechai Limon with a new urgency: Israel wanted the last of her missile boats.

But the Cherbourg naval and customs authorities had been stung by the allegations of negligence leveled at them from Paris. As a result they were very much on their guard: the Israeli boats were kept under close surveillance. They could no longer simply be sneaked out one weekend.

In November 1969, Mordechai Limon was summoned to Tel Aviv for urgent consultation with Moshe Dayan, other military men, and a number of intelligence officers. They had to find a way of getting their missile boats from France—everyone agreed on that. But the means of doing so provoked fierce debate.

The preferred way, obviously, was to get the French government to honor its legal commitments. Agreements had been signed and the boats paid for. They belonged to Israel. But no one knew better than Mordechai Limon—who had held to the conviction that the French would change their minds about the embargo longer than most of his colleagues in Israel—that the official line was set. The embargo was a reality, something to be lived with and not changed. They would not get their boats through diplomatic means. Something else—something more devious—seemed the only solution. But this solution involved a moral compromise about which many participants in the debate had grave doubts. All remembered the criticism leveled at Israel for violating the sovereignty of Argentina by sending agents to kidnap Adolf Eichmann. No one wanted Israel to acquire the image of a lawless nation of pirates that violated international principles whenever it suited her own interests.

The prevailing view, however, was expressed by those who

pointed to the equally lawless bombardment of Israeli ships and property by the well-armed Egyptian forces. They argued that the very survival of their country was in doubt. The missile boats (not to mention the embargoed Mirages) could tip the scales between victory and defeat. "Piracy" was an unpleasant accusation but it was better than seeing the Egyptian army marching unchallenged to Tel Aviv.

After days of argument the group of military and intelligence leaders decided that extraordinary methods were the only way of getting their missile boats.

After that, the only decision left was: how to do it?

In close consultation with Admiral Limon, Mossad and military officers worked long hours considering and reconsidering a number of schemes. When they had ruled out all but one, they set to work planning it in every last detail. Every forseeable problem was ironed out, every contingency taken into account. The Mossad knew that the plan would be unusually difficult to carry off because it involved not experienced agents but technicians and sailors unused to intelligence work. Moreover, it would require from everyone concerned the utmost discretion.

Mordechai Limon promised that everyone under his command would play his part perfectly. Operation "Noah's Ark," as it was code-named, would have to succeed.

Limon returned to Paris after about ten days in Israel. When he arrived he telephoned Felix Amiot of the Cherbourg shipyards and officially informed him that Israel no longer wanted the missile boats. There would be too long a wait for them, he said, and Israel didn't need them enough to be able to afford that wait. They were now ready to sell them off to any suitable buyer. The only condition of sale was that Israel be reimbursed the money it had already spent. Amiot agreed to the request. "That seems very reasonable," he told Limon.

Not long after their phone conversation Felix Amiot received a visit from a man who identified himself as Martin Siem, a construction company owner and director of the Norwegian shipping company Starboat and Weill. Siem had recently met Amiot in Paris, and the Frenchman reminded him of the occasion. "You are from Oslo, as I recall," said Amiot.

"Well, yes and no. My company is registered in Panama but I call Norway my home."

Soon they got around to the purpose of Siem's visit. He told

Amiot that he heard of the Israeli ships which were being offered for sale, and was interested in buying them.

"That type of vessel is just what my company needs for some oil-exploration work we are doing off the coast of Alaska. The only problem is time: I would like the boats as soon as possible. We are in something of a hurry."

The two men easily settled the financial terms for a deal and closed it with a gentlemanly handshake. Amiot prided himself on being a man of action, and was happy to make the deal quickly.

The next day Amiot wrote a letter to the Minister of Defense, who had to approve the deal. Amiot reported that he had a serious client who was willing to pay a good price for the boats.

The request went to a committee called the CIEEMG (Inter-ministerial Committee for the Study of the Export of War Materials) for approval. They saw no reason to oppose the sale. Felix Amiot had a letter from the Israelis saying they no longer wanted the boats, and since the vessels were unarmed they could not be considered as war materials any longer. Norway was not in the Middle East, and therefore not covered by the embargo. So on November 18 the CIEEMG approved the sale to Starboat and Weill.

Had they examined the matter more closely, the French would have discovered that Starboat and Weill had been created only a few days before, on November 5, in the offices of a Panama law firm called Arias Fabrega y Fabrega. They also could have learned without much trouble of Martin Siem's connections with an Israeli shipping executive named Jacob Meridor, and with another Israeli, Mila Brenner, who was the director of Maritime Fruit Carriers, Ltd. They might have questioned Siem's contention that he needed high-speed boats designed for military uses to assist in oil drilling operations; or the fact that a man who was president of his own construction firm couldn't build boats designed to his own specifications.

But the French were relieved to be rid of the boats at all. Selling them to a Norwegian businessman and giving the Israelis their money back would solve an irritating problem for government policy-makers who were tired of the whole embargo question. No one even considered referring the matter to the President or his cabinet.

Working with uncharacteristic speed, the Civil Service completed all the necessary documentation for the sale within a few weeks. These were dispatched to Cherbourg by express mail. At the Cherbourg post office it was decided to take the official-looking parcel (which was over a foot in thickness) direct to Felix Amiot's office in a special van. The local postal officials didn't want any further criticism of their slow delivery.

Meanwhile, young sailors started arriving at Cherbourg in increasing numbers. This puzzled the locals, who had been told that Israel was no longer interested in the boats, until it was explained to them that some Norwegians had bought the vessels and were coming to take them away. That explained why so many of the arriving seamen were blond and blue-eyed.

It quickly became apparent that the Norweigians would be leaving soon. No one noticed this as acutely as the owner of Tabac Dumont, a small shop near the harbor. He did a roaring business with the sailors, who were buying cartons of cigarettes instead of single packets, and large quantities of food and other supplies. When he wasn't busy he watched from his store as the sailors carefully painted out the Hebrew lettering on the sides of the boats and replaced them with their new names: Starboat 1, Starboat 2, etc.

The Israelis, on the other hand, seemed to be staying put for a while. As Christmas approached, some of them told their French friends that they were planning to go to Paris over the holiday to see friends or relatives there. Many others, over seventy in all, reserved tables at the Cafe du Théâtre for their special Christmas Eve dinner. The Israelis showed every sign of going on with business as usual, even though their boats were being sold and they no longer had any reason to stay in Cherbourg.

Some citizens of Cherbourg did, however, notice unusual behavior among their Israeli guests. At a local casino an Israeli sailor who regularly placed small bets at the roulette table was suddenly playing for huge amounts. The croupier, who knew the man well, asked why he had suddenly changed his betting pattern. The sailor replied: "It doesn't matter. I won't be here much longer." This brought forth a stream of Hebrew from the sailor's two companions, who were clearly angry with their friend for what must have been an inadvertent—and foolish—slip. The croupier could tell that the man regretted what he had said.

Other locals noticed that some of the "Norwegians" were such accomplished linguists that they included Hebrew among their repertoire of languages.

Even more unusual was the regular appearance by the harbor of Lt. Colonel Ezra Kedem, who had commanded the first missile boat to sail out of Cherbourg some eighteen months before.

On December 18, the final paperwork was completed on the sale of the boats to Starboat and Weill. That very night, the citizens of Cherbourg heard the sound of motors as the Norwegian crews began testing their boats. The tests continued for several nights afterwards, and soon everyone was used to them.

At least one resident of the port city had good cause for knowing exactly what the truth was about the imminent departure of the missile boats. This was a woman named Stephanie, the wife of a local café-owner. For many months she had been having an affair with an Israeli named Nehemiah, a handsome Algerian-born sailor who was to command one of the missile boats.

Stephanie and Nehemiah were in love, and they talked of going back to Israel together. The woman was willing to leave her husband, she said, for the twenty-eight-year-old Israeli. But as December wore on, it became obvious to her that Nehemiah was going to be leaving soon; and though he never told her the circumstances of his leaving, it wasn't difficult for her to guess the truth. Faced with the necessity for an immediate choice, Stephanie concluded that while a love affair was one thing, breaking up a marriage was quite another. She would not leave her husband for Nehemiah.

Instead she presented the young Israeli with a white terrier puppy. Nehemiah was nonplussed: he didn't know what his fellow crewman would think of having a dog on board for their perilous 3,000-mile journey to Haifa. But they all liked the dog immediately, and accepted her as a sailor like themselves.

From the 18th to the 23rd the Israeli crews worked feverishly at night inspecting, testing, and generally getting their boats ready for a long voyage. When Christmas Eve finally came, all was in readiness.

That morning, Mordechai Limon kissed his wife Rachel, his daughter Nili, and son Zvika goodbye at their Paris home. After stopping off at his office in the Boulevard Malesherbes, the Admiral headed west for Cherbourg.

Observant passersby in that town could notice Ezra "the Shark" spending most of his time either staring out to sea with high-powered binoculars or closely inspecting the harbor layout. Of special interest to him seemed to be the two channels used by ships coming in and out of Cherbourg. The western channel, some sixty-five feet deep and guarded by a lookout, was the more commonly used. The eastern channel, narrower and less often used, seemed to get more attention from Ezra Kedem. Ships' captains disliked this channel not only because it was narrower than the other but because of the unstable submerged rocks which had accumulated in it for years. Conditions had never been good there but recently they had become worse than ever.

Nonetheless, this was the channel through which the three missile craft had escaped earlier in the year. It had the advantage of possessing several blind spots, areas where the radar surveillance equipment used by the harbor authorities was unable to spot any movement. (Ezra knew this from his friendly conversations with the French authorities themselves.) It was obvious that the Israelis had to use the same channel this time. The prospect was daunting.

Ezra Kedem occasionally had other worries to contend with. He received a bad fright on December 12, when Michel Debre, the anti-Israeli Prime Minister, traveled with five other ministers to Cherbourg for the launching of France's new nuclear submarine *Le Terrible.* An observant military aide noticed the five missile boats docked together and suggested that they be dispersed. "You can never trust those Israelis," he said; "they may become a target for Arab terror attacks."

Felix Amiot put the official's mind at rest. Security was very tight, and anyway, the Israelis were no longer interested in the boats. They had been sold to "some Norwegians." Just to be on the safe side, however, Amiot paid a visit to the editor of the local newspaper *Le Phare de la Manche* to remind him of an agreement they had struck earlier about maintaining strict silence over the presence of the missile boats. As a result of their agreement, local reporters were ordered never to write about the boats.

"Operation Noah's Ark" was now reaching its final, critical stage.

Limon reached the harbor area of Cherbourg at 4 PM and immediately went to check in at the nearby Hotel Sofitel. Then he walked down to the harbor area, where he met Lt. Colonel Ezra Kedem and one of the blue-eyed Norwegians—a soldier he had known and fought with for the past twenty years named Lt. Colonel Hod. The three men shook hands and went to inspect the boats.

Aboard each one were twenty Israeli sailors.

As the three men discussed their situation, they were deeply worried. A strong wind was blowing even in the protected harbor area. At sea a full-scale storm raged. A large ship designed for long trips on the open sea would have had a rough time of it in those conditions, but the missile ships were *not* so designed.

Someone joked nervously that "It might be good practice for our oil-prospecting venture off the coast of Alaska." No one laughed.

Limon said grimly, "If this wind keeps on blowing, you won't be able to sail tonight. And if you're not off tonight, there's a good chance these boats will never reach Haifa. We aren't likely to get such an opportunity again."

Lt. Colonel Hod agreed. "The wind is blowing in exactly the opposite direction required. That's really bad. It will be a rough business."

Ezra the Shark had been silently staring at the sky. He shrugged his shoulders and said simply: "Head wind. Side wind. Back wind. What difference is it? We have no choice. We have to sail tonight.

"In the meantime, I have to go to town to buy a *jambon* I promised someone back home. I'd better go for it now."

With affection and admiration at his friend's bravery, Mordechai Limon put a restraining hand on Ezra's shoulder.

"You have more important things to do now than go shopping," he said. "I'll go and buy your *jambon*." And off he went.

The next hours were spent in feverish but methodical preparation.

Each crew checked its supplies of food, tools and other necessities. The fuel tanks were filled to absolute capacity and extra stores were taken on. Ezra Kedem, who was commanding the lead boat, maintained till the last moment his careful watch on harbor and weather conditions.

At 9 PM the engines were started up.

In town, preparations of a different sort were going on. It was Christmas Eve. The citizens of Cherbourg were putting up last-minute decorations and opening bottles of champagne. As they sat down to their Christmas dinners, they couldn't help noticing the roaring engine noises. That noise had become part of their lives in the past few days, so they weren't surprised to hear it.

The only surprise was among the staff of the Café du Théâtre, where the large tables reserved for the Israeli sailors went unfilled. It didn't take them long to guess what was going on.

In fact, the Israelis were unaware that even their careful security measures—laid out in detail by the Mossad—had failed to deceive entirely the French intelligence service. They had noticed the sudden departure of so many Israeli families—ostensibly for holiday visits to Paris. They had been picking up frequent two-way messages passing in coded form between the radio operators and Israel. They also heard about slips of the tongue like the one that occurred in the casino, and about the Norwegians who spoke Hebrew. It was impossible not to notice all these "coincidences."

On December 20, intelligence agents sent a message to Paris reporting the coincidences. The boats and the Israelis were clearly leaving at the same time. But this was just five days before Christmas and no one was paying much attention. The warning was destined to lie on some official's desk, unopened and unread.

At midnight, the roar of the missile boats' engines was drowned out by the peal of church bells and by the sirens from all the other boats in the harbor. Cherbourg was celebrating Christmas. Congregations all over town began their midnight masses.

Five minutes later the Israeli boats slid their moorings and gingerly made their way through the treacherous obstacles of the eastern passage. Once clear they gave their engines full speed and headed out into the English Channel.

Two men watched the boats leave. One was Mordechai Limon, the other Felix Amiot.

For the first time that his family could remember, Amiot had decided at the last minute not to celebrate Christmas with them at their house on the Côte d'Azur. He did not confide to them the urgent business that brought him secretly back to Cherbourg. In reality, he had known about the operation virtually from the beginning.

Amiot and Limon watched until the boats were beyond the range of eyesight. Then, shaking hands warmly, they parted. Limon drove back to Paris and Amiot sped through the night to be with his family on Christmas day.

Early the next morning, a few men wandered down to the dock area for a breath of sea air. Immediately they noticed that the quay where the missile boats had been revving their engines a few hours before was quite empty. Without exchanging a word they agreed to "forget" what they had seen. In a dockside café, the barman remarked to customers huddled over their glasses of red wine: "I see the Norwegians have set off for Alaska." His audience roared with laughter.

In Paris, Mordechai Limon was not so jolly. The final responsibility for sending the boats off had been his. Because of his decision, a hundred young Israelis were at sea in vessels never designed for the sort of rough Atlantic seas they must be encountering now. Crews of twenty were handling boats that theoretically required forty-five men to run them efficiently.

Limon sat anxiously hour after hour by his radio, waiting for weather reports, or for first news of the mysterious disappearance of five boats from Cherbourg harbor. He knew that as soon as the disappearance was reported he would be in for a heavy storm of his own . . . but at the moment he was more worried about the 100 brave young men for whose lives he felt responsible.

The diplomatic storm that Mordechai Limon was expecting might have broken at midday on Christmas, when a reporter for *Le Phare de la Manche* received a tip that the boats had gone. But the conscientious newsman respected the vow of silence that his editor had made with Felix Amiot, and as a result withheld the scoop until further notice.

Unknown to Felix Amiot, unknown to the Mossad, and certainly unknown to the reporter who "spiked" the story, a rival newspaper called *Ouest France* had decided a short while before to send a team of reporters to Cherbourg in order to compete more effectively for local readership. The best way to do this was to dig up local gossip on the spot.

Thus, on December 26, a day after *Le Phare de la Manche* was tipped off, one of the rival reporters got wind of the story. Under no constraints not to publish, he immediately telephoned the story through to his head office in nearby Rennes. Soon after that, both Associated Press and United Press International picked up the story through their stringers in Rennes. They passed it on to their offices in Paris, and the next morning it was in newspapers all over the world.

Throughout the day, the telephone never stopped ringing at either the French Ministry of Defense or the home of Mordechai Limon. The harried information officer at the Ministry had to deal with a barrage of questions from journalists of every nationality: "Have the French lifted the arms embargo?" "What Norwegian bought the boats?" "Why are they using missile boats for oil exploration?" "Can we quote you as saying that the boats are headed for Alaska?"

If the Frenchman was flustered, Admiral Limon by contrast presented a polite face to all his callers.

"I wish I could help you," he said. "I understand from the French government that the boats were sold to some Norwegian company. I don't happen to remember their name right now. I am at home, not in my office. Perhaps you could ask the French government. . . ."

During the day came a news flash: the boats had been sighted heading for Gibraltar. Clearly they were not taking the most direct route to Alaska.

President Georges Pompidou, who had replaced General de Gaulle after the General's resignation in April, was called at his country home where he was celebrating Christmas with his family. The man who had to break the news to him, Secretary General Michel Jobert, reported that Pompidou was furious. So was Maurice Schumann, the Foreign Minister who had just come back from a successful tour of Algeria and Egypt, where he had promised friendly relations and large supplies of armaments in return for Arab oil. Now it would seem to his North African hosts that France had allowed Israel to grab the boats. Schumann repeatedly told members of his staff: "I have been humiliated." And he demanded immediate action against the Israelis.

President Pompidou, however, was a realist. Whether the missile boats were being navigated by Norwegians, Israelis, or Panamanian pirates, there was nothing much he could do about it. He said to Schumann, "Do you suggest we bomb them? Torpedo them?" French naval authorities had already reported with some embarrassment that there were no French surface vessels in service at the time with sufficient speed to catch up to the missile boats.

Maurice Schumann, still seething with anger, telephoned the residence of Israeli ambassador Walter Eytan at 5 PM on Sunday the 28th. He demanded that Eytan come and see him immediately. Unfortunately, however, Eytan was in Switzerland visiting friends. His address was not known. Schumann demanded that *someone* come to see him if the ambassador couldn't make it personally.

So at 6 PM two minor diplomats called on the Foreign Minister at his office in the Quai d'Orsay. Schumann raged at them for over an hour.

"What have you done with the missile boats? I demand to know. I demand a very rapid reply, because the boats are capable of very high speeds. It is totally unimaginable that they are heading for Israel. But if they *do* happen to turn up there, the consequences will be very grave indeed for Israel."

As calmly as possible the more senior of the two Israelis (press officer Avi Primor) pointed out that he knew nothing of the missile boats, but would be pleased to convey the message to his government in Jerusalem.

The next day Prime Minister Golda Meir chaired a meeting of the Israeli cabinet. At the conclusion of the meeting they sent a message back to France saying simply that the French government, as Admiral Limon had already explained, had sold the boats themselves to a Norwegian firm called Starboat and Weill. Of course, they pointed out, there was always the possibility that the Norwegians had hired out the boats to some Israeli firm.

The calm and ingenious statement from Jerusalem gave no indication of the heated debate that had taken place in the Cabinet meeting. Golda Meir and Moshe Dayan had wanted to come right out and admit that the boats were on their way to Haifa. The more traditionally-minded Abba Eban wanted to stick to protocol and deny everything. In the end they decided on a measure of compromise.

At the same time, Nasser of Egypt was meeting with Colonel Muammar el-Qaddafi of Libya. Knowing the boats to be unarmed, they discussed the idea of intercepting and sinking them. A submarine was dispatched for this purpose—but the Israelis had anticipated the move, and had already sent their own vessels to meet the unarmed boats. The Egyptian submarine returned to base without firing a shot.

While no one tried to sink the missile boats, they did receive a great deal of attention. French Mirages flew overhead repeatedly, as did American and other NATO forces. The American Sixth Fleet sent an aircraft carrier to take photographs. The Russians also got into the act, sending several ships to play a kind of cat-and-mouse game with them. Once, near Cyprus, one of the Soviet ships came dangerously close to ramming one of the Israelis, but this was almost surely an accident.

The international attention lavished on the Israeli boats paid an unexpected dividend. On the boat commanded by the young Nehemiah, everyone on board admired the way Milou, as the white terrier puppy had been named, became accustomed immediately to being on the open sea. She never got seasick like other members of the crew, and learned how to walk with a wide gait to steady herself when the boat was in rough seas.

It wasn't until they were well into the Mediterranean that little Milou began behaving strangely. For no apparent reason she started shivering and whimpering; then she broke into a mournful howl. Moments afterwards the operator of the ultra-sophisticated counter-electronic equipment announced that he had picked up the signal which indicated they were being tracked by radar. Within seconds they saw a French Mirage following them. When this happened a few more times—strange behavior by Milou preceding the detection of radar signals—the crew realized that their delightful little mascot was a more effective and fast-acting counter-electronic device than the most advanced technical hardware then in use.

As a result of their discovery, Nehemiah brought Milou into action with him during the Yom Kippur War. On at least three occasions Milou's unfailing reactions warned Nehemiah of impending danger and gave him the fractional but vital edge over his Syrian or Egyptian opponents. In modern push-button sea warfare, where computers and electronics have replaced the human eye, a terrier puppy proved the Israelis' most useful ally.

As soon as the missile boats were near enough to Israel, a group of Israeli fighters flew overhead and covered them on their way. For the rest of the journey the boats were never without their flying escort. Ezra Kedem later said that the first time he really began to feel safe was when he saw the Israeli planes flying toward them.

A few days later the strange convoy arrived at Haifa's Kishon harbor; the boats and their crews were greeted by public jubilation.

In Paris the reaction was not so enthusiastic. Two four-star generals who had approved the sale of the boats to Starboat and Weill were unceremoniously relieved of their positions. Mordechai Limon was asked to leave France, a request which clearly saddened him—he had been there seven years—but with which he had to comply. Limon refused to make an official statement, but when he went to the airport a reporter asked him whether he had ever commanded a missile boat "like the ones built at Cherbourg." With a perfectly straight face he replied:

"No. They are too small for me. Anyway, I have no interest in doing oil survey work."

Even after Limon's departure the controversy raged on. Accusations of complicity were leveled at Felix Amiot, who vigorously defended himself. He said at the time:

"Security is not my problem. My job was to build ships. I got on very well with the Israelis, but as far as I am aware that is not a crime."

Amiot made it clear that he was not going to be bullied by Georges Pompidou or anyone else. He made no apologies.

As for the good citizens of Cherbourg, an official government investigation stated: "There appears to have been a vast conspiracy of silence among the people of Cherbourg over the whole affair."

Undoubtedly this statement has some truth in it. The feeling among the townspeople may have been summed up by Madame

Giot, the concierge of the hotel where so many of the Israelis had stayed. She knew they were going to leave on Christmas Eve when one of the sailors, little older than a boy, kissed her before he went out for the evening ". . . I sensed it was *adieu*," said Madame Giot, but "I kept their secret. . . . They had done us no harm—in fact they provided work here. They had paid for their boats. I never understood the problem."

The only resident of Cherbourg who had a grudge against the Israelis was the owner of the café where seventy-four of them had ordered Christmas dinners which they left without eating—or paying for. His anger lasted only a couple of weeks. In the mail came a check, with apologies for the uneaten dinners.

The café-owner couldn't have known it, but the check was signed at Mossad headquarters.

Alfred Frauenknecht and the Paper Planes

ALFRED FRAUENKNECHT WAS a troubled man. It was the beginning of June 1967, and he had just heard about General Charles de Gaulle's declaration of an embargo on the shipment to Israel of "offensive weapons." With Israel on the verge of war with its powerful Arab neighbors, Frauenknecht knew, the embargo could have disastrous effects: if the French Mirage fighter-bombers on which her air force depended sustained any damage in battle, there would be no spare parts to repair them.

Frauenknecht was in a better position than most people to appreciate Israel's dilemma.

As chief engineer of the jet fighter aircraft division of the Swiss firm of Sulzer Brothers, he had responsibility for supervising the construction of Switzerland's own Mirages. The Swiss government had bought the planes from the French Dassault armaments firm on the condition that they be built in Switzerland, and had awarded the contracts for doing so to Sulzer Brothers of Winterthur. As supervisor of the project, Frauenknecht often had occasion to meet Israelis when he went to Paris for discussions with the Dassault engineers. He had become quite friendly with some of the Israelis and often discussed with them their political and military problems.

Frauenknecht was naturally relieved when Israel won the war so quickly.

But, as he soon discovered, Israel's problems were far from over. The intransigent de Gaulle maintained the arms embargo even after the war was over and showed no signs of lifting it.

In December of that year, representatives of the various countries who had bought the Mirage were invited to Paris to discuss improvements that could be made on the plane as a result of the experience gained by the Israelis during the Six-Day War. Frauenknecht was invited as representative of Sulzer Brothers.

The Swiss engineer was shocked by what went on at the meeting. He saw that the French were happy to benefit from everything the Israelis had learned about the Mirage's performance in combat, but wouldn't even consider recommending that the embargo be lifted in exchange. To Frauenknecht this was a blatant violation of the rules of fair play.

More profoundly, it offended Frauenknecht's sympathy with the Israeli cause. Like many German-speaking Swiss citizens, he had supported Germany in the days leading up to the Second World War. And like many of his countrymen, he felt a deep sense of shame afterwards for what he had done. It was partly for this reason that he had become a staunch supporter of Israel. Europe, he believed, had to atone for its sins against the Jews. Frauenknecht's contact with Israelis through the Mirage project intensified his support for their cause.

One evening early in 1967 he was dining at a restaurant with some of his Israeli friends, and found himself with one of them in the men's washroom. While the two men were washing their hands, Frauenknecht noticed on his companion's forearm a small tattoo of several numbers. Innocently he asked what the tattoo meant.

"It is a souvenir from an enforced stay in Dachau," replied the Israeli.

Anyone who has met a survivor of Hitler's death camps knows how difficult it is to respond to such a statement. It was especially difficult for Frauenknecht, who had always carried with him a sense of war-guilt.

Soon after this disturbing encounter, Frauenknecht made a point of visiting Dachau himself. It was a symbolic gesture for him, but a traumatic one. He was brought face-to-face with the most inhuman consequences of the way Jews had been treated by the Nazis.

Thus, when he saw France "stabbing Israel in the back," as he put it, his conscience was deeply troubled.

At lunch with a Parisian colleague he argued Israel's case in the strongest of terms. The embargo, he said, was unforgiveable. France was holding on to fifty "Jewish Mirages" which the Israelis had already paid for; their action was a threat to the tiny nation's very survival.

"It is a matter of honor," he told his companion.

"What can we do?" replied the French businessman. "You know what it is with politicians. It is out of our hands. Anyway, let's order another bottle of wine."

Frauenknecht was not willing to let matters stand that way. He was determined to help Israel in whatever way he could. And not long after that crucial meeting in December, he got his chance.

In the latter months of 1967, the Israelis were investigating every means of getting their hands on spare parts for their Mirages. Some of the engineers who had worked with Alfred Frauenknecht knew that he was sympathetic to their cause and thought it would be worthwhile enlisting his aid. One evening before he left for Paris a couple of his Israeli friends met him and asked point-blank whether he could get them the spare parts they needed.

"They are worth their weight in gold," one of the Israelis said.

Frauenknecht was sympathetic, as they knew he would be.

"I will do all I can to help you," he said, "but it is beyond my power to make such a deal. I will have to refer to my superiors. And you will have to make a direct approach to the Swiss government."

In January, the Israeli government did just that. As discreetly as possible they asked the Swiss whether they could supply the spare parts which the French were withholding from them.

In February they got their answer: No. They were back where they had started.

In Tel Aviv and Jerusalem the alternatives were reviewed again and again. Even though the French security and military establishments tended to favor the Israelis' cause, the government refused to budge from its embargo. Friendly French pilots, many of them trained at the same schools as Israeli airmen, offered to fly the planes to Israel. That offer was turned down, with regrets, because of the necessity of refueling the planes somewhere en route—a process that would have been dangerous and difficult. An even more outlandish plot that would have had the Israelis steal their own planes was ruled out immediately.

At Mossad headquarters, it was suggested in desperation that someone have another crack at Alfred Frauenknecht. Perhaps he would be able to think of a way of getting at least some of the spare parts.

So, at the beginning of April, 1968, two Europe-based Mossad agents paid Frauenknecht a visit. The agents, Colonel Zvi Allon and Colonel Nehemiah Kain, met him in a room at Zurich's Ambassador Hotel and, introducing themselves by different names, once again presented their case.

The reply they got was sympathetic but not much more encouraging than what Frauenknecht had told the other Israelis who approached him five months before. He said simply that he would do what he could to help, but he made no promises. Allon and Kain got the next flight back to Israel. They didn't expect much.

Early one evening the telephone rang at the Israeli embassy in Paris. The switchboard operator answered with a sprightly "Shalom." In that terse businesslike manner that foreigners often mistake for rudeness she informed the caller that the man he wanted to speak to, Zvi Allon, had gone home for the night.

"Can you call him again in the morning, please?"

But the man on the other end of the line was insistent. In his German-accented French he explained that he was calling from Zurich, and his business was important. Was there no way to reach Colonel Allon?

Sensing the urgency in the man's voice, the operator managed to put his call through to Allon's home. When the officer got on the line, he heard two sentences from a voice that sounded familiar.

"I am Alfred Frauenknecht. I would like to see you soon, please." The line went dead.

At the embassy that night there was a frantic buzz of activity. Within hours Zvi Allon was heading for Orly airport to catch a flight to Zurich. Flying from Rome to meet him was Nehemiah Kain. Coded messages were transmitted to Mossad headquarters informing them of Frauenknecht's telephone call.

The Mossad men were excited. They knew that Frauenknecht would not ask them to see him if he didn't have something substantial to say. He was not that sort of man.

Dared they hope that Frauenknecht had a way of getting them their spare parts? Might he even—as he said he would try to do— have convinced the Swiss government to sell off superfluous material from forty-seven Mirages they had decided they didn't need?

When they met Frauenknecht at the Ambassador Hotel, as they had arranged they would at their last meeting, the two Israelis could hardly wait to sit down and talk. But the Swiss engineer suggested they go to a place where they could be more private.

To their astonishment he took them to the Wiederdorf, Zurich's tiny and rather tame red-light district. Had Frauenknecht gone nuts?

In fact, he knew exactly what he was doing. The Wiederdorf caters mainly to the hordes of foreign visitors who make use of Zurich's many banking institutions. The prostitutes who ply their trade there carefully study the financial papers each morning so they will know what rates to charge in any currency offered to them. And, as Alfred Frauenknecht knew perfectly well, no respectable *Swiss* businessman (or government official) would be seen there. Thus it was safe to talk there with his Israeli visitors. They took a taxi to the district and found a well-hidden corner table in a strip joint. While a rather sedate Italian "danseuse" gyrated on stage, the three men talked.

Without any preliminaries, Frauenknecht came to the point.

"You are wasting your time looking for spare parts. I can get you the complete Mirage."

Colonel Allon promptly replied, "That's impossible. How can we steal your Swiss Mirages? We know they are stored in tunnels bored into the Alps. They have metal doors of a thickness that will withstand an atomic blast. Anyway, even if it *were* possible, we have no quarrel with the Swiss government."

Impatiently waving his hand, as if to brush aside the Israeli's line of thought, Frauenknecht cut Allon short.

"I would never betray my country," he said. "To take our own Mirages would be treason. And I am not a traitor."

The two Mossad agents looked at Frauenknecht blankly. Had he wasted their time by inviting them to Zurich?

Sensing their bafflement, Frauenknecht spoke again.

"I am thinking of the *plans* of the Mirage, which will enable you to build the machine yourself. I know your Mr. Al Schwimmer, the president of the Israel Aircraft Industries. I know that he is capable of building such a sophisticated plane. But it would take years to design a complete aircraft and then tool a factory to manufacture it.

"If you had the blueprints, *all* the blueprints, including the vital ones which enable you to build the machine tools necessary for the job, then you would have a short-cut method of solving your problem. In addition, these tools I have mentioned will enable you to construct the spare parts you so desperately need within a matter of months."

Now the Israelis were listening to Frauenknecht's every word. As they looked at him in amazement he paused, then said softly:

"You will want to know the price.

"I would like you to clearly understand that I am not doing this for the money. I am doing it to help you. But I need some cash in case I get caught, to protect my wife. What I am offering to undertake for you will be dangerous and difficult. I warn you of that. The blueprints take up enough space to fill a railroad car."

Frauenknecht went on: "I will need $200,000 for my work, as a kind of insurance. That is all."

The two Mossad men looked at each other in complete amazement. They knew, and Frauenknecht knew, that he could have asked for five million, ten million, anything he wanted. The money would have been difficult to raise, but it would have been found somehow. No price was too high for the Mirages.

To offer them the plans for a mere $200,000 was practically to give them away. All three men knew it. But Frauenknecht had named his price, and he would stick to it. Nothing would have to be paid in advance. When "all was ready," as the engineer put it, he would need the money. But not a penny until then.

Frauenknecht told the Israelis nothing whatsoever of how he was going to get the plans. They would have to trust him.

"I will contact you again," he assured them. And the meeting was over. The Israelis walked away astonished, but more hopeful than they had been in months. This Frauenknecht, they agreed, was a serious fellow. The short, dapper engineer seemed to know what he was doing.

Now all they could do was wait.

Early summer, 1968. Alfred Frauenknecht was breakfasting in the Sulzer cafeteria with Dr. Schmid, the firm's managing director. Casually, quite out of the blue, Frauenknecht said:

"Herr Doctor, I have a plan whereby we can save at least 100,000 francs a year."

Schmid's eyes opened wide. There is nothing more certain to set the adrenalin flowing in the veins of a businessman—Swiss or any other nationality—than the prospect of saving money. Frauenknecht continued:

"As you know, the crates containing the blueprints on the Mirages are taking up a lot of valuable space. Now that the construction program has come to a halt, we have no further use for them—unless there is an emergency.

"I propose that we have the plans microfilmed. The bulky blueprints can then be destroyed in an incinerator, and the storage space thus released could be more profitably employed. I calculate this would save us 100,000 francs a year."

The top management of Sulzer was extremely impressed with the idea. Business was booming and they were having to hire warehouses to store extra material. They not only agreed to Frauenknecht's plan but left the organization of it entirely to him, as he modestly suggested.

At Frauenknecht knew, security had to be air-tight. Because the factory did so much top-secret work for the government, the highly efficient Swiss military intelligence organization kept the place under close watch. When Frauenknecht proposed to them his plan to burn the blueprints in the town incinerator, they discussed the project in detail with him. They agreed that this seemed the safest way of disposing of the material, but stipulated that the operation had to be carried out in the presence of a senior intelligence official.

They further demanded that only one microfilm copy of each sheet of paper be made, and even laid down which type of copier was to be used. Once the machine was purchased the intelligence men chose the place where it was to be installed—a little-used, windowless room carefully sited away from the areas where unauthorized personnel worked.

Just as Frauenknecht anticipated, the installation of the microfilm apparatus, and its work schedule, were carefully supervised by Swiss intelligence men. They also approved Frauenknecht's plan to buy an unmarked Fiat van to be used for the sole purpose of transporting the copied documents. Every Thursday at a precise time they were to be driven to the town incinerator by Frauenknecht himself. The cautious engineer specifically asked that armed police guards be present during both loading and unloading of the documents.

Ever thoughtful and conscientious, Frauenknecht had even thought about the security risk during the brief journey from factory to incinerator. He personally chose a reliable man—his own cousin —to act as driver. Frauenknecht's cousin had perfect credentials: during the week he worked as a bus driver for the municipal transport authority. Thursday was his day off, and he would be paid for undertaking the extra work.

The whole operation was carried out with clockwork efficiency. Special crates measuring exactly 120 by 80 by 50 centimeters were built by a local firm, and these were used to transport the papers to the incinerator. Once inside the incinerator building, an inspector counted the cartons, to make sure that the number unloaded was the same as the number specified to him by the inspector at Sulzer Brothers' factory. He watched as each carton was opened to make sure that all of them really contained blueprints. Only after seeing all the blueprints tumble into the roaring furnace did he sign receipts. Each receipt had to be completed in duplicate, as demanded by Frauenknecht on behalf of the Swiss military authorities.

The plans covered all the parts of the aircraft, and details of how it was to be constructed. Of special importance were the designs and blueprints for the tools needed to build the frame and engine of the airplane. For one of these elaborate machines alone there were over 45,000 blueprints.

Day after day the microfilm operator toiled away.

Laboriously unfolding the acres of instructions and diagrams, some measuring nearly ten feet in width, he carefully copied every last scrap of paper. At all times he worked under the unblinking eye of a security officer. He also had to put up with being searched every time he left the room.

It was slow work. There was something over two tons of documents and the operator managed to get through about 110 pounds a week. At the end of the day the copied documents were packed into their cartons and stored behind locked doors until the following Thursday, when Frauenknecht and his cousin drove them to the incinerator.

The Swiss are known throughout the world for the neat efficiency with which they work, and the blueprints operation lived up to their reputation. The plan devised by Frauenknecht was foolproof, and it pleased his employers immensely. They even went so far as to promise their diligent engineer a special bonus at Christmas time.

When Zvi Allon and Nehemiah Kain left their meeting with Alfred Frauenknecht they joked about his excessive formality, saying that they half-expected him to pull a contract from his pocket and ask them to sign. They couldn't help wondering how this mild-mannered engineer was going to pull off the amazing feat he had promised them.

Frauenknecht proved how ill-placed their scepticism was.

Understanding the Swiss business mind better than any foreigner could have, he set up his plan in a way that would never attract the slightest suspicion. Not even a sharp-witted professional security officer would ever imagine that the weak link in the security chain was precisely that link which they trusted most completely: Frauenknecht himself. The engineer deliberately devised the plan himself, and arranged things so that he would have maximum responsibility for it. He knew that no one would ever think of questioning his motives, and therefore his actions.

Frauenknecht's self-assurance may seem foolhardy, but he knew exactly what he was doing. As an important and trusted official he was well-known to the Swiss police and security forces. A report on him stated, in part: "This man can be totally trusted. His private and professional life are impeccable. He is a loyal citizen, a devoted husband and a conscientious employee. He goes to church regularly. . . . His employers trust him completely both on a technical scale and also with financial matters. They have total confidence in him. . . ."

Frauenknecht had never seen the report from which these remarks are quoted, but he knew what such a report would contain. With his own credentials thus impeccably established, he relied on himself to carry out personally the appropriation of the blueprints.

The plan he devised was simplicity itself. Long before the first shipment of blueprints was to be consigned to the flames, Frauenknecht had hired a private garage in Winterthur. The garage had its own entrance, and it was very close to the route that the van would take from factory to town incinerator.

From the same company that Sulzer had employed to manufacture the cartons used for transport of the papers, Frauenknecht ordered his own cartons—identical in every way to Sulzer Brothers's. He had them delivered to his garage and kept them there.

Finally, for weeks before the operation was to begin, Frauenknecht had been making frequent trips to the capital city of Berne. By making discreet inquiries he had learned that the Swiss Federal Patents Office was permitted to get rid of papers that had been there for more than fifty years. Introducing himself as a scrap paper merchant, he told the clerk at the Patents Office that he was interested in buying any paper for which they no longer had any use. Of course, the clerk was only too happy to cooperate. He sold the old papers—blueprints and plans of various kinds—for next to nothing.

The clerk explained to Frauenknecht, "Space, like time, is money. That is why you are getting this material so cheaply. We are very, very cramped here."

Frauenknecht nodded sympathetically, and in the course of several weeks loaded huge quantities of paper into his van.

With the "fake" blueprints in hand, Frauenknecht and his cousin began practising a crucial step in the operation. They planned to turn off their prearranged route from factory to incinerator and head speedily for their garage. Once inside they were to do a simple switch operation: unload cartons of the Mirage blueprints brought from the factory, and replace them with the cartons full of papers that Frauenknecht had been purchasing in Berne.

For weeks in advance they practised the scheme. By the time they were ready to start doing it for real, they could complete the whole switch in five minutes. No one at either end—factory or incinerator— would ever notice the missing time.

As Frauenknecht had expected, the plan worked perfectly. The official who witnessed the unloading of the cartons inside the incinerator building never dreamed of actually *reading* documents which he knew would be marked SECRET. All he had to do was verify that the cartons of paper were flung into an incinerator working at a precise temperature—and that is exactly what he did. Everyone was happy: Sulzer Brothers were freeing their storage space, the security men were insuring that the papers didn't fall into the wrong hands, the inspectors were certain that the operation worked smoothly.

And Alfred Frauenknecht was obtaining a complete do-it-yourself kit for an advanced jet fighter-bomber.

Unknown to anyone, the engineer and his cousin paid another visit to their garage every Saturday after making their trip to the incinerator. Working quickly and silently they prepared the following week's load for the incinerator by ramming old blueprints into the cartons stored there. Then the preceding week's consignment of Mirage blueprints was reloaded into the van, and they drove it the thirty or so miles to the town of Kaiseraugst.

Situated on the Rhine near the Swiss-German border, Kaiseraugst was built by the Romans as a walled city to protect their empire from the Germanic tribes to the north. Today, with its spectacular views and notable ruins, it is immensely popular with tourists. Thus, the presence of two more strangers would not be noticed—even though their visits turned out to be weekly events.

Without stopping anywhere, Frauenknecht and his cousin drove the van to a warehouse on the edge of town owned by the Swiss firm of Rotzinger and Company. The warehouse was located in an industrial zone where no one worked on Saturdays; thus there was little chance that anyone would notice either the arrival of the van or the rapid unloading of its contents into the warehouse.

Their unloading job completed, Frauenknecht and his cousin would drive back into town. There they always went for a well-earned bottle of German lager at the crowded Hirschen restaurant. While they were enjoying themselves, Frauenknecht's eyes would subtly seek out those of another man who always sat by himself at a corner table. Frauenknecht's would give the man a signal—a brief nod of his head—and then turn back to his companion. The crowds of workers who had come for their traditional Saturday drink would certainly never notice Frauenknecht's unusual behavior. He and his cousin continued to enjoy themselves for an hour or so while they chatted and drank.

The man to whom Frauenknecht gave his discreet signal, however, rarely waited around. He was a German whom Frauenknecht knew as Hans Strecker, a "friend" of Colonel Nehemiah Kain. Strecker had been employed by the Rotzinger company for only a year, but already he was a trusted and respected employee whose job it was to ease Rotzinger trucks on their way to destinations all over Europe and handle the paper work this entailed. His employers knew him to be a diligent and conscientious worker: he even came in on Saturdays to prepare for the following week's workload.

As soon as Strecker received the signal from Alfred Frauenknecht he drove straight from town to the Rotzinger warehouse. There he would load the cartons full of Mirage blueprints into the trunk of his Mercedes 220, lock up the warehouse, and then drive toward the German border.

Strecker never had any trouble with customs officials. A good and thorough agent, he had made many trips across the border long before he began carrying top-secret documents in the trunk of his car. The customs men soon came to know him as a friendly and cooperative fellow who never lost his patience over bureaucratic delays and even helped them by doing some of their chores for them. Moreover, he was generous in the extreme when it came to buying the occasional beer at one of the many cafés in the border area, or doing favors either in Switzerland or Germany.

Thus, Strecker's black Mercedes was a familiar sight at the customs house. His pals always waved him through cheerfully.

Once in Germany Strecker put his foot down on the accelerator as he sped through the Black Forest toward Stuttgart. Just before reaching the city he turned off the autobahn to head for a small air-field where the more affluent residents of the area keep their private planes and gliders.

Within minutes the Mirage documents would be loaded onto an Italian-registered twin-engine Cessna and the plane would be flying toward Brindisi, in the south of Italy. Here they were transferred to the hold of an El Al plane. By Sunday morning—twenty-four hours after leaving Winterthur—they were being unloaded at an airfield in Israel.

So eagerly was the shipment awaited that an armored truck was always standing by, with engine revving, to rush them into the hands of a technician at Israel Aircraft Industries.

Frauenknecht's first shipment arrived in Israel on October 5, 1968.

Every week after that the operation followed the same smooth pattern. Never once did Frauenknecht or his cousin show any signs of strain or hesitation.

Week after week the microfilm operator ground away; signed and countersigned receipts were carefully checked, hundreds of pounds of paper were dumped into the Winterthur incinerator. Frauenknecht kept going back to the Berne Patents Office for more supplies of fake blueprints, and, with his cousin, paid a weekly visit to the delightful old town of Kaiseraugst.

It took the engineer almost exactly twelve months to complete the operation. The only break he took was his annual vacation.

Late in September 1969, Frauenknecht delivered his very last consignment of blueprints to the Rotzinger warehouse. He admitted to his cousin that he might now sleep easily for the first time in a year. He had certainly earned the cognac that he and his cousin ordered on what would be their last visit to the Hirschen restaurant.

As they sat chatting in the bar, Frauenknecht had no way of knowing that, at that very moment, Hans Strecker was being caught red-handed in the act of piling cartons into his Mercedes.

The two owners of the Rotzinger company, Karl and Hans Rotzinger, had been alerted by a suspicious passerby who was puzzled by the stranger he saw every Saturday hanging around the warehouse. The passerby, who was in the habit of walking his dog nearby, reported that the man was always loading boxes into his private car.

When the Rotzingers heard about the mysterious stranger they decided to investigate. They drove to the warehouse on that Saturday morning and parked some distance away. To their astonishment they realized that the stranger was none other than their faithful employee Hans Strecker, whom they saw placing cartons into the trunk of his car. Relieved but still puzzled, they called out to him in greeting.

The moment he saw the Rotzingers, Strecker jumped into his car and drove off at full speed.

Now the Rotzingers were really baffled. They went into the warehouse and saw the single carton that Strecker, in his haste, had left behind. They decided to open the box. Stamped in huge letters on the very first blueprint were the words: TOP SECRET. PROPERTY OF THE SWISS MILITARY DEPARTMENT.

The Rotzinger brothers drove straight to the local police. Within the hour a full alert went out all over the country to apprehend at all costs a certain Hans Strecker.

But by then the tiny Cessna was already airborne, heading high over the Alps. No one at the Rhine crossing has seen or heard of Strecker since.

Anyway, the Swiss police had other things to do besides look for Hans Strecker. How had top-secret blueprints pulled out of an incinerator at Winterthur made their way to the Rotzinger company warehouse?

It took them seventy-two hours of non-stop investigation to put the finger on Alfred Frauenknecht.

The engineer had already learned of Strecker's fate from an unidentified man who telephoned with the news. He did not panic, but went about his business normally. Monday morning he was at the Sulzer offices exactly on time. He worked a full day and went home at the usual hour. Tuesday morning he drove out to the military airport at Dübendorf near Zurich to keep an appointment with some officials who wanted to discuss the future needs of the air force.

At the airport a squad of five security and police officers, including a senior officer from Swiss counter-intelligence, were waiting to arrest him. Frauenknecht calmly accompanied them to Basle prison, where he was placed in a cell by himself.

Once in the cell, Frauenknecht showed that he had not lost a bit of his composure. He proposed a deal. He would never breathe a word, he said, about the whole business of the Mirage plans if the authorities agreed to his terms.

"I am ready even to overlook the indignity of being handcuffed and taken to prison in front of a lot of people who know me," he said.

"The French," continued Frauenknecht, "will be furious. For if this matter becomes public knowledge I will be forced to reveal that the entire plans of the Mirage have 'disappeared.' You know what the French are like: they will provoke a political crisis which will sour relations between our countries for a long time to come."

"Anyway, the Swiss have the plans on microfilm. They were quite useless to us since we are not going to make any more planes."

Legally, Frauenknecht admitted, he had committed a crime; but morally he was blameless. Switzerland had not suffered in any way. The interrogators, who had expected from Frauenknecht a groveling plea for mercy, were told instead:

"If you promise to keep the whole thing quiet and let me go free, then *I* promise not to tell the French either. Nobody need know about it."

When Frauenknecht told the police and security men that the plans had gone to Israel, he defended himself stoutly.

"I did it to help Israel on moral grounds of conscience. For them it was a question of survival. For myself, a devout Christian, I am still haunted by the memory of Dachau and Auschwitz."

The authorities, however, were unmoved by Frauenknecht's motives. The law was the law, and he would have to be brought to trial. In the meantime he would remain in their custody.

Frauenknecht stayed in jail for a full eighteen months without being charged or brought to trial. Even so, his jailers treated him with kid gloves. He was given the privileged job of prison librarian and even managed to get a television set installed in his cell. Claiming that since he had not been charged with any crime he was not a criminal, he petitioned the prison authorities to supply a TV set. They refused, so he took his case to the local court. When the judge there turned down his request he fought it all the way to the Supreme Court, and finally won. He got his television set.

Frauenknecht even brought a smile to the face of the prison director when he told him in perfect seriousness: "I think I have worked out a method of saving space here. . . ."

When he was finally brought to trial, Frauenknecht made no attempt to deny that he had violated Swiss law. But he also maintained that he had done so for good reasons—and did not regret his actions in the slightest. The motives behind his actions won him a great deal of sympathy in the court.

The Swiss intelligence service had a slightly harder time trying to deny the accusations against them of negligence. A representative of the service claimed in court, "We checked Frauenknecht thoroughly. We had no reason to suspect him."

In the end, however, the law was not on Frauenknecht's side. On April 23, 1971, he was convicted of industrial espionage and violating Swiss military secrecy. The court sentenced him to four and a half years of hard labor. Afterwards the engineer admitted that he was expecting a full twenty-year stint behind bars—the maximum sentence for the crimes of which he was accused.

Frauenknecht spent his term in Basle Prison, where he continued to be treated as a special prisoner. He reorganized the prison library and read a great deal.

In October 1971, some seven months after his sentence began, Frauenknecht noticed a small item in a newspaper he was reading. The article concerned the trial flight of a new Israeli aircraft called the "Nesher" (Eagle). Through the details he gleaned from that article and a few others that appeared in newspapers over the next few days, Frauenknecht was able to tell that this was the Israeli equivalent of the Mirage, the plans for which he had so laboriously helped smuggle from Switzerland to Israel.

Not long after Frauenknecht's release from prison in 1975, a friend in Israel invited him and his wife to pay their first visit to the country. Their visit "coincided" with a major demonstration of the new pride of Israel's aircraft industry: the Kfir ("Young Lion"), a Mach 2.2 fighter-bomber. Observers from all over the world had come to see it. All of them recognized immediately that the plane was closely modeled on France's Mirage V. A West German military expert poked his French companion in the ribs and quipped:

"Son of Mirage."

Standing nearby, the short man with closely cropped hair and a distinctive pallor—as of someone hidden from the sun too long—overheard the joke and smiled faintly. Alfred Frauenknecht understood better than anyone else the discomfiture with which the Frenchman had received his companion's remark. The French were still extremely touchy about the entire incident.

As the Kfir streaked through the sky above Tel Aviv, Frauenknecht felt considerable pride at seeing the results of his espionage work for Israel. But mixed with the pride was bitterness: Frauenknecht had recently discovered that a spy's glory is a lonely glory.

He had expected on arrival in Israel to be greeted at the airport by marching bands, bouquets of flowers, cheering throngs. Instead he was studiously ignored by Israeli officials. No one seemed to know who he was. The Jerusalem government had not even paid his fare to the country—it had been picked up by a sympathetic hotel owner. The only official he was able to meet with told him discreetly that neither the Mossad nor any other state agency could acknowledge the role he played in the creation of the Kfir. To do so would have been to admit Israeli espionage on Swiss territory.

Back in Switzerland a lawyer friend of Frauenknecht's told him: "That's the way it is with the spy business. Nobody ever admits anything."

Today Alfred and Elizabeth Frauenknecht live in a five-room house at number 15 Flora Street in the Swiss village of Aardorf, not far from Winterthur.

To the neighbors their house is known as "Little Israel" because of the wealth of books about the country and souvenirs sent by Israeli admirers. There are books in German, French, English and Hebrew; glasses sent from the glassmaking center of Hebron; and, occupying pride of place, an album of photographs given as a gift by the Israeli Air Force.

At the café near his home where Alfred Frauenknecht goes for a weekly beer or two, he is immensely popular. Despite his stay in jail his drinking companions treat him with a certain awe. As one of them said: "As far as we are concerned, his only crime was that he got caught! Normally we do not forgive that crime in Switzerland—but with Herr Frauenknecht we make an exception."

Since leaving prison the engineer has had several jobs, including positions in an electronic company and a plastics factory. Now, however, Frauenknecht makes his living from inventions. One of the most successful of these is a cheap air-conditioning unit for small cars.

But he gets particular pleasure from another of his inventions. This is a device for use in offices which automatically bundles up discarded documents without removing them from their wire basket trays, and quickly disposes of them in bulk. Cost-conscious Swiss businessmen have bought over 15,000 of these useful gadgets.

Not too long ago, Frauenknecht sent a sample of the document-discarding device to the French Ministry of Defense. Apparently, no one there much appreciated his thoughtfulness: they neither thanked him nor sent the model back. They are still somewhat touchy about the subject of discarded documents.

Frauenknecht takes their rudeness in his stride, however.

"Just like the French," he says solemnly.

"And people think we Swiss have no sense of humor!"

Spies Against Israel

Just as the Mossad makes a point of keeping up to date on what the enemies of Israel are doing, so those same enemies keep watch on what goes on in Israel. Thus the Mossad—as well as the other arms of Israel's intelligence service—must engage in a constant war of counter- intelligence.

The following chapters deal with only a few of the counter-intelligence operations in which the Mossad has played a role.

Israel Beer
Ben-Gurion's Friend

ISRAEL BEER, "Pipke" as he was commonly nicknamed, bitterly resented the summons he had received from Isser Harel. The message was blunt and peremptory: come to my office.

As an acknowledged expert on military affairs and a close confidant of David Ben-Gurion himself, Beer was a leading personality in Israeli public life.

Having emigrated to Palestine in 1938 from Austria, Israel Beer joined the underground Haganah army and served with distinction for many years. With his sharply analytical mind and academic military training he rose quickly in rank, eventually becoming a colonel, and at the end of the War of Independence he was chosen to be head of the planning and operations department at army headquarters. He was often to be seen sitting with the Prime Minister at official functions.

Beer left the army in 1950 for a career in politics, but he maintained his interest in, and contact with, the military world. He attended top-secret staff meetings and had access to whatever information he asked for. Army plans, blueprints, defense documents of the highest importance all passed through his hands. In 1955 he was asked to write the official history of the War of Independence and was given a special room in the Ministry of Defense where he could conduct his research.

Beer's fame as a military expert even extended outside of Israel itself. He lectured on war-related subjects in several European countries, particularly Germany, where he deeply impressed such important figures as the politician Franz Joseph Strauss and General

Reinhardt Gehlen, head of the intelligence service. On lecture tours in Germany he gave young audiences stern warnings about their duty to the homeland and the need to make Germany a strong democratic state in the face of "the Communist menace from the East."

Beer's brilliant analyses of the strategy required in the event of a ground war in Europe won him the admiration of many commanders at Europe's NATO headquarters. French Defense officials openly praised his wide-ranging grasp of military problems.

Thus, when Israel Beer found himself being curtly summoned to see Isser Harel on an autumn evening in 1960, it is understandable that he was irked. Harel was hardly showing the respect due to such an important figure.

Beer made no effort to hide his annoyance as he walked into Isser's office with cigar in mouth and plopped himself down in a chair across the desk from the Mossad chief. Knocking the ash from his cigar with a contemptuous flick of the thumb, Beer leaned forward in his chair and said simply:

"Come to the point. I am in a hurry."

Isser stared straight into the unblinking eyes of the balding Professor Beer. All over the face of his visitor—with its distinctive yellow moustache stained by stale cigar ash—he could read the disdain that was directed toward himself. But Isser was not a man to scare easily. He continued to stare back into Beer's face as he asked him two short, concise questions.

"Why have you continued to make visits to East Berlin?"

"Why did you travel to Poland?"

Then, assuming the dictatorial manner that he sometimes indulged in, Isser raised his voice.

"Have I not warned you before about mixing with communists?" Crashing his fists down on the desk in front of him, Isser exploded:

"I warn you, Beer. I forbid you ever to go to Europe again!"

With that the professor leapt angrily to his feet. Nobody—not even Ben-Gurion—ever dared to talk to him like that.

"Mind your own business," he yelled back. "I will complain to the Prime Minister! What is more, I will report you to the party!"

And with that, he stormed out of Isser's office.

For several minutes the Mossad chief sat in silent thought. He had had instinctive doubts about Israel Beer for a number of years. He had noted the series of anti-American articles that Beer wrote at the time of the Korean War. He knew that Beer, though now a member of Ben-Gurion's Mapai party, had earlier joined the more radically left-wing Mapam Group. The professor took a vigorously pro-Communist line at the time, and argued so vehemently with the moderates in the group that he finally quit. It was only later that he had joined Ben-Gurion's ruling coalition. His new line became: "Long live Ben-Gurion and you can do whatever you want."

Isser had no quarrel with Beer's political affiliations, but he wondered how a man could change his loyalties so drastically—and so quickly. The Mossad chief belonged to no party himself, but he did know what he believed in. Beer's opportunism made him suspicious.

Now, sitting at his desk after the military expert's abrupt departure, Isser was once again troubled by something he had said. That warning that Beer had made as he left—"I will report you to the party"—what could that mean? Beer knew that Isser had no party; and even if he had, even if he belonged to Ben-Gurion's Mapai, Israel was a democratic state: People were free to join whatever party they chose; this did not control their lives.

Every bit as surprising as the content of the bizarre statement was the impulsive way in which Beer had thrown it at him. The warning seemed like a pure mental reflex from a man who was accustomed to presenting the image of a logical, dispassionate analyst. Instinct had leapt through the veneer of sophistication.

Isser was worried about Israel Beer, and he felt he had to tell Ben-Gurion about it. He had voiced his concern to the Prime Minister before, yet Ben-Gurion now trusted Beer more than ever. The Prime Minister seemed to think that Isser was simply jealous of Beer's prestige and influence. But Isser couldn't let that stop him. He went immediately to see his boss and laid out all the reasons behind his suspicions.

"Beer has been gathering military information which is of no concern to him. He has been visiting communist cities on his trips through Europe. He has been too friendly with the Russian diplomats serving in Israel. He meets them frequently.

"Beer's social life also has had some peculiarities recently. He spends a lot of money in Tel Aviv nightclubs—more than he earns. When he was in Munich recently he picked up a $200 tab without showing the slightest concern. He has been buying himself and his lady friends—some of them pretty dubious characters—a lot of expensive clothes. He is on very bad terms with his wife Rivkah and spends his evenings drinking heavily in bars. Bars like the Atom in

Ben Yehuda Street." Isser's voice was filled with moral outrage. He never indulged in such vices.

"It is clear to me," he announced, "that Beer is a man undergoing some kind of strain—the sort of strain which an agent leading a double life suffers from. Recently he was involved in a public scandal: the husband of a woman he associates with punched him in the face and knocked out some of his teeth."

Beer had told the Prime Minister that he had lost the teeth in a car accident, and Ben-Gurion chose to believe this version of events. He remained steadfastly unconvinced by Isser's claims.

"It is your job," he calmly replied, "to be suspicious of everybody. For my part, I trust Beer completely."

That ended the interview—but not the problem as far as Isser was concerned. It was one of his great virtues that he was never simply a "yes" man with Ben-Gurion. A weaker character might have steered well clear of criticizing a man so close to the Prime Minister. Isser took the opposite tack: he ordered his agents to watch Beer even more closely. Research staff began to delve into Beer's past to ascertain whether there were gray areas of deception or half-truth in the story of his life as he told it to friends and colleagues.

Isser Harel was following another of his famous "hunches."

It was the night of March 28, 1961, some eight months after Isser Harel and Israel Beer had their dramatic confrontation in the Mossad chief's office. It was also Passover, one of the richest and most treasured of all Jewish holidays—the celebration of the deliverance from bondage in the house of Egypt. At Jewish homes all over the world, families were seated at the table for their *seder*, the traditional Passover meal at which the story of deliverance is told.

At eight o'clock that evening, a man stepped from his apartment at 67 Brandeiss Street in Tel Aviv. The night was warm but a cool Mediterranean breeze compelled him to button the jacket he was wearing. In his hand he carried a briefcase.

Walking quickly down the deserted street, the man glanced around him repeatedly as if to make sure he was not being followed. He turned into a small side street and stopped in the shadow of a telephone booth. Although he had covered a mere 200 yards from his apartment he was clearly breathing heavily. Pausing for a few moments to catch his breath, he looked around again. Seeing no one in the vicinity he darted down the street to a small café situated at the nearest street corner.

The owner of the café was sitting behind the bar, and he was glad to see a customer—his first of the evening. The man ordered a cognac and took it to a seat at a table in the corner, far from the bright lights of the street. He kept his briefcase on a seat next to him. When the café owner tried to strike up a friendly conversation, the customer answered curtly, indicating that he didn't care to talk. In silence he sat drinking his cognac.

Lighting a cigarette, he looked nervously at his watch.

About five minutes later another man walked into the café. He was dressed in a dark, somber-looking suit and wore a broad-brimmed hat. Waving to the only other client in the place, he sat down opposite him at his table.

Not a single word was exchanged between the two men. Moments after he had sat down, the newcomer got up and walked out.

In his hand was the other man's briefcase.

Seconds later, the original customer got up and paid for his drink. Without saying a word he walked out into the night as the owner started sweeping up.

Outside, the tall man looked around again before walking home again. He took exactly the same route he had used before. This time, however, he carried nothing.

At the door to the building where his apartment was, the tall man entered without bothering to look around again. He was sure that he had not been followed. Climbing the stairs to his apartment he walked in and made straight for his library with its walls lined with books in many languages. There he sat down and waited.

Midnight. The silence of Brandeiss Street was broken by the sound of a car driving fast down the street. It came to a halt in front of number 67 and out stepped the stranger with the hat, the second man to visit the nearby café several hours before.

In his hand was the briefcase he had picked up from the other man.

Now he walked up to the door of number 67 and entered without knocking. Obviously he was expected. Obviously, he did not expect to stay long, for he left his car engine running. . . .

At the home of Isser Harel, the telephone rang. Isser picked up the receiver immediately; he had been expecting the call. He recognized the voice of one of his top agents. No apology was necessary for calling on this holy night.

"Our man has just seen the Russian contact for the second time this evening. They met in the small café you know about. Our man had a briefcase with him which he handed over to the contact, and they parted.

"I followed our man home, I am outside the place now. The Russian has just walked in with the same briefcase he took in the café. He is inside with our man now."

Isser was desperately worried, but he was not surprised. 67 Brandeiss Street was the address of Israel Beer.

He decided that now was the time to strike. But everything had to be done properly, delicately. To arrest the professor now, caught red-handed while passing documents to a Soviet diplomat who was known as Russia's top spy in Israel, would have international repercussions and might even bring down Ben-Gurion's government.

Isser decided to wait until the diplomat had left before making his move. In the meantime, he told his agent to get a search and arrest warrant for Israel Beer.

This was going to be done legally or not at all.

After putting down the phone Isser immediately picked it up again and placed a call to Ben-Gurion. Their conversation lasted less than ten seconds. Isser said simply:

"I am acting against Israel Beer tonight."

Ben-Gurion hesitated only a moment. Then he said:

"Do your duty."

The conversation was over.

At 2:30 AM Israel Beer sat reading in his library. The leather briefcase was lying on the table nearby, exactly where he had left it after his visitor's departure, its contents untouched.

Suddenly there was a knock on the door.

Before Beer had a chance to hide the briefcase, or even get up out of his old armchair, the door came crashing in. A single, expert kick had knocked it half off its hinges.

Seven men came filing into the apartment and stood around the figure now sitting stiffly upright in his chair. One of the men said quietly, "You are under arrest. We have a search warrant."

Beer saw the officer glance in the direction of his briefcase. He calmly responded with exactly the same words used by David Ben-Gurion a few hours before on the telephone with Isser Harel.

"Do your duty."

Beer knew full well the identity of the counter-intelligence officer who had spoken to him. He had been on a first-name basis with the man for several years. All he said was: "Do you mind if I smoke?"

The Mossad officer in charge of the arrest knew that he was dealing with one of the country's most eminent men. Beer was a lecturer at the officer's training school of the army, a full colonel in the reserve, a counselor and adviser to the Ministry of Defense and to the Prime Minister himself. This was a traumatic moment for all present. The agents could hardly believe that the man they had come to arrest was really a Soviet spy. What if they were mistaken? They almost hoped they were. . . .

Whatever doubts they may have had were quickly dispelled when the senior officer opened the briefcase that was lying on the table near Beer. Inside the briefcase he saw a number of top-secret documents, including a detailed list of Israel's major armaments factories. And, to top it all off, they saw Ben-Gurion's private diary. The Prime Minister had lent it to Beer when the professor expressed an interest in writing a series of articles about Ben-Gurion's philosophy of government and leadership. The diary contained not only his most private thoughts but also a number of state secrets, some of them not even known to cabinet members.

Beer was taken into custody immediately.

When Isser Harel handed Ben-Gurion his diary, the Prime Minister commented wearily: "I have been surrounded by lies." The news had clearly shattered him. Isser refrained from mentioning that he had voiced suspicions about Beer as early as 1953. It was on record that both he and Moshe Dayan had opposed Beer's wish to rejoin the army, and that Beer had used his friendship with Ben-Gurion as leverage to get himself appointed an official adviser to the Ministry of Defense with access to all its documents.

Now Isser was certain that Beer had been working for Moscow for years. But for the first few days of his interrogation, Beer admitted nothing. He simply repeated the same version of his life story that he had been telling friends and colleagues for years.

According to that version, Beer was born in Vienna in 1912. His parents had emigrated to the United States but returned shortly afterwards to Europe. Beer had studied humanities and German literature at the University of Vienna, where he claimed to have been a pupil of Max Reinhardt, the famous man of the theater. While at the university he joined the students who were revolting against the dictatorship of Englebert Dollfuss and participated in street fighting against the Nazis in 1934. He had attended the famous Wiener-Neustadt military academy, he said, and became an officer in the Austrian Schutsband.

In 1936, said Beer, he had gone to Spain to fight with the International Brigade against the Fascists in the Civil War. Because of his military training he was made an instructor and got to know all the greatest Communist military men. With them he took part in the famous battles of Madrid and Guadalajara, and helped in the ferocious fighting at Teruel. In early 1938, when the war seemed lost, he escaped from Spain and was asked to go to Moscow to undergo further training.

Instead he decided to go back to Vienna. It was there that he came under the influence of Zionist thinking, and shortly afterwards decided to emigrate to Palestine. Defiantly Beer told his captors: "That is my story, as you all know."

On the fourth day after his interrogation began, Beer received a visit from Isser Harel. Isser knew that the prisoner was not being cooperative, and he planned to do something about it.

He looked Beer in the face, just as he had done at their first meeting so many months before. In a calm but unyielding tone of voice he said to him:

"I know you are a Soviet agent. Tell me the truth. If you are cooperative you will make it easier on everyone, including yourself. Tell me your story."

Challenged in this way, Beer proceeded to go through the whole story one more time. When he was finished Isser calmly told him:

"You are a liar."

"We can find no trace of your parents in Austria. If they were typical Jewish parents, as you make them out to be, then why aren't you circumcised?

"We have checked all the records in Austria. You never fought on the barricades. You never received a doctorate, as you claim you did, nor did you even attend the university. You did not go to the military academy because Jews were not allowed to at that time. They have checked their lists for us and your name is not there. The Schutsband has no record of your membership either.

"We have gone through the records of the International Brigade and your name is not there. You never fought in Spain—in fact, you have never taken part in any military campaign anywhere.

"Now tell me: who are you? We want the truth."

It was obvious to Beer that the Mossad had caught him out. He was broken. For the next three days he dictated a full account of his espionage activities.

Isser suspected that Beer had been "activated" by Moscow shortly after the Suez Campaign in 1956 and pressed from that time on for every bit of information he could lay his hands on. When the French were supplying Israel with arms, Beer passed on details of the weapons and the quantities that Israel was receiving. He did the same thing for the armaments bought from Germany, and also gathered whatever information he could about Germany's role in NATO during his trips to that country. Israel's own scientific research—particularly in nuclear technology—was another of the subjects on which Beer's bosses in Moscow had probably asked him to supply information.

Even while Beer was making his confession, he continued to mingle fact with fantasy. Everything he said was checked, when possible, by Mossad agents and their allies in Israel and Europe (including the Communist countries). Several of his claims were demolished by the patient researches of these agents.

Beer's trial began in June 1961 and, because of the nature of so much of the evidence, was held partially *in camera*. Thus, to this day, many of the revelations of exactly what he passed on to Moscow remain a secret. It is known, however, that he gave the Russians secret army plans relating to battle tactics and lists of secret military installations, in addition to information about Israel's foreign arms suppliers.

At his trial, Beer defended what he had done on patriotic grounds. "I felt I had to play a part in saving Israel from falling into the hands of the western powers," he said.

"My belief is that Israel should be allied to the Communist countries. I never betrayed Israel. I was trying to save my country. All my efforts were aimed at altering her path to political disaster."

In the end, Israel Beer was sentenced to ten years in prison. On appeal his sentence was raised to fifteen years.

While serving his term at Shatta Prison in the Jordan Valley, Beer wrote a book justifying his espionage on ideological grounds. He claimed once again that he had been trying to serve Israel. His bosses in Soviet intelligence, unlike their counterparts in Israel, made no attempt to help him or secure his release from prison. He remained there until May 1968, when he suffered a heart attack, and died soon thereafter.

Israel Beer never revealed his true identity. Nor did he even admit that he had worked for the KGB. But the way he was carefully planted within Israeli society fitted perfectly into a pattern of espionage laid down by the Soviet Union's intelligence services as early as 1917. It was decided at that time to make Palestine, then under British mandate, a major center for espionage. Accomplishing this aim was made relatively easy by the vast numbers of Polish and Russian Jews who were emigrating at the time. Many of the emigrants were idealists who combined an ardent Zionism with an equally strong socialism. It proved easy to include ordinary secret service agents in this mass movement, or to convince some of the genuine emigrants to engage in spying.

Later, in the 1930s, when refugees from Germany and Austria fled to Palestine as Hitler's power grew, other German-speaking Soviet agents joined the ranks. It is almost certain that Israel Beer was among this "second wave" of Soviet agents.

The Soviets took immense trouble in establishing a fool-proof cover for him, indicating that they regarded him as one of their most important agents in the Middle East. Only after Beer's imprisonment did Mossad agents in Austria discover that there had, in fact, been an Austrian named Israel Beer. He was a poor Jewish student in Austria who bore a vague resemblance to the agent who became Ben-Gurion's trusted friend. But the real Israel Beer disappeared in 1938—the year that the agent emigrated to Palestine—and was never heard of again.

The Russians waited almost twenty years, an exceptionally long time, to send their man into action. Clearly they expected great things from him—and they got what they expected. Beer fed a vast amount of military information from Tel Aviv to Moscow.

But to this day no one is certain of Beer's exact identity. Where did he come from? How was he recruited? Who gave him his orders?

The answers to these questions lies buried in the files of the KGB, and in the grave of the agent who called himself Israel Beer.

The Spy in the Sarcophagus

IT WAS THE EVENING OF November 18, 1974. On runway 6 of Rome's Fiumicino Airport, a group of customs men were overseeing the departure for Cairo of a United Arab Airlines passenger jet. To protect themselves from the light drizzle that was falling they stood under the wing of the plane. They tried to keep warm by stamping their feet and blowing into their cupped hands.

The men were getting impatient. Already the aircraft's departure had been delayed two hours.

Suddenly a van belonging to the airline came speeding toward them across the runway. With a screech of its brakes it stopped under the other wing of the plane; two men leapt out of the front seat, opened both rear doors and began unloading a metal trunk. The trunk was stamped with the words DIPLOMATIC LUGGAGE in French, English and Arabic. It was obviously heavy, for one of the Egyptians struggling with it asked the Italian customs men for a hand.

"Please hurry. We want the airplane to take off as soon as possible.

"And be careful: don't drop the trunk."

Turning to his companion he said in Arabic: "It has to go in the animal hold."

The Egyptians didn't realize that one of the Italian officials was fluent in Arabic. He didn't let on that he had understood, but naturally the man's statement aroused his curiosity. Why should a trunk that size, marked DIPLOMATIC LUGGAGE, have to go in the animal hold? Normally it would go in the ordinary luggage compartment.

As the Egyptians continued to struggle with the cumbersome trunk, the Arabic-speaking customs man casually strolled over to them. The trunk was clearly labeled: "Minister of Foreign Affairs, Cairo. Property of U.A.R. Ambassador, Rome." This meant that the customs men had no right to search it except in the presence of the ambassador or his representative.

On the other hand, the same Convention of Vienna that laid down the rules about diplomatic immunity from luggage searches also stated that such luggage should contain only official documents or material used in embassy work. It seemed unlikely that a trunk over three feet long would be used to transport documents. With perfect politeness the customs official asked one of the Egyptians what the trunk contained.

"Musical instruments which the ambassador is sending to Cairo," was the curt reply.

Then, switching back to Arabic, he shouted at the ground crew: "Come on! Get this damned thing on the plane."

The Egyptians were clearly nervous. It had stopped raining and the customs officials could see beads of sweat glistening on their foreheads. Their leader, the one who spoke Arabic, stepped closer to the trunk. As he did so, one of the Egyptians pushed him away.

"This has diplomatic immunity," he barked. "It is none of your business."

But the customs man was politely insistent.He thought he heard a strange sound coming from the trunk. If it contained violins or oboes or whatever, they must have been peculiar instruments. Placing a hand firmly on the trunk, which was now leaning precariously halfway out of the van, he stopped the Egyptians who were trying desperately to lift it.

The customs man put his ear right up to the trunk. Now the sounds were unmistakable. First in English, then in Italian and finally in French, someone was shouting:

"Help! Help! Save me! Assassins!"

The customs man stood up and announced: "The plane will not have authority to leave until we look into this matter more closely." Then he joined his colleagues who were standing at some distance and joked, "They have a very strange talking musical box in there!"

Just as he was reporting his find, one of the Egyptian airline officials suddenly thrust the trunk back into the vehicle. The driver dashed to the front of the van, jumped in behind the wheel, and went hurtling off toward the nearest airport exit.

The customs men acted fast. The second Egyptian was grabbed as he began to run away and was flung to the ground. Two other Italians leapt into a red Alfa-Romeo that happened to be standing nearby and went roaring off in pursuit of the van.

It was no contest. The speedy Alfa caught up with the other vehicle at the entrance of the highway connecting the airport with Rome and forced it to stop. The Italian officials took the Egyptian into custody and brought him to join his friend at nearby Ostia police station. While one of the officials drove the handcuffed airline employee in their little sportscar, the other traveled to Ostia in the van, still carrying its peculiar cargo in the rear.

When they arrived at Ostia, the Italians carried the trunk inside the police station and began breaking its diplomatic seals. They intended to find out what or who was crying for help. Ignoring the Egyptians' protests, they unlocked the trunk and swung open its lid.

When they saw what it contained their eyes opened wide with amazement.

Inside the trunk was a half-dazed man. He was jammed into a jack-knife position with his knees touching his face and his hands were tied tightly behind his back. His bare feet were strapped into a pair of bright yellow oriental slippers which in turn were screwed down firmly to the base of the trunk. He had been tied to a low wooden stool built into the inside of the trunk.

As the officers stepped closer to the open trunk they were repelled by a disgusting odor of human excreta, perspiration and chloroform. They had to don masks before they could bring themselves to untie the prisoner, whom they had already nicknamed "the mummy in the sarcophagus."

The prisoner, who wore only a thin shirt and underpants, could barely stand up from stiffness and fatigue. He was taken immediately for medical care.

Meanwhile, one of the police officers closely examined the trunk, which had clearly been used as a portable prison before. The built-in attachments to which the victim had been tied showed evidence of considerable use. The officers also discovered a moveable helmet which could be slid over the head of the victim, and saw that cushions to protect the occupant's spinal column had been sewn in. The cushions were deeply stained with long-dried perspiration.

In their report about the victim they had found in the box, the police said: "Right now he is not in a very good condition and is clearly still under the influence of drugs. He has vomited repeatedly, but is being attended by doctors, who say he is in no great danger of permanent harm. He was delirious at first but must have had his wits about him, for he had worked the gag around his mouth loose with his teeth. He was then able to call for help.

"That is all we know about him now."

When the "mummy" had recovered sufficiently, he was interrogated first at the local police station and then at headquarters in Rome. The story he told the police failed, however, to inspire much confidence in his forthrightness.

He claimed that his name was Joseph Dahan, born in Morocco in 1934 but now a naturalized Israeli citizen. In his pocket was a Moroccan passport issued at Damascus in 1961.

This much of the man's story made sense enough. It was what followed that made the Italians sceptical.

"I arrived in Rome a few days ago," said Dahan. "I went to the Café de Paris in the Via Veneto. That is a street situated in the center of the city," he told his interrogators with a straight face.

"Yes, we are aware of that," they responded gravely.

"Anyway, I was approached by some Egyptian embassy officials who knew me. They said they recognized me from the days when I worked for them as an interpreter. They were very friendly and gave me lots to drink. Finally I got drunk.

"Suddenly, right there in the Via Veneto among all these film stars and society people, the Egyptians grabbed me. They pushed me into a big car. Nobody came to help me.

"The Egyptian fellows drove me off at great speed and took me to a big house on the outskirts of the city, but I don't know where. They fed me this liquid which they said was tea. It tasted terrible; I don't think it was tea. After that they injected me three times.

"Next thing I knew I found myself in that coffin tied up like an Egyptian mummy. I was in a car and it was moving, so I managed to get the gag out of my mouth and kept shouting again and again for help. Finally you found me."

The doctors reported that Dahan had been lucky. It was intended that he be loaded onto the plane unconscious. Had he not woken up the plan would have worked. He'd have been in Cairo by now.

But it was also abundantly clear that the man was lying, or withholding part of the story.

"Why did they go to all that trouble to kidnap you?" asked one of his interrogators.

"I can only guess," replied Dahan. "Maybe they believed I had learned a lot of their military secrets when I was translating for them. They must have feared I would pass this information on to their enemies."

As the "mummy" talked on, he seemed to gather inspiration for new fantasies.

"I knew all about their secret service organization in Europe and how they operated in every capital. They decided to take me to Egypt to shut me up. They were going to kill me."

The Italians, still dissatisfied, tried to probe deeper. Though the prisoner didn't know it, they had already discovered through a medical examination that his blonde hair was the result of a skillful dyeing process. Its original color was black. What else had the man done to cover up his past?

"How is it that a simple interpreter like you could have learned so many secrets?" asked one of the policemen.

"That's a good question," said Dahan. "I don't really know."

Dahan was clearly trying to put off his interrogators, and they were getting more and more frustrated by him. One moment he declared that he had come to Rome from Frankfurt, ten minutes later he said he had made the journey from Naples. The purpose of his visit was to collect some money he was owed; but he couldn't seem to remember the man's name.

Outside the cell where he was being held, Dahan was causing even greater controversy and befuddlement.

Both the Moroccan and Israeli embassies denied any knowledge of him. No such person had ever been a citizen of either country.

In the newspapers, meanwhile, the wildest stories were circulating about "the man in the trunk." Headline-writers outdid each other for lurid appeal: at first the mummy was a "double agent"; later he became a "triple agent." He was working for Morocco, Egypt, Israel or the United States, depending on whose story one believed.

The two Egyptian diplomats who had taken the trunk out to Fiumicino Airport, identified in the papers as Abdel Moseim El Neglawy and Selim Osman El Sayad, were expelled from the country. The ambassador became so tired of the abuse heaped on his head that he claimed publicly:

"The trunk now in the hands of the police is not ours. We have never seen it before. It was planted on our two senior diplomats by the Italians at the airport.

"*Our* trunk contained harmless material. The Italian authorities placed the dangerous Israeli spy Joseph Dahan in the false coffin for their own obscure reasons."

The ambassador's claims were a little excessive even for the Italian counter-intelligence, who by that time were used to anything, however crazy, that might be said about their mysterious Joseph Dahan. Count Guerino Roberto, the Chief of Protocol, summoned the Egyptian ambassador to the Foreign Office and rapped him over the knuckles for broadcasting this false version of events.

Meanwhile, Italian counter-intelligence had little to say about the man in their custody. All they would say to the press was:

"The only certainty about Joseph Dahan is that he is not Joseph Dahan."

The story about Dahan reached the international press and soon photographs of him began to appear in newspapers and magazines all around the world.

Almost immediately, from the town of Petah-Tikva, not far from Tel Aviv, came the angry voice of a woman named Nourit Louk. Born in Iraq, the woman now lived in Israel. And she knew something about the mysterious Mr. Dahan.

She was his wife.

To a newsman who visited her she proclaimed angrily, "That is not Joseph Dahan, he is my husband Mordechai Louk. I want to have words with him. He has abandoned us. I find it hard to bring up the children he has given me without his support. And what is more, in my eyes he is no hero. Nor is he a spy. . . ."

With admirable restraint Mrs. Louk refused to go into the minute details of their private life, except to say that when Mordechai was home he preferred to go out dancing and drinking and generally wasting his time, rather than get a respectable job like other men.

"He was a lazy good-for-nothing," chipped in Louk's mother-in-law.

In Italy, meanwhile, the police were discovering that Nourit Louk had plenty to complain about. Four women from Naples came forward and claimed that they were all "engaged" to Louk. One was a German woman who was known to mix with officers from the NATO base there. Another was a thirty-two-year-old Neapolitan secretary who was ready to dip into her savings to hire a lawyer to help him with his legal troubles. She had apparently forgiven him for neglecting to inform her that he was already married.

But Louk refused all legal aid. He also declined to receive visitors, especially his "fiancees."

At Louk's Naples hotel room, Italian police discovered a wardrobe full of expensive clothing. They were also intrigued by a large ring with a dragon motif engraved into a fancy stone. When closely examined, the ring was found to contain a secret compartment in which microfilm could be hidden.

The newspapers now decided that Mordechai Louk was a master spy, though they continued to disagree about whom he was working for. In any case, his adventures as a latter-day Casanova seemed to interest Italian readers more than his espionage activities.

At Italian counter-intelligence headquarters, the story of Mordechai Louk was hardly a mystery any longer. Though they didn't admit it publicly, the Italians had for some time been receiving full cooperation from the Mossad.

The Mossad knew all about Mordechai Louk. He had served in the Israeli army after emigrating to the country from Spanish Morocco in 1949. Though his profession was carpentry he seemed to prefer other occupations: he had served one prison term for attempted armed robbery, and three others for petty crimes.

Louk was constantly having troubles: if not with the police then with people to whom he owed money, if not with his wife's family then with one of his numerous lovers. In 1961, he decided that he had had enough of Israel. While on maneuvers with his army unit in the Gaza region he slipped across the Egyptian frontier, gave himself up to Egyptian army officers, and asked for political asylum. He was now adding desertion to his other crimes.

The Egyptians promptly arrested Mordechai Louk and threw him into jail. As far as they were concerned, he could easily be an Israeli spy.

In prison Louk met a few other Israelis. Some were petty criminals like himself who had decided to try their luck in Egypt, and one or two were pimps who believed they could do better business in Cairo than in Tel Aviv. Nearly all were extremely disillusioned by the treatment they had received at the hands of their captors. Louk tried to lift their spirits by talking merrily and singing Israeli songs. He took it upon himself to become a kind of unofficial leader of the Israeli group, and made valiant efforts to boost the morale of his fellow countrymen in their inhospitable surroundings.

But Louk himself was prone to depression. One Israeli who was released from the prison and allowed to return to Israel later re-counted: "Louk became gloomy about his stay in jail. He once tried to commit suicide by cutting his veins with a piece of iron which he spent days patiently sharpening. But he was saved just in time and was kept in the prison hospital for a week.

"Then he tried to kill himself again by throwing himself out of a window. Later he tried cutting his veins again, and this time they kept him in the hospital for a full month. He was a very single-minded man."

When the Egyptian secret service heard about Louk's determination they became convinced that they might be able to put him to good use. He was handsome, intelligent and multi-lingual—and he was a Jew. They made a cautious approach to him and asked whether he would be interested in doing some work for them.

Louk was an active and fun-loving fellow, and languishing in a Cairo jail he was going slowly mad. The opportunity of becoming a spy immediately struck his fancy. He accepted the offer.

For the next six months he went through a series of tests and training programs in espionage techniques. As proof of his loyalty he was required to make propaganda broadcasts on the Hebrew services of Egyptian radio. His instructors taught him photography and microfilm skills and he became adept at the use of both firearms and radio transmitters. He also brushed up his French, Italian and German, becoming as fluent in these languages as he already was in Hebrew, Spanish and Arabic.

In the summer of 1962, Louk was declared a fully-trained opera-tive and received his final field briefing from a senior intelligence officer. His area of work would be western Europe: France, Switzer-land, Germany and Italy. His primary task: to make contact with as many Israelis as he could and gather from them whatever data he could about economic and political developments in Israel.

"When you meet Israelis," he was told, "you will supply us with their names, their jobs, their addresses. Every piece of information will be of value—gossip, rumors about public scandals, even their opinions about Israel.

"We also want you to find out names and identities of the Israeli secret service agents now operating in Europe. Give us their family background and any other material about them. We will supply you with cameras and you are to take photographs of everyone you come in contact with.

"Your salary will be $150 a month to start with. You will also get necessary traveling expenses, but when you have such expenses they must be authorized by us first, and you must always produce authentic bills and receipts, even for taxi rides. If you do your work well, and if you are not extravagant, we will see that your salary is increased."

Louk was provided with an Egyptian passport in the name of Mohamed Hamdi Habal. His dark hair was dyed blonde and he was then sent to Damascus, where a cover for his future operations was set up. No sooner did Louk arrive in Damascus than he was taken in hand by Egyptian secret service agents operating there. They took away his Egyptian passport and provided him with a Moroccan one, in the name of Joseph Dahan. Once the Egyptians were satisfied that Louk was a genuine convert to their cause, they returned his Egyptian passport and told him to use both when traveling in Europe. Wishing him good luck, they put him on a plane—and Mordechai Louk began his spying career.

No one in the Egyptian intelligence service knew it, of course, but the Mossad had been keeping an eye on Mordechai Louk from the moment he deserted his army unit and crossed the Egyptian border. It did not take long for the Mossad network in Egypt to get wind of the Israeli soldier who had deserted to the enemy: such an occurrence was a rarity and naturally it caused widespread comment.

From that time on, the Mossad kept abreast of every move that Louk made. When they learned that he was being activated as an Egyptian spy in Europe, they decided that he would be of more use to them in the field than in prison—which is where they could have put him. If they let him operate freely, he would surely lead them to some of his Egyptian contacts.

Thus, everything that Mordechai Louk did in Europe was closely watched by Mossad agents. He traveled all over the continent for nearly three years. During 1962 and 1963 he worked chiefly in Germany and Switzerland, living at various times in the cities of Munich, Coblenz, Zurich, Frankfurt and Basle. He worked as an assistant to full-time Egyptian agents who were then busy recruiting Germany scientists for Nasser's armaments programs.

In January 1964, Louk was transferred to Naples; for the rest of his brief career as a spy he was based there, though he traveled periodically to Germany and Switzerland.

It was in Naples that Louk began to make trouble for his employers. They certainly didn't pay him well, and he was only able to afford pretty miserable lodgings in a poor part of the city. To eke out his meager income he had to moonlight as a tour guide. When he began to get involved with his various fiancees, he had no scruples about letting them make further contributions toward his income. Thus he was able to afford the fancy clothes which Italian police officers found in his hotel room.

After less than a year in Naples, however, Louk decided that he wasn't being treated (i.e., paid) in accordance with his needs or his value. In early November, 1964, he set up a meeting with his immediate supervisor, who worked under the name of Selim Osman El Sayad, and informed him that he was going to get tough. "Either you increase my salary and stop making my life a misery by querying every tiny expense," he said, "or I'll stop working for you.

"And what's more," added Louk, "I know a lot about your organization. I can sell this information for a very high price indeed —and you know very well who will be interested."

El Sayad was somewhat amused by Louk's estimation of his own importance, since he had been complaining for months about the scarcity of Louk's intelligence reports from Naples.

The errant spy seemed to spend more time with his female companions than he did on the job. But Louk presented a real danger nonetheless: a dissatisfied spy can be nothing but trouble. Something had to be done about him.

El Sayad extended an invitation for Louk to "come and discuss this matter with us in a friendly way" at the Egyptian embassy in Rome.

Louk was clever enough to refuse the invitation. He knew a thing or two about the law, and about the methods then in use by Egyptian intelligence officers. Once he set foot in the Egyptian embassy he was legally on Egyptian soil, and they could do with him what they pleased. Louk insisted instead on meeting in a public place, where he could be certain of safety. El Sayad suggested the expensive Café de Paris on the Via Veneto. They could sit quietly and talk things over there.

Louk accepted. When he arrived for the meeting with El Sayad and two other intelligence officers, he was sure that he would be safe in this crowded café with its wealthy and famous clientele.

What Louk did not know was that El Sayad had several accomplices waiting in a car that was parked nearby. At a signal from him, they would discreetly but persuasively take the recalcitrant agent away with them.

At their meeting, El Sayad was brutally candid with Louk.

"In view of the poor quality of the information you give us, and also its infrequency, we think you are paid too *much*, not too little. Perhaps you could spend a little less time with your women and a little more time on the job for which you were trained. Unless you try harder we are going to cut your salary."

It is not clear why El Sayad took this hard line with Mordechai Louk. Perhaps he thought that Louk would be frightened enough to start working harder, or that he was bluffing all along.

One theory espoused in Mossad headquarters is that the Egyptians never had any intention of letting Mordechai Louk leave his rendezvous in the Via Veneto. According to this theory, the Egyptians already suspected that their Israeli agent was working secretly for the Mossad. For months the Israelis had been scoring success after success against them in Europe. Hardly a move could be made by the Egyptians without news of it reaching Tel Aviv almost before it reached Cairo.

Whatever the truth is, however, Louk was no more cooperative than he had been before. El Sayad gave the agreed signal to his men and they swooped in to march the horrified Louk to their car. By that time he was too drunk to respond quickly. Before he knew it he was being held in the back seat of a car which was speeding off to the Egyptian Embassy. There he was drugged and put in the "sarcophagus" in which the Italian customs men found him.

Mossad agents watched the whole thing: the meeting and subsequent abduction to the embassy. After a quick consultation with headquarters in Israel the agents decided to save Louk from execution, the fate that surely awaited him in Egypt. They informed Italian counter-intelligence of what had happened and worked together with them to keep watch on the Embassy. Airport officials were warned that Egyptians were likely to smuggle a man out of Rome, and customs men were put on the alert.

Thus, it was no accident that when the Egyptians made their move, two days later, they were being watched closely by Italian airport officials. Nor was it by chance that the officials had an Alfa-Romeo standing nearby in case a chase should be necessary.

Even so, it is to the Italians' credit that they reacted so quickly to the suspicious-looking trunk. Until that moment they had no idea of its existence, though it had obviously been used for people-smuggling many times before.

Quietly and discreetly, Italian counter-intelligence intervened with the police and saw to it that Louk was free from any criminal liability. When Louk realized that they knew who he was, he put in a request to meet with the Israeli consul. He wanted to confess all and make a clean start. He had no illusions about what faced him if he returned to Israel: a trial and certain imprisonment—not to mention the wrath of his family.

"Let me go back," he pleaded. "If I go anywhere else on this globe I am a dead man. I know all about the Egyptian secret service and their methods."

Louk's request was granted. The next day, wearing a blue suit with a red tie and dark sunglasses, he was driven to the airport. This time, however, he was transported not in a trunk but in a comfortable and well-protected police car.

Despite his harrowing experiences of the previous weeks, Louk had lost none of his nerve. Asking on arrival at the airport to meet with the press, he declared: "I want to thank the police for saving my life. I want to apologize to my country and to my wife and children for behaving so badly. I am ready to pay for my crimes. Then I would like to re-start my life with my family if they will forgive me.

"I am a carpenter. From now on that is the only profession I ever intend to practise."

Thus, on November 4, Louk flew back to Israel in a first-class seat on an El Al jet liner. His trial was conducted soon after and held partly *in camera*. The prosecution spelled out precisely how he had been tracked all over Europe during his adventures as a spy there.

Louk was sentenced to thirteen years in jail. When he was released he kept the promise he made at the airport to mend his ways. Today he lives with his wife and children—and works as a carpenter.

His spying days are over.

Invisible Spies

A MAN'S MOVEMENTS can be followed by simple observation. Israel Beer and Mordechai Louk, spies for Russia and Egypt respectively, were caught because they were seen talking to other men known to be enemy intelligence agents.

Not all spy activity is either so easily detected or so easily dealt with. While the individual agent will never be completely replaced, new ultra-sophisticated espionage methods are now playing an increasingly important role in the gathering—not to mention the analysis—of information. This is particularly true when an intelligence service is generously funded by the government it serves. And the more important a country's secrets are considered, the more likely it is to be subjected to the most advanced espionage techniques.

The Mossad and its partners in the Israeli intelligence community learned just how susceptible they are to espionage in Moscow, on a fine spring morning in the early 1960s.

Since 1948 the Israeli Embassy had been housed in a small building which, though large enough at first, had become, over the years, completely inadequate to its needs. For a long time the Israelis had been pressuring the Moscow government to allow them to buy or rent larger premises. Finally the Russians agreed.

But instead of offering the Israelis a choice of ready-built houses which were suitable for diplomatic purposes, they suggested that a brand-new building be constructed. With reluctance the Russians agreed that the architect could be Israeli, but they insisted that the manual laborers all be Russian. The new embassy would include the ambassador's private residence and living quarters for several other high officials, in addition to the usual run of offices.

The building went up in record time. Within months the embassy staff began moving their furniture to the new quarters.

It was on the first day of the move that a woman staff member noticed something odd.

Walking in stiletto-heeled shoes over the splendid new parquetry floor of the lobby, she suddenly stopped dead in her tracks. Tapping a certain place in the floor, she remarked to a colleague who was passing by, "There's a funny noise. It kind of sounds hollow just there."

As a crowd of onlookers gathered around, she demonstrated what she meant by walking over the area again. Everyone agreed: there *was* a hollow sound at the point where she stopped.

The ambassador was alerted and a security official brought in. Working with a hammer and crowbar, he lifted the area of flooring from where the sounds had come. The circle of onlookers gasped in astonishment as there appeared beneath the floor a large black hole. It seemed to be a tunnel of some sort.

Two young officials decided to explore the tunnel. Climbing down armed with flashlights, they gingerly made their way through the dark passage and soon discovered that it grew larger and larger as they went along. From the fresh plaster work and smell of paint, they knew that it had been built recently. About fifteen feet below the surface the chasm widened out and was soon ample enough to allow the two men to walk side-by-side.

Coming to a fork in the tunnel the two men chose to stay together and follow one branch. They explored for what they later estimated to be a full ninety feet before finding their way barred by an iron grill. They were nervous about what lay on the other side but curiosity overcame apprehension, and pushing against the grill they discovered that it rolled back on well-oiled hinges. As they poked their heads into the sunlight they were startled to discover themselves in the courtyard of an adjacent building long suspected to be a KGB headquarters.

That was enough. They dropped back into the tunnel and hurried back to the Embassy as fast as they could.

When they reported on their find to their colleagues at the Embassy, the ambassador immediately telephoned Jerusalem to consult with his government.

It was obvious, he said, that the Soviet authorities had planned to engage in intensive spying. The tunnel was large enough to provide both physical and electronic access to the entire embassy.

No sooner had the ambassador hung up the receiver than there was a telephone call from the Soviet Foreign Minister. Apologetically he informed the Israeli official to whom he spoke that there had been a problem with some of the water pipes in the vicinity of the Embassy.

"You may notice some flooding shortly," he said. "Please don't be worried; we have the matter under control."

And almost as he spoke, water began to seep into the embassy from the tunnel. Within minutes the beautiful parquetry floor was inundated. Furniture had to be moved out hastily to protect it from permanent damage.

Obviously the two Israelis had been spotted while exploring the tunnel, and KGB officers, alarmed at the prospect of any more explorations, decided to flood it. When repair men came to fix the water damage inside the embassy, they blocked off the hole. Very simple.

In Israel, however, there was intense debate about what to do. The Soviet government had been planning the espionage tunnel ever since they agreed that the embassy should be housed in a new building.

Should an official complaint be lodged?

While Levi Eshkol was conferring with his cabinet about what to do, Soviet Ambassador Mr. Zoubakhine, known as "Spy Number One" among Israeli intelligence officers, took the initiative. He threatened Prime Minister Eshkol with "most dire consequences" if a word was breathed about the tunnel under the embassy. He made no attempt whatsoever to hide the fact that the tunnel was designed solely for espionage purposes.

The affair was hushed up, but it soon became common knowledge in Moscow. In the weeks ahead there was a lot of careful examination of the floors in other western embassies. In diplomatic circles the joke went around: "Are they tunneling *in* at your place, or are you trying to tunnel *out*?"

Despite the tunnel incident, the major Soviet espionage effort against Israel is, and always has been, in Israel itself. Israel Beer was only one of many Soviet agents working in the country. A goodly number of the "diplomats" at the Russian embassy spend most of their time in espionage work. With its severe limitations in personnel, the Israeli counter-intelligence service could never hope to deal with all the spying that goes on within its own borders.

When Isser Harel once complained to Ben-Gurion about the threat posed by the Jewish agents planted by Moscow in the guise of genuine Zionist settlers, Ben-Gurion took the news with relative equanimity.

"If they are Jewish spies," he said, "then let them at least spy in Israel!"

Today, however, the techniques—and perhaps the threat itself—cannot be so easily shrugged off or dealt with. For the most powerful Soviet spy of all cannot even be seen, let alone put out of action, from Israel itself.

In the eastern Mediterranean, just beyond the range of the naked human eye, lies a fleet of three nondescript-looking Soviet vessels. Every day, around the clock, they patrol Israel's shores. Though without offensive weapons themselves, they are protected by powerful naval forces armed with scores of helicopters and missiles.

The sole mission of these Soviet vessels, the *Caucacus*, the *Crimea* and the *Yuri Gagarin*, is to spy on Israel. They bristle with the most sophisticated electronic equipment, and their crews consist of experts in computers, communications, and Israeli affairs. Between them they can monitor every radio and telephone message sent in, from, or to Israel.

Ordinary telephone calls are their prey, as are messages that come from military, civilian, and even police radios. The commercial jet liners that use Tel Aviv's Lod airport have every radio message intercepted and taped. Radar installations and other tracking devices can be pinpointed with perfect accuracy. It is also believed that the Russians have on board their spy ships devices capable of interfering with Israeli communications systems. The *Yuri Gagarin* maintains contact with Soviet spy satellites. Constantly supplied by ships that rendezvous with them at regular intervals, they can keep their vigil indefinitely.

Though the Soviet experts on board do some of their own analytic and interpretive work on the spot, most of the material they gather is sent back to Moscow by the helicopters that regularly fly out. Radio contact with Moscow is maintained twenty-four hours a day.

It was for this reason that when the Entebbe rescue operation was being planned in 1976, orders went out to everybody concerned: "Keep your mouth shut—and your radio turned off!" Had the Russians picked up advance warning of the operation, they could have radioed it to Entebbe—with obvious results.

Occasionally the Russians decide to take a closer look at activities in Israel. In 1977 they dispatched a number of KE 25 helicopters, equipped with cameras and radar units, inside Israeli air space to observe and photograph ship movements. When the Lebanese civil war was raging in 1975, Israeli missile boats patrolling off-shore were followed constantly by Soviet ships. At night the Russians kept high-power searchlights trained on the Israelis.

On the eve of the Yom Kippur in 1973, the Soviet ships made a hurried departure. At that time, however, they were militarily defenseless. Now that they have a strong protective force with them at all times, they can stay on the scene even in periods of military crisis.

This security makes their presence all the more threatening to Israel's military leaders. In the event of war, the Soviet ships could pass on what they glean from their electronic surveillance to Egypt, Syria and the other Arab states. Anything telephoned or broadcast in Israel would quickly fall into the hands of their opponents. Moreover, if the Russians decided to, they could institute a complete jamming operation on all radio communications between Israeli military forces. Front lines would be cut off from headquarters.

It isn't difficult to see why the Soviet spy ships are so worrying to the Mossad, as well as to the rest of Israel's intelligence organization and military leaders. An omnipresent Soviet spy network could tip the scales in an all-out war. This being the case, the spy ships might well be a top-priority target for Israeli attack. With the American Sixth Fleet anchored not far away, the consequences of a shooting war between Soviet and Israeli forces could be disastrous.

In the meantime, there is nothing that the Mossad, or anyone else in Israel, can do about the super-spies patrolling her shores.

"Michdal"
The Yom Kippur War

IN THE WAKE OF THE Six-Day War, it seemed to observers all over
the world that the Mossad could do no wrong. Operations thought
to be impossible were carried out with a speed and efficiency that
seemed effortless. It was generally accepted that Israel's crushing
victory in the Six-Day War was largely the result of brilliant behind-
the-scenes intelligence work. With such a flawless organization
behind them, the people of Israel could virtually conclude that their
security was inviolable.

In 1973, however, a streak of bad publicity began to change that
image. Early in the year it became clear that the Egyptians and
Syrians were preparing for war. The vast armada of tanks, planes
and missiles with which the Soviet Union had been reequipping the
Arab forces was being made ready for action. Massive troop movements were reported as division after division rolled toward both the
Syrian and Egyptian fronts. President Anwar El Sadat of Egypt
spoke of "impending hostilities."

The weight of the evidence was overwhelming. As a consequence,
the Israeli army held large-scale maneuvers in which thousands of
men were called away from their jobs and ordered to report to their
units. Industry and agriculture came to a halt.

But nothing happened. There was no war.

The mobilization cost Israel ten million dollars, not counting the
lost production. It resulted in considerable criticism about "mis-
leading" information supplied by the intelligence services.

Shortly afterward came news from Norway of the assassination

of the wrong man by a Mossad revenge squad despatched to elimi-
nate terrorists responsible for attacks against Israel. The Mossad
had long held the conviction that terror could only be fought with
terror, but it wasn't until the slaughter of eleven Israeli athletes at
the Munich Olympics that Golda Meir would agree to such strategy.

Zvi Zamir, who replaced Meir Amit as head of the Mossad in
1968, pursued this policy with a vengeance that surprised others in
the Mossad who had thought him too susceptible to ministerial
pressure. At the top of his "hit list" he placed a thirty-nine-year-old
Palestinian named Ali Hassan Salameh, who was the leader of the
Munich group of assassins.

Mossad agents took their first victim in October, 1972, a matter of
weeks after the Olympic games. He was Wadi Abdul Zwaiter, a
Palestinian poet who had brought to Rome the three Japanese Red
Army gunmen who later flew on to Tel Aviv and sprayed bullets and
hand grenades around the arrival building of Lod Airport, killing
twenty-four people. He was tracked down to Rome and killed by
gunfire at the entrance to his apartment building. The execution
went perfectly, and his killers were out of the country within hours.

Over the next ten months, Europe and the Middle East became a
battlefield of terror and counter-terror. The Mossad execution
squads claimed a large number of victims, but in the process lost
some of its finest agents.

Finally, in July 1973, they got what seemed like a definite lead on
Ali Hassan Salameh. He was said to be in the small town of Lille-
hammer, Norway, and a team of killers was despatched to take care
of him.

But the operation went disastrously wrong. The team, which
included a number of amateurs, killed the wrong man, and they
proceeded to get caught. At their trial the agents revealed very full
details of the revenge operation, thereby giving the Mossad a pleni-
tude of what they fear most: publicity. Newspapers all over the world
carried stories of how the ruthless Mossad had been carrying out an
illegal murder campaign.

A month later the growing list of disasters was added to when an
Israeli fighter flew over Lebanese airspace and, singling out a civilian
airliner that had taken off from Beirut airport, forced the plane to
leave its normal route and land instead at a military base in Israel.
There the passengers were asked politely to disembark; after being
carefully screened, all were allowed back on again, and the plane
returned to Beirut.

The air force carried out this illegal hijacking because George Habash, leader of the terrorist group PFLP, was supposedly on the aircraft in question. As it turned out, he wasn't.

The mistake caused a furor in Israel. The Mossad protested that they had not recommended seizing the aircraft and were not even sure that Habash was actually on board. The orders for its capture had been given personally by Defense Minister Moshe Dayan.

But the Mossad got the blame.

At this point the Mossad's secretiveness worked to its disadvantage. It could have used a subtle public relations exercise to boost its standing in Israeli public opinion. But it was established policy never to draw attention to the organization or any of its activities; and that policy continued to prevail. The quiet and reserved General Zvi Zamir was hardly the man to change it.

Thus, the Mossad's reputation reached an all-time low.

The Mossad's own blunders were reinforced by another development that had, for the last six years or so, been altering radically the balance of power within the intelligence community. The net result of these trends was to leave the Mossad with less and less power and credibility.

Since the Six-Day War, the military intelligence service had subtly begun to elbow out the Mossad and replace it as the dominant arm in security affairs. Before that, military intelligence had concerned itself exclusively with military matters. With the powerful figure of Isser Harel making sure that each security agency stayed firmly in its place, the division of responsibility had been clear and unquestioned. Harel controlled the different branches as precisely as a good conductor controls a symphony orchestra.

Soon after the Six-Day War, military intelligence came under the leadership of Major General Aharon Yariv, an extrovert personality who completely overshadowed the more retiring Zvi Zamir. Yariv simply ignored the tradition of secrecy surrounding the names and activities of intelligence commanders and was more than ready to promote himself—and his department—to the press.

At the same time, under Yariv's initiative the military intelligence service began to widen its sphere of influence. Not only did it continue to gather military information but it concerned itself with political, economic, diplomatic, demographic and scientific research. It also expanded its activities in the analysis of data. These moves were encouraged by Moshe Dayan, always suspicious about the civilian Mossad. With Dayan's blessings, Yariv raised his section of the secret service to dominance in Israeli intelligence affairs.

With the Mossad discredited in public opinion and military intelligence so unreasonably powerful and self-assured, the ingredients for the disaster of the Yom Kippur War were all prepared.

The prime ingredient was something known as "the concept." This was a fixed notion, universally held in the military establishment from Moshe Dayan downward, that there was a very low possibility of war. The Arabs, the military men thought, were unprepared for battle.

They held on to this "concept" rigidly, in spite of the floods of data that indicated otherwise. Not only the Mossad but other observers gathered a wealth of information about large-scale mobilization in the Arab countries. They fed all their data into the research and evaluation departments of military intelligence.

Their reports were studiously ignored or argued away by officers who already had their minds made up. These officers had a vested interest in their thesis, and they would not let it be swayed by mere information. The "concept" was unquestioned and unquestionable.

Throughout September 1973, the reports of war preparation kept coming in from all sources. Israeli military journalists who visited the Sinai and the Golan Heights were staggered by the growing volume of armed forces massing on the other side of the border. Desperately worried, they wrote dozens of dispatches warning of the menace: but the military censor, taking his orders from the men who had concocted the "concept," slashed his blue pencil through their articles.

At army headquarters in the Sinai Desert a junior officer had been working through the data and evaluating it on a mathematical point-by-point basis. Taking into account all the factors that might indicate a renewal of mass conflict, he toted up the score daily in the light of the information just received from the front. One day in September he leapt up from his seat and hurried in agitation to his commander.

"There is going to be a war," he told him. "I know it for a fact—I can prove it!"

His superior ignored him.

Day after day the junior officer was seen running around the headquarters building with his data sheets in hand, begging senior officers to take action. Nobody paid him any attention.

By another stroke of bad luck, Aharon Yariv had retired as head of military intelligence and been replaced by General Eliahu Zeira. Zeira had served as military attache in Washington and then as Yariv's deputy. He had very little direct experience of Arab affairs and less in security work. But Zeira was the personal choice of Defense Minister Moshe Dayan, and his word therefore carried considerable weight. Less cautious a man than Yariv, he had a reputation for never changing his mind once he had made it up.

This can be a dangerous flaw in any field commander, but it is fatal in an intelligence environment where a constant flow of incoming reports requires continuous reassessment and an open mind.

The Soviet intelligence advisers to Egypt had meanwhile evolved a publicity ruse to fool the Israelis, and in September they worked with the Egyptians to put it into action. Thinking that the Israelis would never expect them to declare their hand so openly if they were really planning to go to war, they deliberately stepped up their battle cries. The aim was to enhance Israel's false sense of security.

To feed that sense of security further, the Egyptians orchestrated a campaign of whispers directed at foreign journalists who were visiting Cairo. "The Egyptian army is incapable of fighting." the journalists were told. Hearing it from formerly reliable sources, they easily fell for the trick. Even the independently-minded newspapers like *Le Monde* were duped. Their correspondent wrote: "the young, inexperienced soldiers of President Sadat are incapable of using or controlling their sophisticated Soviet equipment."

Israeli commanders, normally cautious and mistrustful, played right along. They were convinced there would be no war. And to order another mobilization, with all the disruption it would cause among the civilian population, would be not only uncalled-for but economically disastrous.

At Mossad headquarters, Zvi Zamir was hardly so complacent as his military colleagues. He was, in fact, deeply uneasy. By the second week of September it had become obvious to him that Syria and Egypt were planning a full-scale war. Information pouring in from agents all over Europe and the Middle East confirmed it unanimously. Some said war was ten days away, some said two weeks. But all agreed on one thing: there would be war.

One Mossad communications officer said, "We are riding into the valley of death."

This much was obvious to the Mossad because they listened to their agents. And those agents were producing vast numbers of documents and coded messages about the approaching conflict.

They gave precise details of how the Egyptians and Syrians intended to attack: where the commando units were going to land their helicopters in Sinai, where fighter-bombers were going to strike.

In all, the Mossad received over four hundred messages, four hundred pieces of information that predicted in detail the outbreak of hostilities.

Four hundred messages, all of which were passed on to the military authorities and ignored.

Just how the two branches of the intelligence service were moving in different directions was demonstrated on September 13, when a patrol of Israeli planes was sent on a reconnaissance mission to the Syrian ports of Latakiye and Tartus. This patrol was initiated in response to information about the growing number of heavy Soviet weapons arriving at the ports every day.

As the planes approached their targets they were met by a swarm of Migs. The Israelis had their own air cover, however, and in the ensuing battle thirteen of the Migs were shot down. One Israeli plane was lost but the pilot was rescued by helicopter from the sea.

The jubilation over this victory only reinforced the feeling of complacency at army headquarters. General Zeira's intelligence evaluation department produced a report that said, in part: "The Syrians realize more than ever that they cannot win a war against us. The activity now being witnessed on the Golan Heights is aimed at a limited retaliatory blow in low-key. That is why their forces are gathered there—to make a token strike, and to insure that if we hit back they will be able to block us."

The Mossad's version of events was totally contradictory. They viewed the dogfight over Syria as a preliminary to the real battle to come. They based their belief on the reports that continued every day to reach their desks.

And still the warnings they issued were ignored. "The concept" was not to be argued with.

While the reports continued to pour into Mossad headquarters, military men urged newspaper editors to be "moderate" in their reporting. They didn't want to stir up fears of war among the civilian population. As late as October 2, the editors—to their everlasting and bitter regret—cooperated with the military leaders and toned down their reports from the front.

By that time, even some generals had sensed they were on the wrong track. When Zeira told one of them that he could guarantee forty-eight hours advance warning of any possible major attack, a senior man on his general staff said bluntly: "Frankly, I am worried. I have the impression there *is* going to be war. I feel it in my bones."

In Washington the CIA had come to the same conclusion. On October 4, two days before the invasion began, they warned the Mossad: "We believe the Arabs are going to attack you."

When the report was passed on to military intelligence, they replied, as coolly as ever, "We do *not* believe they will attack."

Still somewhat in awe of Israeli intelligence capabilities, the Americans allowed themselves to be convinced. "It's their own fate," said one CIA official. "One assumes that they know what they're talking about."

It is known that after the war was over, three top CIA officials were fired.

Mossad chief Zvi Zamir had meanwhile gone on a secret mission to Europe to try and check on matters for himself. On the morning of October 6 he sent a frantic cable to Prime Minister Meir: "The war will start today."

He was too late.

"The concept" was so firmly engrained in the minds of military men that at noon on the sixth, General Zeira walked into a press briefing in Tel Aviv still convinced of its truth. As he spoke calmly and self-assuredly to the assembled newsmen he repeated once again:

"There will be no war."

At 2 PM, an agitated major entered the briefing room and handed General Zeira a telegram. Zeira read it and without a word left the room. He did not return.

The journalists learned why immediately. All over Tel Aviv the sirens began sounding, and the newsmen rushed back to their offices to find out what was happening. They knew that the last place to get reliable information was the military intelligence service.

At noon the Egyptians had swept over the Suez Canal with tens of thousands of men. Syrian forces had struck from the Golan Heights with the greatest concentration of heavy tanks ever assembled in a single battle.

The small number of unprepared, inexperienced youngsters on

the Israeli front line took a terrible battering. On the first day the army suffered 500 dead and over 1,000 wounded. By contrast, in the whole of the Six-Day War, only 850 men had fallen.

Several Mossad agents who had warned of the attack days in advance literally wept through sheer frustration at the way they had been ignored.

Within days, however, the superb Israeli forces had turned the tide of battle. After halting the Syrian and Egyptian advances, they counterattacked and were able to inflict heavy losses on the armies of both nations. On October 15, General Ariel ("Arik") Sharon carried off his daring plan to bridge the Suez Canal at the precise point where, according to tradition, Moses crossed the Red Sea some 4,000 years before. Under heavy fire he and his forces penetrated well into Egypt and eventually encircled the entire Egyptian Third Army.

At this point the Russians stepped in and warned of direct intervention if the Israelis went any further. Secretary of State Henry Kissinger pressed Golda Meir to accept a ceasefire; this was broken once but then reestablished. With his usual style of superpower diplomacy, Kissinger negotiated an uneasy peace settlement.

Though the Yom Kippur War was a victory for Israel in a purely military sense, psychologically it was a terrible blow. The rest of the world had seen the supposedly ever-vigilant state caught napping: her armed forces could no longer be considered invincible. Her intelligence service was obviously not as infallible as was once thought.

Within Israel itself, the disillusionment and loss of morale seeped into every level of society. Some turned for guidance to the story of Belshazzar, King of Babylon, which is told in the book of Daniel. Belshazzar had received a message in writing on the wall of his banquet room; the only man able to interpret the message was the prophet Daniel, who told him that it warned of coming disaster. No one believed him, and disaster struck.

Now, in 1973, disaster had struck again. Why had no one heeded the warning of the 400 messages received from Mossad agents all over the world? Why had Israel's leadership, like the thousand lords of King Belshazzar, ignored the voices of doom? Were they drinking too deeply from the cup of self-esteem and reveling in their own importance?

In the anger that followed the Yom Kippur War, it became

popular to sum up Israel's failure with a single Hebrew word: *michdal*. This colorful expression is best translated, politely, as "mess-up" or "foul-up." To this day it is the taunt hurled at Israeli leaders whose names are connected with the mistakes that made disaster possible.

Nobody escaped the wave of recriminations. Golda Meir resigned as Prime Minister. The Agranat Commission of Inquiry, appointed to investigate the reasons for Israel's unpreparedness, recommended that a number of senior officers, including General Eliahu Zeira of military intelligence, be removed from their posts. It also recommended a reexamination of the structure of power within Israel's intelligence services.

The intelligence community came in for heavy criticism like nearly everyone else involved in political and military affairs. It is clear, however, that though the evaluation procedures employed before 1973 were woefully inadequate, no one could reasonably claim that the Mossad was negligent in the performance of its duties. Yet public opinion did claim exactly this. It was forgotten that the Mossad had warned again and again—400 times—of the coming invasion.

If the army had listened to them, the Mossad would today be basking in a glow of universal admiration. Instead they have had to bow before the storm of reproach. It is not enough for them to plead innocence to the charge that their inadequacies led to the *michdal* of the Yom Kippur War. Nor is it in their nature to defend themselves publicly. The men and women of the Mossad remain today as secretive as ever about what they do. On hundreds of fronts all over the world they go quietly about their business of arming Israel with its most valuable weapon: knowledge.

Epilogue

NOT FAR FROM Tel Aviv there is a village called Kefar Habad. It is a poor village and a tiny one, inhabited mainly by pious Hasidic Jews who support themselves through farming.

The synagogue of Kefar Habad is as stark as the village itself. The ceiling is full of holes and the benches inside are of plain wood. Sparrows fly in and out of the gaps in the ceiling as they wish; many of them have their nests inside. Outside, on the door, is posted a schedule of the rotation for armed guard duty. The pious men of the village take turns patrolling with machine guns slung over the shoulders of their long black coats while the others work in the fields.

On July 29, 1977, the synagogue at Kefar Habad was filled to capacity with visitors. Nearby a number of important-looking cars were parked. There was a bar mitzvah going on.

Normally a bar mitzvah is a gay, festive occasion; well it should be, for it marks the day that a boy turns into a man.

This bar mitzvah, however, was different from most. Every year the Hasidim of Kefar Habad invite up to 100 boys to celebrate with them their passage into Jewish adulthood. These youngsters come from all over Israel, but all have in common one tragedy: they are the sons of men killed in war.

Thus, the atmosphere among the congregation that hot July day was tinged with sadness and solemnity. As the sparrows flew and chirped overhead, the eighty-six boys—many of whom had never known their fathers—went through the traditional ceremony of reading from the Torah.

When they had finished their reading, one of them walked to the front of the synagogue. His birthday was actually not until September but his bar mitzvah date had been advanced two months so that he could take part in the special occasion. He had been chosen to make the customary speech with which the ceremony ends.

This slender, fragile-looking boy had been given the nickname "Shai"—Hebrew for "gift"—by his mother. She remembered painfully well the last time father and son had seen each other. It was in October 1964, when her son was only two weeks old. That was also the last time she had seen her husband: hence the name "Shai," a living gift from the dead man she had loved so much.

The boy's name was Shaul Cohen. His father, a spy for the Mossad, was Eli Cohen.

Among the congregation were several men, strangers to the Cohen family and to most of the others present, who had known this boy's father well. Some of them had worked with him closely on the mission which sent him, alone, to the Syrian capital of Damascus. Some had been present when he sent from Damascus the terrible radio dispatch that signaled his capture. All had mourned his death by hanging.

Now they watched as the nervous brown-eyed boy who looked so much like his father gathered strength and began the speech he had written himself.

"I would like," he said, "to have been like all the other children. I would have liked my father to be a simple man, and not a hero. Then he would be alive and I would have had a father whom I knew and who lived with us like other fathers.

"I have read everything about my father's life and what he did for our country. I have collected all the books and articles and photographs. But I have hesitated to talk about him before now, for I knew that it still hurt my mother when my father's name was mentioned.

"I will now make my vow. I promise you, father, that in my life I will never fail you. I will do my duty with all my strength and my devotion for the nation of Israel."

The synagogue was still and silent as Shaul Cohen added:

"I will be a faithful son of an admired hero. I will try to be like you, father. That is my pledge."

The most honored member of the congregation, Prime Minister Menachem Begin, wept openly as Shaul finished his speech. When it was over he bent down and kissed him on both cheeks. Shaul also shook hands with other distinguished guests like Motta Gur, Israeli Chief of Staff, and Defense Minister Ezer Weizman. Prime Minister Begin presented the young Shaul with a copy of his own autobiography, *The Revolt*, and Shaul showed the book proudly to his mother. The ceremony broke up in a flurry of handshakes and animated conversation as the congregants went outside to where the pious Hasidim had set up tables for a party. As they walked out, Shaul Cohen confided to Israel's leaders that although his father had been a soccer fan, he himself preferred basketball.

Outside the guests drank cognac and vodka, and everyone joined in a frenzy of singing and dancing. Though this day had its origin in sorrow, they would end it with celebration. For out of sorrow would be born new life, new hope for a peaceful future. As they danced in the fields around the humble synagogue, all sang the famous words of Jewish celebration:

"Lechaim, Lechaim—to Life!"

Index